By Influence & Desire

By the Same Author

La Famille Necker, Madame de Staël et sa Descendance
The Emperor's Talisman: The Life of the Duc de Morny
Napoleon III and Eugénie: The Story of a Marriage (in manuscript)

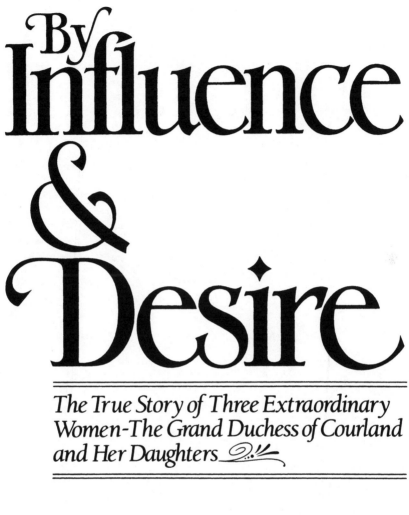

By
Influence
&
Desire

The True Story of Three Extraordinary
Women–The Grand Duchess of Courland
and Her Daughters

By
Rosalynd Pflaum

M. EVANS
Lanham • New York • Boulder • Toronto • Plymo. 'h, UK

M. Evans
An imprint of The Rowman & Littlefield Publishing Group, Inc.
4501 Forbes Boulevard, Suite 200, Lanham, Maryland 20706
http://www.rlpgtrade.com

10 Thornbury Road, Plymouth PL6 7PP, United Kingdom

Distributed by National Book Network

British Library Cataloguing in Publication Information Available

Library of Congress Cataloging-in-Publication Data Available

ISBN 13: 978-1-59077-394-9 pbk: alk. paper)

☻™ The paper used in this publication meets the minimum requirements of American National Standard for Information Sciences—Permanence of Paper for Printed Library Materials, ANSI/NISO Z39.48-1992.

Printed in the United States of America

Design by Diane Gedymin

"But," said Talleyrand with a smile, "what are politics if not women?"

Anna-Dorothea von Medem, the grand duchess of Courland
"I do not believe there was ever a woman more deserving of adoration."

TALLEYRAND

Wilhelmina, the duchess of Sagan, her oldest daughter
"If ever the world were lost and you remained to me, I would need nothing more."

METTERNICH

Dorothea, the duchess of Dino, her youngest daughter
"You belong to me. Don't ever leave me."

TALLEYRAND

AUTHOR'S NOTE

AS A DISTINGUISHED AMERICAN biographer once said: "A biography is not an encyclopedia." The author has not consciously taken liberties with the facts—except in describing occasional incidents that we know must have occurred, but about which information is lacking. This is especially true with the grand duchess's early years when intimate detail is not available about certain recorded events; unfortunately, Anna-Dorothea's diary has been lost. As in most attempts at recreating the past, there is frequently no way of knowing the exact words that were spoken in certain circumstances, but care has been taken to see that the feelings represented are accurate. The extensive correspondence of some of the leading protagonists has been extremely helpful in this regard.

CONTENTS

ACKNOWLEDGMENTS

THERE ARE SO MANY PEOPLE deserving of my grateful recognition. I should begin with the late Theodore Purdy, who gave me the courage to start when I first broached the subject of the Courlands to him. Then I must single out Mrs. Katherine Taylor Rood for her untiring advice on the manuscript in its original form; Mrs. Gisella Amberg, who helped with the initial translations; and Mrs. Jenny Holtzermann, who has always been available whenever I needed assistance with the German sources. I wish to thank Mme. Gaston Palewski, the grand duchess of Courland's direct descendant, and her husband for their gracious reception of me as well as for permission to quote from the family's collection of Talleyrand letters, letters which M. Palewski, a member of the Institut de France, has published (*Le Miroir de Talleyrand: Lettres Inédites à la Duchesse de Courlande pendant le Congrès de Vienne*).

I am indebted more than I can say to Dr. Maria Ullrichova, the Czechoslovakian literary scholar whom I have never had the pleasure of meeting. Dr. Ullrichova inadvertently set me on the trail of the Courland women some fifteen years ago, when she wrote to me, a stranger, suggesting that we exchange copies of our latest books and sent me hers, *Clemens Metternich–Wilhelmine von Sagan: Ein Briefwechsel, 1813–1815* (the correspondence of Metternich and the duchess of Sagan), on which I have drawn heavily. Dr. Ullrichova was the discoverer of this correspondence, now reposing in the Prague Central State Archives, which spelled out, in detail, the hitherto unsuspected true significance of the relationship between the two. I also want to express my indebtedness here to Dorothy Gies McGuigan's *Metternich and the Duchess*. This is the only book pulling together still unpublished correspondence of the pair from public archives in Central Europe, and is invaluable to anyone working in the field. Even someone using the identical source material—as my truncated Bibliography indicates that I, to a large extent, have—must be grateful to Ms. McGuigan for her scholarly research, encyclopedic knowledge of the period, and intuitive grasp of her subject.

Permission to quote from the letter written by the duchess of Sagan and Baron d'Armfelt to Vava, their daughter, was graciously granted by one of Vava's descendants, Miss Wava von Essen, who is the administrator of the d'Armfelt archives in Finland.

This work could not have been written without the unstinting efforts of various personnel at the University of Minnesota's Wilson Library, especially Erika Linke, the head of Interlibrary Loans, and her predecessors and colleagues there and in the Reference Department. On the other side of the ocean, I owe an enormous debt to the entire staff of the Bibliothèque Nationale in Paris, where the bulk of my research was done over several years, and where I was made to feel at home in the Salle de Lecture, Salle des Périodiques, Salle des Fîches, and Bureau des Estampes.

Without the help of Jeanne Bernkopf, whose skillful editing has pulled the manuscript together; without Mary Schmidt's perseverance in typing four completely different versions of it; without the enthusiasm of Mary Kling of Paris and Jacques de Spoelberch; without Millicent Jacka's patience; and without Gertrude Howland, who pointed me in the right direction, this book could never have been published.

PHOTOGRAPH CREDITS

WHEN IT COMES TO ILLUSTRATIONS, the people to thank in a work of this kind fall into several categories, and so many were generous of their time and efforts that I trust I have not omitted anyone. Those who helped pinpoint the whereabouts of pictures I was interested in and those who gave me authorization to use them include:

Mme. Monique Bagnole; the Biron de Courland family; Ehrenwirth Verlag of Munich; Günther Elbin; Philippe Entremont; M. and Mme. Rudolf Firkusny; Father John Gibb; and Prince Francis Schwarzenberg.

Space availability necessitated an ultimate, difficult choice, and I wish to thank the following for permission to reproduce those pictures actually appearing here:

François Bonneau, curator, and the administration of the château de Valençay; Ms. Wava von Essen; M. and Mme. Gaston Palewski; Dr. Maria Ullrichova; Philip Ziegler; the Bibliothèque Nationale, Paris; Bildarchiv der Österreichischen Nationalbibliothek, Vienna; the National Museum of Finland, Helsinki; the Historisches Museum der Stadt Wien, Vienna; and the Musée Talleyrand au Marais.

Finally, I want to acknowledge the following photographic credits:

François Bonneau (Talleyrand's boot); Emmanuel Pagnoud (Peter, the grand duke of Courland); P. O. Wellin (pictures from the National Museum of Finland, Helsinki); Dr. Maria Ullrichova (the views of Nachod and Ratiborzitz); and the staffs of the previously listed museums.

FAMILY TREE

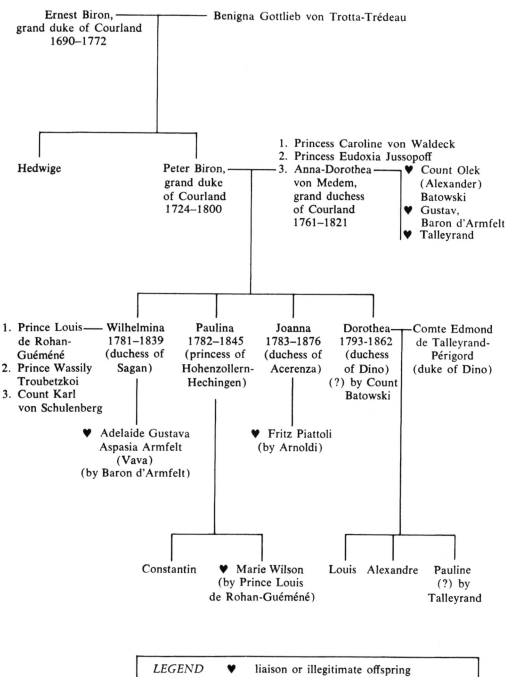

LEGEND ♥ liaison or illegitimate offspring
        (?) father in doubt; possible father indicated

PROLOGUE

1710

WHEN PETER THE GREAT cut the two huge pâtés that served as the centerpiece of the wedding feast for his niece, Anna Ivanovna, that late fall day, out popped a pair of drolly attired dwarfs. The tsar threw back his head and laughed at their comical twistings and turnings and strange grimaces as they danced a minuet amid the clutter of gold vessels strewn upon the vast, candle-lit table. Dwarfs were greatly prized in Russia, so a highlight of the continuing festivities for Anna was the marriage of the tsar's favorite dwarf, Ekime Volkov. The seventy-two dwarfs who participated were dressed after the German fashion and had been recruited from Peter the Great's and the tsarina dowager's own services, or else fetched from the farthest reaches of the realm. The six-foot seven-inch tsar held the garland of fragrant-smelling flowers over the tiny bride's head during the church service, exactly as he had for his niece, and the ritual and pomp of the two services were identical throughout.

Because Anna Ivanovna (who was later to become tsarina) was the first Russian imperial princess to marry a foreigner in over two centuries and because her marriage was the first public ceremony held in Saint Petersburg, the city the tsar had conjured out of the marshes on the banks of the Neva River, Peter the Great had decreed that the events be appropriately celebrated. There were elaborate processions to astound the general populace. Lapps, Finns, Bashkirs, and representatives from every other Russian province participated in their colorful native dress; carts were drawn by bears, hogs, and dogs; and there was even a huge cloth

xv

sea serpent, its tail supported on numerous smaller wagons linked together to undulate as it moved. There were fireworks. And at court there were rough-and-tumble orgies, masquerades, and all-night balls.

Peter the Great had every reason to be in a jovial mood. His dramatic victory over Sweden, the mistress of the North, at Poltava the previous summer had permanently shifted the political axis of the Continent. European statesmen, who had thought of the tsar of Russia as simply a remote, exotic Eastern potentate, if they thought about him at all, awoke to the realization that henceforth they must reckon with His Imperial Majesty's interests. And the union of Peter's seventeen-year-old niece with the sixteen-year-old grand duke of Courland, the titular ruler of a strategic piece of Baltic real estate—a barren buffer strip in what is now Latvia—symbolized this recognition and allowed Peter the Great to bring Courland, with its ice-free deep-water ports, into the Russian orbit, in spite of Courland's feudal ties in Poland.

The young groom proved his extraordinary capacity as a drinker and lecher in the week-long merrymaking. But he had the misfortune to die forty-eight hours out of Saint Petersburg at the village of Doderhof, on the couple's homeward journey.

The grand duke's untimely demise was not allowed to interfere with Peter the Great's far-reaching plans. The reluctant new grand duchess was ordered to continue on and assume control at the Courland capital, Mitau (today Jelgava). But the real ruler of Courland was the Russian resident Alexius-Petrovitch Bestuzhev, whom the tsar placed at his niece's elbow as an adviser.

A large, unattractive woman with lank locks, brows, and lashes dyed black to imitate the raven-haired beauties of Russian folklore, Anna, who was lazy and possessed of an indifferent education, lolled away her days, bored and dreaming, on a bearskin rug and soon became the resident's mistress—as her uncle had intended. Unbeknown to Anna, Bestuzhev was sharing his bed with a Westphalian woman of modest background, who utilized her influence to place her brother in the Russian resident's office. Ernest Bührein (Biron, as he later spelled his name in order to claim relationship with the distinguished French family of marshals) was endowed with a splendid, towering figure, a large measure of sex appeal—and sheer determination. He rose rapidly and became Anna's private secretary, then her paramour. He proved a capable administrator, and when the Russian resident was recalled, Biron assumed his post and for a decade ably governed the duchy—and Anna.

To still the scandal, Anna wedded her lover to one of her impoverished, aristocratic ladies-in-waiting, Benigna Gottlieb von Trotta-Trédeau, a little, pockmarked hunchback who was in love with the bluff, hearty Ernest. The ménage à trois took their meals together daily and had adjoining suites throughout Anna's lifetime —first in the Annenhof, her palace outside Mitau, and later in the various imperial residences in Russia.

Childless Anna treated Peter, the oldest Biron child, as her son. Was he? Anna lavished time and affection on little Peter, as well as on his younger brother and sister; she spoiled them outrageously, ordering them toys from Moscow and tops from Holland, playing shuttlecock and ball with them herself. On state occasions, when etiquette demanded the tsarina dine in solitary splendor, young Peter had the signal honor of serving her. And only Peter was permitted to shoot the muskets the tsarina had stationed at every window of her summer residence at Peterhof.

If Peter was a Romanoff, he probably never knew it, for the three most involved, Benigna, Anna, and Ernest, died with their lips sealed. Perhaps Peter was favored solely for his childhood role in helping Anna retain her full authority. When the Russian Supreme Council called her to the vacant throne of the tsars, Their Sublimities, in an attempted power play, discreetly isolated her in one wing of Moscow's Imperial Palace. It was only through messages courageously smuggled to her in the lining of Peter's clothes, when the six-year-old came to call daily, that Anna was able to thwart their attempt to limit her autocratic powers before she was crowned tsarina.

No other imperial favorite in Russian history, with the exception of Potemkin, ever wielded as much influence as Ernest Biron, and the ten years when Anna sat on the Russian throne are still known as the Age of Biron—*Bironovishtchina*. The only aspect of sovereignty Ernest lacked was the title. He was never far from the tsarina's side, and when she had him elected grand duke of Courland, he filled that post in absentia. Grand Duchess Benigna's diamonds were the envy of the Russian princesses, the magnificence of the Birons' silverplate astonished even the blasé

French ambassador, and Ernest's liveries and carriages were almost as costly as the tsarina's.

When the time arrived for Anna Leopoldovna, the tsarina's niece and heir presumptive, to marry, Ernest suggested his son Peter, but the twenty-year-old girl haughtily replied, "I should rather be shot than marry either one but, if marry I must, I choose the duke of Brunswick." To save Biron's pride, Anna featured Ernest's family and especially the rejected Peter at the elaborate, never-ending nuptial festivities. The grand duke led the opening polonaise with the tsarina, Peter served the bride at the wedding supper, and Grand Duchess Benigna was in charge of undressing her.

Within the year, Anna had convulsions and never left her bed again. Rallying briefly, she signed a ukase naming the infant son of her niece her successor, but she hesitated to name Biron regent. Common sense dictated that the one way to protect her lover from his many enemies was to have him descend from power quickly once she was gone.

"Duke, Duke, my heart is sad for thee, for thou art encompassing thine own ruin!" she cried impatiently, thrusting the petition for the regency that Biron kept handing her underneath the pillow. Five anxious days passed before his tears and entreaties prevailed, and she signed what she considered his death warrant. But she was reluctant to hand it to him and cached it away with her diamonds in the jewel chest she kept within easy reach of her bed. Two nights later, she died.

Anna was right. Trouble was not slow in coming. Ironically, it was on the night of Ernest's greatest triumph—the betrothal ceremony uniting the Biron daughter with the duke of Holstein and thereby indirectly with the Romanoffs—that a palace coup erupted.

Ernest was dragged from bed, naked and bleeding from multiple wounds, and trundled off in the predawn light to the dread Schüsselbourg Fortress prison. Benigna, still in a nightgown stained red with her husband's blood, and Peter and the rest of the regent's family were tossed in on top of him. The mother of the little tsar, Ivan VI, was declared regent, and the Birons were packed off to external exile in Pélim, in the province of Tobolski in Siberia.

After atoning a full year in hell for each day he served as regent—twenty-two years in all—Ernest was pardoned. In 1762, when another bloody coup killed Tsar Peter III and made his wife,

Catherine II, tsarina, she replaced Biron on the Courland throne and restored all the family possessions, even the Grand Duchess Benigna's jewelry. For Catherine the Great shared Peter the Great's dream of making Russia the mistress of the Baltic and reasoned that the grateful grand duke would prove a convenient puppet.

Biron lived for nine more years. But in those years he faced the problem of major misunderstandings between the throne and the Cour nobility who sat in the Diet and filled the duchy's administrative posts and, to a man, considered the Birons upstarts. During the twenty-two years the Biron family had been in exile, those in the Cour power structure had strengthened themselves politically at the expense of their absent ruler, whom they had never expected to see again. To them, Ernest was as welcome as Banquo's ghost, and the nobles refused to disgorge any usurped privileges.

His son, Peter, succeeded him, but he did not possess the practical political ability so badly needed in times of stress and strain. He was insensitive to the demands and needs of the day, lacked tact, and was distinctly handicapped by his violent temper.

When Peter divorced his second grand duchess for failing to return from a trip home to Russia—his first wife, a gentle German princess, had died—his astute mother, Dowager Duchess Benigna, wondered whether marriage with one of the best local families, rather than with another foreigner, might not elevate the ignoble Biron dynasty in Cour eyes and strengthen Peter's hand in his dealing with the recalcitrant lords. Anna-Dorothea von Medem, the younger, unmarried Medem daughter, seemed a made-to-order choice.

CHAPTER ONE

The Grand Duchess & The Grand Duke
1779-1790

NOT A GREAT DEAL IS KNOWN about the earliest years of the "divine Anna"—as Peter called her. Her Medem family, which was one of the richest and most cosmopolitan of Courland, boasted of its "seven hundred" years of unblemished blue blood and was descended, like most of the Cour nobility, from the Order of Teutonic Knights. (The order was actually founded six hundred years earlier, but Anna-Dorothea's daughter in her memoirs picked up an extra century somewhere.)

Anna-Dorothea could not have been more than three or four when she made her first appearance at the ducal court, dancing a minuet with other aristocrats' children. Grand Duke Peter was struck, even then, by her auburn beauty and singled her out to honor by insisting that she eat dinner afterwards at his side.

After her mother's death when Anna-Dorothea was a year old, Anna-Dorothea and her sister, Elisa, who was five years older, lived with their maternal grandmother in the country. The *starostikha*, as a rich landowner's wife was called, was a stern matriarch, and the thing Anna remembered most vividly of that period was prostrating herself before her grandmother to ask forgiveness for the smallest trifle: Blows rained down on serfs and granddaughters alike. As a concession to their father's wishes, the girls were taught to read and write, although the *starostikha* kept repeating, "Too much reading makes women stupid." She might have had other, sharper commentaries had she known her granddaughters were using this ability to further their nurse's illicit affair. The nurse was the only person on the vast estate who showed the motherless girls any warmth or affection. The little sisters reciprocated by

1

reading her lover's passionate letters aloud to her and writing her replies.

When their father took another wife, a widow with two older sons, the girls came home. Their time was divided between the Medem town house in the tiny Cour capital, Mitau, and the family manor house, Alt-Aültz, which was situated between impenetrable marshes and vast birch and virgin pine forests, and like the town house, was built of stone, a rare luxury in the north. Anna-Dorothea and Elisa's education was taken in hand by their stepmother and was a far better and more diversified one than many other contemporaries, even in the West, received. Frau von Medem taught them certain subjects herself. A member of Mitau's avant-garde, she had returned after a considerable stay in Paris a devotee of Jean-Jacques Rousseau, and their new regime was based on his famous work *Emile*. They were brought up to be independent; if they needed something, to request, not demand, it; never to expect service as their due; and, most important of all, to accept people for what they had to offer. This last, revolutionary tenet was to influence Anna-Dorothea throughout her life.

The family had a dancing teacher and a music teacher, and each Medem, old and young, had to sing or play an instrument— Anna sang—to contribute to the different entertainments they produced to while away the long winter months. The sisters also wrote madrigals and composed *bouts-rimés* in excellent French for their half-brothers when the boys came home from the academies of Königsberg and Strasbourg. For the life of aristocracy on the remote Baltic shores was surprisingly sophisticated—and French-oriented, because of the duchy's close ties since feudal times with Warsaw, the Paris of the Vistula.

Because of Mitau's location as a relay post between Saint Petersburg and Europe, travelers headed for Russia invariably broke the long, tedious trip in the Cour capital. The hospitable local saying, "You must stay for tea," was very elastic and often stretched into weeks, for visitors helped break the tedium in that remote bastion of civilization. Casanova came and went, his passage duly noted—both in his *Memoirs* and by the arrival of various Cour progeny nine months later. And when the famous Italian adventurer Cagliostro arrived, he presented himself as an Egyptian Free Mason with magical powers and stayed at the Medems' Bachstrasse house because Anna's uncle was grand master of the local Masonic lodge.

The Medem men were agape at Cagliostro's cabalistic cabinets and transmutation furnaces, magnetized by his extravagant promises to turn dross into gold, and captivated by his wife, a witty young woman who was as accomplished a rogue as he. Perceptive teenage Anna-Dorothea pointed out that no countess could have the poor table manners the "Señora" had, and no true Spanish count would speak so atrocious a French as Cagliostro did. Equally suspicious, Frau von Medem took to sleeping with the key to the family strongbox underneath her pillow.

But Elisa proved more gullible. Anna-Dorothea's sister had recently lost the only child she would ever bear—the one bright spot in a dismal, brief marriage to crotchety Baron von der Recke, a miserly man, old enough to be her grandfather, and whom she subsequently divorced—and Cagliostro convinced her that out in the country at Alt-Aültz, where he hoped to lay his hands on some Medem gold, he would be able to put her in touch with the spirit of the departed infant. Elisa went, but the shades of the netherworld proved uncooperative.

The knave horrified both girls when he suggested that the frail Baroness von der Recke should continue on to Saint Petersburg with him as an acolyte—and alternate bed companion. Later, Elisa's written exposé of Cagliostro brought her name to prominence in literary circles for the first time and helped denounce him for the scoundrel he was; it also won her a pension from Catherine the Great, one of his more exalted victims, who declared "her hands itched to flog him."

When Grand Duke Peter met the eighteen-year-old Anna-Dorothea, her figure was well proportioned to her five feet. She had the delicate skin and ivory complexion so prized in northern women, and perfect teeth, a rarity in that day of no dentists. A fine mouth, a strong chin, soft green eyes, and an aquiline nose—slightly too long, like that of all the Medems—were framed by an oval face, set off by an abundant mass of heavy auburn hair. Craftily, Benigna encouraged Anna's participation in the plays and operas produced at the "Ducal Theater of Courland"—and nature took over.

Peter needed little encouragement. He fell in love with the wisp of a girl and hoped she would provide him with legitimate heirs. He already had three acknowledged illegitimate ones. Anna-Dorothea played the lead the night of the gala celebrating the dowager duchess's birthday, and the grand duke proposed later that same evening, when he managed to get his divine Anna off to himself in the *orangerie.*

Anna-Dorothea's feelings for the grand duke are not known. But brought up as she was to expect the typical marriage of convenience, she must have been well satisfied. After all, the grand duke offered her a crown, and he did not hold her hand over the coals of his pipe to test her obedience to him, as her grandfather had done to her grandmother before agreeing to be engaged. The stocky grand duke had inherited a modified version of his famous father's roughhewn good looks and cut an impressive figure that belied his fifty-five years. He loved to dance. Tsarina Anna had hired the famous Landé to come from Paris to teach the three Biron children—and her court—the minuet.

Anna apparently decided that the solicitude and affection the grand duke showed for his hunchbacked, pockmarked old mother more than offset his towering rages and his black moods when he went for days without speaking to anyone, and she could not help but be pleased to see her beloved father, Johann, elevated to the role of unofficial middleman between the throne and the opposition. The grand duke also sent a fast courier posting to Vienna to purchase for Johann the esteemed title of count of the Holy Roman Empire. Anna's stepmother was equally satisfied. Anxious to save the large Medem estate for her own two boys, she had brought up her stepdaughters to heed the dictum "An old husband makes a young widow," and successfully wedded off Elisa and now Anna-Dorothea to rich older men who took them without dowries.

Secrecy concerning the engagement of Peter and Anna was of the essence because of the equivocal status of the grand duke's divorce from his second grand duchess. Catherine II had pushed that match between Peter and one of her ladies-in-waiting because the tsarina shared the ancestral dream of absorbing Courland and getting a toe in the Baltic. She had ordered their wedding held in the Winter Palace and even attended it, a signal honor, so anxious was she to pursue her foreign policy strategy through Hymen. But Peter's second wife disgraced herself by drinking too much—she had to be carried home before the finish of the inaugural ceremonies of the new Academia Petrina in Mitau; another time, she smashed Benigna's prized Meissen on the floor in a drunken tantrum. Conceivably, Peter's moods and treatment of her may have been a contributing factor. Nevertheless, when she went to Saint Petersburg, after four years of marriage, for the baptism of Catherine's grandson and did not return, Peter divorced her. His action was not recognized either by the Greek Orthodox Church in which they had been married or by the formidable tsarina, who labeled Peter's mistreatment of her lady-in-waiting a personal insult.

Since there was no telling what the powerful Catherine II might do, were she alerted in time, Peter ordered elaborate security precautions and hurried his third marriage through with unseemly haste.

The Cour Court and officialdom were convoked on shockingly short notice with a sparsely worded communiqué that was tantamount to a summons. Carriages from the four corners of the duchy convened in the great courtyard of the ducal palace on the island in the River Aa in the late afternoon of a blustery, snowy, November day in 1779 to unload the cream of Courland society. They were mystified and asked one another indignantly, as they crowded up the huge oaken Staircase of Honor between the ducal guards posted two to a step, Why were they there?

They did not have long to wait. At 5:30 P.M., the grand chamberlain tapped the floor three times with his great cane of office and bawled out, "His Highness, the Grand Duke of Courland." There was a sudden hush. The Throne Room doors were flung wide and Grand Duke Peter appeared. Raising his hand for silence, he announced his imminent marriage. Anna-Dorothea joined him in the adjacent smaller salon. A court official performed the short service under the ducal canopy, a Lutheran minister said the blessing, and Anna signed the registry "Anna-Dorothea von Medem, the Grand Duchess of Courland" with a firm hand—and, no doubt, a sense of relief.

Anna-Dorothea had felt the tsarina breathing over her shoulder ever since she became engaged and half expected to see Catherine II stride in, an uninvited guest, to break up the proceedings. But with the ceremony a fait accompli, even the formidable Catherine could not dissolve Anna-Dorothea's marriage.

Dinner was served in a long gallery, underneath pictures hung there by the Tsarina Anna depicting Peter the Great's naval battles.

The meal went on interminably, for the Cours, like other Balts, were notorious trenchermen. Then, according to protocol, the young bride was undressed by the dowager duchess's ladies-in-waiting, the hautbois and trumpets sounded the traditional notes to announce that she was on her way, and the dowager duchess herself led Anna-Dorothea to the vast bridal chamber and Grand Duke Peter. They were tucked into the great canopied bed set high on a platform, and the court priests emerged from the shadows and stalked solemnly round, circling with the thurifiers swinging their fragrant, smoking censers, to dedicate the bed to the serious business of begetting young dukes. The hoary ritual of the public bedding down followed. After the last gawking courtier left, the court chamberlain signaled a page to extinguish the guttering candles and himself drew the silken bed hangings.

Anna-Dorothea knew what was expected of her, and a year and a half later, after several miscarriages, she lay back exhausted but triumphant while one of her smiling ladies nestled a tiny squawling bundle in her arms. Her daughter was healthy—and pretty. There was nothing of the beet-red, puckered look; instead, she had a delicate complexion, perfectly formed features, and silky blonde wisps of hair.

Although the Biron heir had not been expected before the following week, the midwife who was to deliver the baby and the wet nurse who was to suckle it were already installed nearby weeks before, at Peter's request. He did not want to take any chances. Throughout Anna's twelve hours of hard labor, he remained in the adjoining room, pacing to and fro, perspiring and fidgeting, like any expectant father. Thankful the infant had finally arrived, Peter was so impatient to see Anna-Dorothea that he pushed his way in against the protests of her mistress of the wardrobe, who begged him to give the maids time to tidy Anna-Dorothea up. Peter leaned over the bed and kissed her. Carefully Anna pulled back a corner of the lace-edged blanket—as if the baby were made of the most fragile porcelain—so Peter could take a peek at the girl. Her ladies-in-waiting clustered round, as anxious as Anna-Dorothea for the grand duke's verdict. Would he be disappointed—or displeased—that their firstborn was not a boy?

"She's a beauty! She really is!" he announced, beaming, and

with one finger tentatively touched an exquisite little hand. Then, a tiny foot.

"Never mind. The next one will be a prince," Anna-Dorothea reassured him, relieved he was so happy. "What will you call her?"

"You decide, my divine Anna. I can already see that she is going to resemble you." Peter's remark visibly startled Anna and was a good indication of his love for her. For the naming of his offspring was always the father's prerogative—and an important consideration when a reigning sovereign was involved.

Anna looked up to see if Peter was serious. He was standing alongside, holding her hand and stroking her head. Encouraged by his wide smile, she suggested, "Let's call her Catherine—to please the tsarina. And Wilhelmina, after dear Prince Friedrich-Wilhelm" (the Prussian crown prince, who was their good friend). Her quick response indicated that she had already given the matter considerable thought.

"This way, Your Excellency," said the mistress of the wardrobe, hovering at Peter's elbow, anxious to show him out. His mother, the Dowager Duchess Benigna, bustled in. Ignoring the parents, she peered myopically at her new grandchild, who was being hurried to its wet nurse. "Oh," she said in a disappointed voice. "It's a girl."

The lady-in-waiting looked at her. "A princess, Your Excellency," she corrected.

Peter concurred as he stood proudly at the head of the great ducal bed beside Anna-Dorothea, who was propped up amid a sea of pillows, when the entire body politic of Courland called the next day. The officials had come, hats tucked underneath their arms, dress sabers and decorations in place, to pay their respects and to inspect the infant who lay sound asleep in an elaborately carved crib, her white lace coverlet slashed by a red ribbon on which was pinned the glittering diamond cross of the Order of Courland.

Home for the ducal family was the palace on the River Aa, which also housed the administrative offices of the duchy and its law courts. "Can you imagine," the Prussian crown prince had written home from there in amazement, "it's thirty-two meters longer than ours in Berlin and has one hundred and eighty rooms."

Peter's father, Ernest Biron, had razed the original thirteenth-century Teutonic Knights' castle on this site and replaced it with the present one, which Tsarina Anna's chief architect, Rastrelli, designed for him down to the Italian frescoes on the wall. Because of Courland's close ties with French-oriented Warsaw, the Cour palace exuded a pronounced Parisian flavor. It was decorated in Saint Petersburg–Louis XVI style, with furnishings brought back from Russia by Grand Duke Ernest and Benigna, as well as with numerous wall hangings which had been embroidered by the dowager duchess during her years of exile with scenes of Siberian natives plying their crafts and trades. There were also pieces from the great German cabinetmakers, including several marquetry models from David Roëntgen, with secret compartments like those he was making for Marie-Antoinette; mirrors from Venice; and a number of chandeliers from Vienna and Hamburg.

The many bleak years of deprivation Ernest and Peter Biron had endured in harsh, bleak Siberia had left them with an unquenchable thirst for beauty. They were compulsive collectors, and scattered everywhere were Biron acquisitions: portraits, including several of the Birons' benefactress, Tsarina Anna, sculpture, mineral specimens, the finest Baltic amber carved into superb Renaissance cups and goblets, rare Limoges enamel ware, objets d'art from East and West. And assured a place of honor amid so much grandeur was a simple, nail-studded chest that had belonged to Anna-Dorothea's paternal grandmother. The single possession Anna could call her own, she had brought it along for a good-luck talisman.

Yet, with all this splendor, the rooms in the ducal private quarters had remarkably little comfort. ("Papa considered a room furnished if it had a table and twelve chairs," Wilhelmina was to comment, years later, when she was grown up.)

In rapid succession Anna-Dorothea produced two more girls, Paulina and Joanna. But the tsarina still refused to acknowledge her existence. Anxious to please his petite duchess, Peter successfully bribed Prince Potemkin, Catherine the Great's lover. And the tsarina curtly acceded.

Peter also moved his growing family out to spacious Würzau, one of his country estates which lay twelve versts beyond the capital's gates, far enough away, he hoped, to discourage some of the opposition's spies and informers. Determined to dispense with the formality of court life and assure a modicum of privacy for Anna and himself, Peter claimed that the white rococo dwelling did not have sufficient room for both his and the grand duchess's retinue of servants and reduced their number as much as he could.

Anna-Dorothea was determined to make a success as grand duchess. She liked the glamor attached to being a sovereign and found her new duties easier to learn than her former starring roles in the ducal theater—a diversion that was beneath her dignity now. She needed little practice to wave graciously at her loyal subjects when she rode through the streets of the minuscule capital, or to nod pleasantly at the Cour guards as they snapped to attention, presenting arms, every time the drums rolled and her carriage swept in or out of the River Aa palace courtyard on her occasional visits there.

The high-spirited young woman was depressed by the long faces and sour expressions of the bored, dour courtiers. Determined to revitalize the somber court, she persuaded Peter to break with precedent and open wide their doors—in Mitau as well as at Würzau—to the more eminent of the many travelers passing through en route to Saint Petersburg. To please her, Peter did not frown when the grand duchess, following the precepts learned from her avant-garde stepmother, included artists and writers. Nor were they the only newcomers Peter saw.

Anna was soon bored by officiating at social functions, opening still another hospital or school. She was ambitious and intelligent. She knew how her father longed for an end to the discord between the crown and the Cour lords, and how he had hoped that the union of the ignoble Biron dynasty with the illustrious Medems might achieve this. To mend Peter's political fences appealed to Anna-Dorothea, and through her untiring efforts, an increasing number of Cour aristocrats crossed the ducal threshold, not to mention any number of Medem relatives who had never set foot inside there since her father-in-law, Grand Duke Ernest, came to power. But the political détente which Anna-Dorothea worked hard to accomplish was of relatively short duration.

The ministers objected to the grand duke's continued living at Würzau. They complained of his inaccessibility there, increasingly evaded his orders, and frequently neglected to advise him of their actions. Technically, Peter had to approve each privy council decision but, as his power eroded, they managed to circumvent him.

The Diet was in an uproar over a new flour tax which was causing the millers to riot, and Peter had another particularly bitter session with his court advisers and cabinet the morning of Wilhelmina's third birthday. However, nothing was allowed to interfere with the scheduled celebrations in honor of the heir to the throne. There were fireworks, a parade, and street dancing, in spite of the February cold, and in the evening, Peter led Wilhelmina in the opening polonaise at the court ball in the dainty blonde princess's honor.

Anna-Dorothea highly disapproved. As she matured and grew surer of herself—and of her hold on Peter—she was speaking out more frequently if she felt strongly about something. But since Peter gave her no say in the upbringing of the three little girls, she held her tongue until they were alone. The minute Peter saw the set look on her face, he recognized the signs: Anna wanted to talk. But he was tired and ready for bed.

Anna-Dorothea had her speech all prepared. "Wilhelmina belongs in the nursery with her governess and sisters at this hour, even if it is her birthday. You shouldn't have kept her up so late. It's not good for a child of her age."

Ignoring the edge in her voice—he'd been arguing most of the day with recalcitrant officials and was not about to start with his wife—Peter replied sharply, "Wilhelmina might as well get used to irregular hours.

"Pray tell me why."

"I've decided we're going abroad. Nothing is going smoothly. If it's not the nobles, it's the cabinet. Or the Diet. Or the prime minister. I'm surrounded by enemies." Peter sounded petulant. "It's time to be off. I've seen little of the world and you have never left Courland. Your father can act on my behalf with the government while we're away. Perhaps my absence will cool tempers here at home." He put his arm around her and added, "What could be more enjoyable than to show off my beautiful young wife?"

"I don't see what going away has to do with Wilhelmina." Anna-Dorothea stuck to her point.

"I intend to take Wilhelmina with us."

"She's only three!" Anna-Dorothea was shocked. "That's madness!"

"I can't bear to be separated from her. My mind is made up. Don't get so upset."

Nevertheless, Anna-Dorothea must have been upset. For once Peter had made up his mind to take Wilhelmina, nothing she could do or say would change it, any more than she could change the direction in which he intended to travel. The obvious place to go was east—to visit Courland's powerful neighbor and obtain Russian goodwill and support for his ongoing domestic struggle. Peter's stubborn decision to go west indicated how little Courland already meant to him.

Few people went very far in those days, especially on pleasure. Travel was too difficult and uncomfortable. Preparations were of necessity extensive, and as there was no deadline for their return, clothes of every conceivable description and for every climate were packed, from furs to sheer muslins; from brocade court gowns and uniforms to weatherproof hunting and riding clothes. Household goods went along, elaborate kitchen equipment, spice boxes, wine barrels, table settings, and that most important household necessity—a close stool. A doctor and complete apothecary store were a must, especially since Wilhelmina was accompanying them. Also crates and suitcases, a portable desk with ink, quills and other writing necessities, Anna-Dorothea's traveling dressing table, crammed with gold-lidded jars, bottles, and brushes, the paraphernalia—like rice powder and scented rouge—necessary to maintain her reputation for being à la mode. There were boxes of books and maps to help pass the long hours on the road.

At last they set off on the trip that was to mark Anna-Dorothea's debut on the Central European scene—and result in profound changes in her life. A fleet courier preceded them to make the necessary arrangements in advance. Then came Anna and Peter in their comfortable travel coach, its interior lacquered a dull gold and elaborately decorated with mythological figures of Pallas Athena, Europa and the bull, and others, each encased in scrolls and curlicues. The reclining seats were upholstered in red velvet, the driver's box was decorated with red hangings to match, and everything, including each horse's saddle blanket, was embroidered with the Biron coat of arms. They were followed by Wilhelmina in her own berlin with the lady-in-waiting assigned to her; next, the two ducal households, the gentlemen and demoiselles of honor, with Anna's two poodles, the chefs and their assistants, assorted staff, and servants—a sum total of eleven carriages with fifty-four horses to transport them. Insecure at heart, Peter did not intend to forgo a single appurtenance of his rank. He had no intention of letting foreigners forget he was a sovereign—and far richer than the rulers of all the small German states put together.

The pace was slow, but they were in no hurry. It was obligatory to stop in friendly courts, and the various estates and castles along the way welcomed the Courlanders, for distinguished visitors were few and far between. Skirting the Baltic with its wide stretches of gray sand, they proceeded by way of Königsberg, where Anna-Dorothea had family, and eventually reached Berlin. Because the old Prussian king was ailing, he delegated his nephew—the grand duke's friend, Crown Prince Friedrich-Wilhelm—to do the honors of his capital. When the crown prince took the visitors to tea at Sans Souci, His Majesty, Frederick the Great, a tiny man for so great a soldier, with a wrinkled parchment face touched up with rouge in the French mode, asked Peter if he needed a watchman who could be relied on never to fall asleep. "If so, I'm your man," he confessed ruefully. The septuagenarian king passed many a sleepless night, sitting bolt upright in a chair because he suffered great pain whenever he lay down.

Frederick the Great was the first in an impressive array of European sovereigns to succumb to the petite Anna-Dorothea's charm. She fussed over him, and although his health did not improve throughout their stay, the ducal pair were invited back frequently, and an aide-de-camp arrived daily at Friedrichsfeld, the royal palace they were renting outside the city gates, with baskets of the finest fruits and flowers from the king's greenhouses.

At the sovereign's insistence, Anna-Dorothea and Peter postponed their departure in order to attend the army's great annual parade at Templehof. Astride mounts from the royal stables—Anna was a superb horsewoman, even for a native of Courland, where everyone rode—they were included in the party which followed the king's open barouche; His Majesty was still too lame with gout to sit a horse. According to custom, Peter, as guest of honor, appeared in a Prussian officer's uniform. Anna-Dorothea did the same in her personal adaptation of the Leibhüssaren Regiment's picturesque outfit, though women did not usually. Her dolman with gold cords, tassels, and buttons, and narrow standing collar of embroidered blue was worn above a chamois skirt. Draped over one shoulder was the Leibhüssarens' traditional panther skin, lined in red and trimmed in sable and attached with four gold hearts on chains over her breast, and her heavy auburn hair had been restyled to accommodate the tall sable hat with red trim and gold chin strap. She created a sensation.

The Courland trio then headed south. They were received everywhere as traveling potentates. Peter played his role to the hilt and gave the lavish gifts expected of him—magnificent snuffboxes to the officials of Venice, Florence, and other cities on their itinerary, and gold watches to the individual members of the various municipal and state honor guards lined up at attention before their doors.

The farther away the grand duke got from Courland, the fewer letters of instruction he sent to the Cour Council and the less he thought about the duchy. Not so Anna-Dorothea. As fascinated as she was with the changing countryside and the different customs and costumes, she never once forgot Peter's problems at home, and pestered her father, old Count Johann, for reports. Determined to impress upon the recalcitrant nobles that their absent grand duke had Courland's interests close at heart, even in far-off Italy, Anna-Dorothea persuaded Peter to establish a scholarship for young Cour artists in Bologna, to be administered by the local Academia Clementina, and wrote her father to see that this was well publicized in Mitau.

She was also concerned about the children she had left at home. She started a diary for Paulina and Joanna, a combination history and geography book, which she sent home to Würzau at regular intervals to be read aloud to her two younger girls by her sister Elisa. This concern, too, was unusual. Long separations were common in princely families, and women in Anna-Dorothea's position rarely spent time with their children from the time they were born until they were of marriageable age.

As was obligatory for any great patron of the arts, the grand duke commissioned the painter of the moment, Angelika Kauffman, to do a double full-length portrait of his wife and daughter while they were in Rome. Then, like other fashionable tourists, they wintered in Naples. Neither Peter nor Anna could stand Ferdinand I, the fat, lazy Bourbon astride the Neapolitan throne, but Peter enjoyed his queen, Maria-Carolina, Marie-Antoinette's sister, though Anna termed Her Majesty dull. She preferred more stimulating company and spent her time with the British ambassador Sir William Hamilton and his fascinating mistress, whom he was shortly to marry and who later became Admiral Nelson's beloved Emma. With Hamilton, an amateur archaeologist and collector, as guide, Anna visited the excavations under way at nearby Pompeii. Like other adventuresome travelers of the day, she, Peter, and young Wilhelmina also ascended Mount Vesuvius, each strapped atop a small, nimble-footed donkey.

The days succeeded each other in leisurely fashion, and spring found the trio still dallying in southern Italy.

Peter had inherited his father's business sense if not his political acumen, and believed in diversified holdings to guard against the future. Continental financiers were making heavy investments in the Low Countries between Utrecht and Amsterdam, so Peter followed suit. Since he was anxious to inspect these extensive additions to his portfolio, in April he ordered the ducal horses harnessed once more.

As they sped toward Leyden and Delft, stories about the old grand duke, rich as Croesus, and his divine Anna, who had so charmed the Prussian and Neapolitan courts, preceded them. Three dashing German counts were determined to inspect close up this beautiful Slav, whose image smiled out at them from the most expensive storefronts—hand-painted on a limited edition dessert service. They bribed some of the staff in an inn near Hanover, where the famous travelers were due to stop, to exchange places with them. When the great berlin clattered up, the trio, clad in extravagant livery, dripping gold and silver braid, ribbon and lace, hurried to let down the steps, getting in one another's way in their haste. Anna-Dorothea had an eye for handsome young men and noticed them at once. She nudged Peter. "Have you ever seen better-looking lackeys?"

"What? No. Frankly, I hadn't noticed them." Peter peered over absentmindedly. In his mind he was hundreds of miles to the west, reviewing details of the new properties he was en route to visit.

The fashionable gallants served the evening meal in the ducal chambers with such panache that they again caught Anna-Dorothea's attention. "Peter! Those footmen! I do wish you'd look at them. They are so well trained and they have elegant manners. Do you think we might prevail on them to join our services?"

"If you wish, my dear. If you wish." Peter acquiesced indulgently, his head already nodding. He had finished a delicious fricassee of the local wild fowl, washed down with fine Rhine wine, and his hands were contentedly folded over his bulging stomach.

Next morning, the imposters continued their good offices, frothing Anna's hot chocolate with a great flourish before letting it cascade from a silver *chocolatière*, held exaggeratedly high, into a wafer-thin, blue and white Meissen cup. By the time the ducal pair were ready to depart, Anna-Dorothea's suspicions were aroused. "I don't know what they're up to, but let's not spoil their game," she whispered good-naturedly and made sure that Peter gave them a generous tip.

And another spicy chapter was added to the rapidly growing legend of the ravishing grand duchess from the frozen Baltic shores.

When the ducal pair finally returned to Berlin, and Peter insisted on buying Friedrichsfeld, rather than renting it again, his complete loss of interest in Courland was manifest. But Anna's suspicions were not aroused because Peter was always buying real estate, and in short order he purchased the domains of Wartenburg in Silesia, Holstein in Kreis Spröttau, and the duchy of Sagan from the heirs of the duke of Lobkowitz.

The wagonloads of statuary and objets d'art Peter had commissioned or collected in Italy were arriving, one after another, week after week, and he enjoyed arranging and cataloguing them. He also discovered a small talent for drawing and designed the "Décor Courland" for a sixty-piece dinner service he had ordered from the royal porcelain factory in adjacent Potsdam—with a gold mosaic trim and a monogram made up of tiny polychrome flowers in the new neo-classic style. In the evenings, royal balls, theatricals, concerts, and sleigh rides succeeded one another in dizzying succession, for Peter and Anna-Dorothea were the stars of the Berlin season. Peter was now the largest landowner in Prussia, and even a sovereign never knew when the need might arise to borrow ready cash from him.

Berlin was far enough away that the vociferous squabbling in Mitau, which had been increasing in volume, was only an echo, and a faint one at that, in Peter's ears. Not in Anna-Dorothea's.

As long as old Count Johann remained on the scene, Anna was not unduly concerned. But her father died, and with his passing, the grand duke lost his principal ally at home. The prime minister and the council proceeded as if the grand duke no longer existed. His correspondence, when he did write, was rarely read, and whatever he ordered was executed half-heartedly at best or not at all. Originally, the Diet found Peter hard to get along with and was happy to have him abroad. Now, with the contrariness of human nature, the same deputies talked indignantly about their absent duke and his neglect in fulfilling his functions.

No one except Anna-Dorothea's sister, Elisa, the Baroness von der Recke, had the courage to send an honest appraisal of the gloomy picture and the grand duke's true position. She urged them to come home. But every time Anna-Dorothea brought up the subject, Peter refused to listen and stalked sulkily away. Courland! That was all Anna talked about. If he wasn't worried, why should Anna be? Whose throne was it, anyway? Besides, in Berlin he was treated with the respect his position demanded. This was no longer true in Mitau, and he had no intention of returning. The thought that Anna-Dorothea concurred with Elisa's point of view outraged Peter and strained their personal relationship, transforming it. Sharp-eyed observers saw increasing signs of this change.

As the pressures built up for Peter to go back and tend his home fires, he turned introvert and spent days in moody silence, tapping ceaselessly on the windowpanes and drumming on tables and other furniture. He no longer took pleasure in Anna-Dorothea's continued success at court, and after one of Their Royal Highnesses' Thursday musicals, there was an embarrassing public scene.

The last strains of Handel were still reverberating and the musicians were filing out. Anna-Dorothea prepared to do likewise, gracefully kicking back her long train and adjusting the folds of her pale pink, flowered silk gown. The color did justice to her green eyes and the magnificent, fiery opal dog collar she was wearing—a gift from a grateful Tsarina Anna to her late mother-in-law for nursing the tsarina's pet rabbit through a serious illness. The crown prince spied her as she wandered into an adjacent salon where lotto was in progress. He beckoned her to his side and handed her a small ivory dish containing markers for the game.

Anna had filled her first card and was starting a second when she noticed Peter approaching with a black scowl. Peter enjoyed music, and he had been looking forward to the evening. But he had not cared for either the visiting soprano or her program. This disappointment, on top of the arrival of a special courier that afternoon with two more pleading letters from Elisa, had put him in a foul mood.

"I want to leave," he growled in her ear.

"Now?" Anna-Dorothea was astonished.

"Yes."

Anna-Dorothea smiled—sweetly, it was noted—and without a murmur, excused herself. The Prussian royal family observed them critically and admired Anna's forbearance—and her obedience. A buzz of indignation at the shocking ducal conduct filled the room, but Anna-Dorothea, head held high, managed to restrain herself until they were in their carriage. As the horses trotted out into the silent, white-coated streets where a few stragglers hastened along, bundled to the ears against the biting north wind, she turned angrily to Peter. "What a breach of etiquette! Leaving before the royal family does! And whispering! In Cour—and at court! There's no excuse for such rude manners."

"I didn't care to have your admirer, the crown prince, understand what I was saying," Peter replied peevishly.

"His Royal Highness was concerned about my comfort, so he asked me to sit with him." (Anna was again pregnant.) "Do you begrudge me that attention?"

"I trust you enjoyed your conversation."

His tone pulled Anna-Dorothea up short. She had long since taken Peter's measure—and knew his moods. He was jealous of fat, balding Friedrich-Wilhelm!

When the Cour cabinet learned that the grand duchess was again with child, the prime minister surprised Anna-Dorothea by writing to her, not Peter, to respectfully recommend that if the grand duke's health did not permit him to travel—an obvious face-saving excuse—she should return without him. It was imperative for the continuance of the Biron dynasty that the expected baby, especially if it should prove to be a boy, be born at home. Anna-Dorothea took her obligations as grand duchess seriously, and this letter galvanized her into action. They must return to Mitau immediately.

Peter disagreed. He had had his fill of Courland's troubles. Most of those causing problems were either Anna's relatives or friends of her family. He had great confidence in her ability. She should go and see what she could do.

Unlike the majority of his contemporaries, Peter had good reason not to underestimate the power of women. It had been his aunt who had maneuvered his father into his first job at Mitau's court. That was how Tsarina Anna and Ernest Biron had met. And had it not been for his sister Hedwige, all the Birons, Peter included, might still be in Siberia. With the help of the local official's wife, Hedwige had wangled a reprieve for herself and returned to Saint Petersburg. Hedwige's fondness for speaking German—she was almost the only one at the Imperial Court who could—made her a favorite of the tsarina's German-born nephew, who loved to play the three-handed card game tredille with her. This young man was the same grand duke of Holstein to whom Hedwige had been engaged, sight unseen, the night of the coup d'état that signaled the Biron family's fall from power. Once he had succeeded to the Romanoff throne as Peter III, Hedwige prevailed upon him to recall the rest of the Birons to civilization.

Anna-Dorothea liked challenges and accepted them all her life. Before Courland's problems had come between them, Peter had always been anxious to please her; so, no doubt, she expected him to follow her shortly, and was sure she could shore up the precarious political situation until he did.

But it was one thing for Peter, the reigning grand duke, to remain behind in Berlin while Anna-Dorothea undertook to act as his substitute. It was another for any woman, let alone a seven-month-pregnant one, to set forth on the hazardous trip east in the dead of winter. During the long, dreary hours of travel, she reflected more than once on the strange reversal of their roles. As she had written Elisa, she could "not condone Peter's neglect of Courland" and the abdication of his duties. But she was surprisingly sympathetic, for she knew how haunted he was by his father's meteoric rise and fall, and by the traumatic experiences of his own adolescence.

Anna-Dorothea had grown up on stories of Peter's fairy-tale youth. A Medem uncle had been present in Tsarina Anna's crowded apartments when Peter and his brother pretended to be Cossacks herding their savage ponies. Roaming amid the swarm of cripples, dwarfs, elaborately dressed blackamoors, dogs, and hundreds of birdcages, the rambunctious pair bore down on dignified Prince Nariatinski, the elderly commander in chief of the imperial army, and snatched off his wig with one of their long-handled whips. When that worthy complained, Grand Duke Ernest rejoined, "If you are displeased, don't come to court any more. Resign. Your resignation will be accepted." Another Medem cousin recalled, more than once within Anna-Dorothea's hearing, the time Peter, age eleven and already a colonel of a regiment of cuirassiers, used troops of the imperial guard to direct a mock battle, with the entire diplomatic corps ordered to appear as a captive audience. Then, at sixteen, his world topsy-turvy, Peter was shunted off to Siberia to live huddled over a stove that was forever going out, in a log cabin with very little light because the entire family was allotted a single candle per day and every chink was stuffed to retain what little warmth there was. With that history, Anna could easily understand why Peter acted the way he did.

The warmth of the greeting awaiting Anna-Dorothea in Courland more than compensated for her arduous but uneventful trip. A Cour honor guard was at the frontier to accompany her the rest of the way home, and the tiny capital was illuminated in her honor. Still, Anna's situation was not an easy one. A sovereign might temporarily abdicate his duties—as Peter had done—but for Anna-Dorothea to step in as other than a figurehead and take charge as he wished her to do was extraordinary. The grand duchess's position was further complicated because it was imperative that no native learn of Peter's genuine lack of interest in his throne.

Anna-Dorothea held an informal reception every Sunday and made it a point to invite different groups of deputies out to Würzau each time. She finessed an official celebration of her own birthday in February and, twelve days later, ordered a military review to fête the absent grand duke's, at which she made her only public appearance. When a minor crisis threatened—the rising bourgeoisie was demanding prerogatives of its own—Anna-Dorothea took a firm stance, and because she did not waver, as Peter was in the habit of doing, the opposing nobles for once coalesced and supported her. By her skillful, tactful handling of the prickly issue,

Anna carried the day—and also converted a number of Peter's enemies.

Peter had still not arrived when their baby was born and thereby missed a made-to-order opportunity to rally the entire duchy to his side in the bipartisan rejoicing at the birth of the long-hoped-for boy. Eight weeks later, with only her sister, Elisa, sitting facing her in the great ducal coach-and-six, Anna-Dorothea led the procession into Mitau's cathedral for little Duke Peter's baptism. The star of the show, a bundle of lace and blue ribbons sound asleep in the arms of a lady-in-waiting, followed—in his own private carriage, as befit his importance in the day's ceremony.

That evening, Baron Howen, the prime minister, respectfully requested a private audience. Anna-Dorothea had taken an instant dislike to the hunched-over little man with the squinty eyes and small pursed mouth the day they met some years before, and had warned Peter against him. It was Baron Howen who had addressed to Anna personally the alarming dispatch that sent her scurrying home from Berlin. The baron's between-the-lines insinuations revived Anna's initial revulsion, and since her return, she had repeatedly refused to meet alone with him. But now she had felt forced to grant the audience. She still distrusted him and noted again, as he bent over to kiss her hand, his thin, pinched lips from which only carefully predigested words escaped. The dignitary wasted no time on preliminaries. Ambitious men were seeking to profit from the anomalous situation that existed in Courland because of the grand duke's prolonged absence. To spare the grand duke the trying domestic problems he obviously no longer cared to be bothered with, would it not be a kindness to persuade him to abdicate in his son's favor? It was only fitting that the grand duchess should place herself at the head of affairs. If she were willing to serve as regent until the infant crown prince was of age, he, the prime minister, would gladly act as her privy councillor. She could leave her worries—and authority as regent—in his hands and spend her time abroad with the grand duke. The prime minister assured her a carefree future, for he was in a position to guarantee no further opposition.

Anna-Dorothea suppressed her anger at his shocking proposal and, to play for time, promised to give it due consideration. The prime minister's carriage was not out the drive before she was writing Peter indignantly. He must come home immediately. The duchy was at stake.

Peter came—and in surly fashion promptly put the wrong foot forward. Instead of cultivating the small amount of goodwill Anna had established, he managed to kill it off in record time. Peter had a violent temper tantrum the day the prime minister came out from Mitau to request permission to convoke an extra cabinet meeting. Anna-Dorothea, who was present, observed the feathers on the hat tucked underneath the baron's arm twitching as if alive by the time the grand duke finished his tongue-lashing. But Howen persisted and left with Peter's reluctant authorization. Needless to say, this performance hardly improved the grand duke's rapport with his ministers—or with Anna, who was understandably bitter.

Her personal relations with Peter had already started deteriorating in Berlin. They had not been improved by his belated, grudging return home, moodier than ever, or by the heedless manner in which he quickly dissipated her few hard-won political gains. Nonetheless, Peter had certain marital rights—and Anna, a duty—and twin girls arrived within the year.

Anna-Dorothea had a difficult time and was still too ill to tell the babies apart before both sickened and died. Shortly afterwards, her son, Peter, caught the same fever. Weak though she was, Anna insisted on maintaining a bedside vigil and watched the frail child slowly waste away. The grand duke sent his fastest couriers to Prague and Warsaw for specialists. But there was nothing anyone could do. The demise of the sole male heir further undermined Peter's shaky position.

To add to Peter's problems, Catherine II's consuming desire to take over Courland's Baltic ports was clouding the domestic picture. An expert fisherwoman in muddy waters, Catherine was roiling the situation to suit her imperial pleasure and undermine Peter's shaky regime. Only recently Peter had confirmed reports that some of the most obstreperous Cour deputies had been receiving substantial bribes—large estates with hundreds of serfs—from the single-minded tsarina.

Anna-Dorothea had a hard time recovering her strength. Another infant, Charlotte, was born and soon followed the little prince to a premature grave. Months dragged by, and she remained so depressed by the death of these four children and the bleak political picture that the ducal physicians, fearful her health might be permanently impaired, recommended a diversion and suggested she take the cure at Karlsbad.

Peter urged her to go and proposed she stop on the way back in Warsaw. For some time he had been weighing an appeal to King Stanislaus-Augustus for help in putting the troublemaking nobles in their place. And this seemed like the perfect opportunity. Though Courland's distance from Warsaw had, for generations, enabled her grand dukes to maintain practical autonomy, the duchy was nominally a fief of the Polish kingdom, and the Cour nobles were honor bound to abide by any decision handed them by the duchy's liege lord, the Polish king. According to the Polish constitution, His Majesty could not himself decide the Courland matter but must ask the Grand Sejm (the Polish quadrennial parliament) to sit in judgment.

With family pride and honor at stake, every effort must be made to get a favorable verdict from that body. And Anna-Dorothea could do so, Peter was convinced, by becoming the toast of Warsaw—as she had in Berlin—and winning the deputies' votes.

While recourse to Poland was the constructive kind of action Anna had been hoping Peter would take, she was dumbfounded to learn that he had no intention of accompanying her. Peter's motives for remaining behind in Mitau—a place he had never wanted to see again, let alone return to—are lost in the swirls of time. All that is certain is that Anna-Dorothea agreed to go without him.

Peter had unwittingly set Anna-Dorothea on the path to freedom when he permitted her to come home without him from Berlin to mollify the ducal council. When he again sent his beautiful twenty-nine-year-old wife off alone to once more fight his battles for him, he gave her the key to the gate. Peter was relinquishing whatever remained of his responsibilities and rights as a husband, and both Anna-Dorothea and he must have known it.

They had arrived at a turning point in their lives.

CHAPTER TWO

The Grand Duchess & Count Batowski
1790-1799

TO ENSURE THAT SHE GOT HER PROPER due as a grand duchess though she was traveling without him, Peter sent off Anna-Dorothea and her sister, Elisa, with the suite of a sovereign, a seemingly endless column of carriages that stretched out behind hers.

April had borrowed a few hours from June, the scent carried on the light breeze was the smell of spring, and the trip west was a pleasant one.

Karlsbad's cure lived up to its reputation. Sipping the mineral waters, which tasted and smelled like rotten eggs, and taking hot baths, suitably covered from head to toe, Anna was soon feeling like her vivacious self. And she was quickly bored. For the aristocracy that congregated at this mecca of the Holy Roman Empire's elite formed a closed society, and Anna-Dorothea found few within its narrow circle to interest her.

Nevertheless, there was a change in Anna—as her sister discovered. Pale, sentimental Elisa, with her perpetually watery eyes and dripping nose—the baroness was allergic as well as asthmatic —may have found Count Karl Kessler, the Prussian ambassador to Saxony, first, but Anna-Dorothea preempted her sister's "soulfriend." The grand duchess enjoyed flirting with the diplomat, and Elisa was properly put out the day she found Anna trying to do justice to a Haydn sonata on the harpsichord with one hand while the ambassador held the other.

The sisters pressed on by way of Weimar, the German Athens, where Anna-Dorothea made another conquest of a different nature. The famous writer Wieland was charmed with the bright, clever young woman, and intimates of the Olympian Goethe reported, "The Grand Duchess is like a fresh breeze blowing through the old man's house. We have not heard him laugh like that in a long time."

Poland's serious economic plight was everywhere in evidence as the sharp-eyed sisters bounced over that country's pitted, poorly maintained roads. In more than one inn along the way, Anna-Dorothea, who knew about farm life from her early years at her grandmother's, was amazed to find that kernels of edible grain had been wasted in the dirty straw over which their own clean mattresses were laid, while the ashen, pinched-faced peasants they passed were clearly starving. She could never get used to the sight, everywhere they went in Poland, of scabby, maimed beggars, both young and old, scrambling like maggots over refuse and fighting one another for the few edible morsels they might salvage. They were even a fixture at the piles of garbage that forever littered the courtyard of Warsaw's Pod Blacha Palace, which formed part of the capital's fortifications and which King Stanislaus-Augustus placed at his distinguished visitor's disposal for the duration of her visit.

Women who dabbled in politics or served as their husband's emissaries were rare, especially beautiful ones, and Anna-Dorothea's debut at the Zamek, the Polish sovereign's palace, was awaited with enthusiasm by the entire Polish court. Because frail Elisa was still suffering from their second spill onto the turnpike in a week—carriage mishaps were occupational hazards for contemporary travelers—Anna appeared alone. Draped around her shoulders was a luxurious stole of snowy ermine, a fur so rare that it was reserved exclusively for royalty, which the monarch had sent to her suite as a welcoming gift.

At her approach, both doors of the great ballroom at the head of the Staircase of Honor were flung wide as befitting a reigning grand duchess—only one door was opened for lesser mortals—and Anna-Dorothea entered a vast gathering, which was multiplied by countless mirrors into an endless crowd. Mournful-eyed King Stanislaus, clad in a diamond-buttoned, oyster-colored, velvet frock-coat with red-heeled shoes à la Louis XIV, hastened forward, his once stately figure stooped with rheumatism. Since he gallantly chose to greet her as a fellow sovereign—a special distinction which boded well for the success of her mission—Anna-Dorothea, instead of dropping in the customary curtsey, held out her hand for His Majesty to kiss.

Anna was nervous for she was on her own in a foreign capital, at a strange court, with a thousand unknown eyes focusing on her. She was trembling so much that a pink bud broke off from her bouquet and fell to the parquet floor. The flower was immediately retrieved by a young officer who emerged like magic from behind the august presence of the king and chivalrously tendered it to Anna-Dorothea on bended knee.

"Everyone is saying you are as beautiful as this rose. But I claim that this rose is only beautiful because it resembles you."

"Bravo! Well said, my nephew!" King Stanislaus chuckled, his eyes twinkling with amusement. It had been a long time since His Majesty had been treated to the charming spectacle of a blushing woman. The sovereign took a pinch of snuff, and before snapping shut the huge gold box on which there was a diamond-encrusted miniature of a Titian, he turned and offered some to the elderly court poet at his elbow. "You're too somber, my poor fellow. Do you fear you have a rival?"

"Oh! Your Majesty, why be so astonished if the Courland Venus has created a new poet. She has so overwhelmed me that I, an old poet, can no longer rhyme."

They were interrupted by the musicians in a small balcony in the far corner who had finished tuning their instruments and burst into a lively tempo. "Would Your Excellency care to dance with me?" Prince Poniatowski, the king's nephew, clicked his heels and bowed low before Anna-Dorothea.

"With pleasure!" Anna loved to dance.

"Be careful, Madame. No one dances a more abandoned version of the mazurka than my nephew," the king warned, as the prince swept her off in his arms.

The courtiers quickly cleared a space to watch. "Faster! Faster!" some shouted, clapping hands in time to the turbulent rhythm. "More! More!" other guests chorused, jumping on top of the chairs for a better view of the famous visitor. For a brief few minutes Anna-Dorothea was no longer a grand duchess who had come to Warsaw to prop up her aging husband's tottering throne, but a pretty, spirited woman thoroughly enjoying herself, whirling and twirling in the arms of a handsome, white-uniformed stranger. The frenzied music urged Anna and her partner on. Repeatedly he pulled her to him with a snap, then deftly released her, and she went spinning around him. The music stopped as suddenly as it began. Anna-Dorothea tried to catch her breath; the prince, too, was breathing heavily, and pulled a large lace handkerchief from his cuff to mop his dripping brow.

The light-hearted, dance-mad Polish court was a far cry from the barrackslike atmosphere of its Prussian counterpart, where lotto ruled. And the palace, with its Vincennes and Sèvres porcelains, its walls hung in Lyons silk, its Parisian furniture and art, was a precious jewel in a French setting. This was not surprising since Poland had had close ties with France ever since Catherine de Medici's son, Prince Henri of Orléans, was elected the Polish king over two centuries before.

Anna-Dorothea and Elisa were so fêted that the British ambassador complained that his feet ached from "too many *entrechats* and mazurkas," and requested a leave of absence. When the weather wrapped Warsaw in the scented sachet of summer, there were also visits to the rhinoceros and leopards at the king's sister's private zoo, and many a delightful afternoon was passed with the king and his morganatic wife, Countess Grabowska, at Lazienski, a tiny museum of a house tucked in the suburbs. Here the sovereign, who had spent a long time in Paris and who was famed as a linguist, liked to read aloud selections from *Candide*.

The varied extravaganzas in Anna's honor momentarily masked the incubating ills that would soon cause the country's demise. Poland, like Courland, was caught in a dangerous crossfire between interference by foreign powers and cabals of the local aristocracy, and, unlike the tiny duchy, it was also cursed with a hybrid government, neither a monarchy nor a republic. An enormous gulf existed between the poor and the rich. Some twenty families possessed twenty million Poles—as serfs—and a small but significant sector of that ruling class already had its eyes opened to the shoals ahead.

Present Russian-Prussian involvement in a war with Turkey offered the enlightened handful a unique opportunity—unmolested by troublemakers from abroad—to set the Polish house in order by pushing through needed parliamentary changes. The past two years had already been wasted in sterile discussions of a revised constitution in the Grand Sejm, but the republican ferment in the west, symbolized by the fall of the Bastille in Paris the previous July, 1789, fired the liberals anew. Their proposed modifications were absorbing a generous share of the conversation wherever Anna-Dorothea went, conversations sandwiched in between discussions of philosophy and the arts, between whist and dancing—or, maybe, betting on an exotic race between a one-legged Bashkir and a large tortoise.

Anna-Dorothea worked hard, winning friends and cajoling people in Peter's behalf, but the Sejm that had to sit in judgment on the ducal case remained bogged down in debate over the revised constitution. Months passed. The seasons were no longer delicately poised between autumn and winter. Towering black clouds brought more than one all-night blow out of the north, presaging the snow to come, but the end was nowhere in sight.

With only the groundwork laid, Anna and Elisa would have to be in Warsaw for the Sejm's next session, when the deputies were scheduled to finish their constitutional travail. Meanwhile, it was time for them to return east.

Peter was happy to have Anna home and pleased with her efforts, although he was more ill-tempered than ever. But Mitau that winter seemed provincial—and hostile—to Anna-Dorothea. Family and friends were turning against her because of her active role in the grand duke's unpopular fight over their ill-gotten prerogatives.

So when in the spring Warsaw beckoned, Anna looked forward to the prospect. She had a mission and a stellar role in a gay capital with a king who treated her as his petted darling. If the grand duchess, earlier, had enjoyed dabbling in politics on the local level, how much more stimulating it was to try her hand at molding affairs and influencing people at Stanislaus-Augustus's glittering court.

When she set forth again, one of the baggage wagons was stacked to overflowing with finely tooled muskets in individual cases to be presented to each lawmaker as a small token of the grand duke's esteem. For Peter had discovered that the opposition nobles had recently sent a powerful delegation to Poland to lobby on their behalf, and he did not want to leave anything to chance.

Contrary to expectations, the sisters' second visit was no better timed than the first. While Anna-Dorothea waited for the Courland affair to be brought onto the Sejm floor, she found herself adopting the habits and manners of the congenial, relaxed Polish court. The line of her admirers lengthened until a whole row of Warsaw's finest stood silently behind her chair wherever she happened to be. They competed eagerly for the favor of fetching the petite grand duchess a cup of tea or perhaps her shawl, or picking up her fan when she dropped it; great was the joy of the lucky man singled out to retrieve a forgotten, cobweb-sheer handkerchief, or to be honored with a special smile.

As Anna-Dorothea continued her impressive lobbying efforts, her suite in the Pod Blacha was so filled with prominent people that it was transformed into unofficial headquarters for the "Patriotic Party." King Stanislaus-Augustus, with Kiopeck, his favorite dog, and Abbé Scipio Piattoli, his confidential secretary, were in constant attendance. The laicized Florentine, a mite of a man whom the king introduced as "My dearest friend. He's a walking encyclopedia," had a principal role in drafting the proposed constitutional changes. The abbé enjoyed conversing with the intelligent, well-read Medem sisters.

The constitution was finally maneuvered through on May 3, 1791, after many of its most bitter opponents had gone home for the Easter recess. By dawn the next day, every church bell in the city was pealing, and the royal artillery fired its cannon. When King Stanislaus and his cabinet, in robes of medieval splendor, traversed the passageway connecting the Zamek with the Cathedral of Saint Jean to celebrate the long-awaited victory with a Te Deum, a joyful contagion engulfed the crowd of onlookers. Anna-Dorothea, who was watching the procession with the black-cassocked Piattoli and other courtiers, was as overcome as they, and she too prostrated herself as the sovereign and his retinue swept on.

As the deputies started to chip away at their huge backlog, Piattoli, who was a man of the world as well as the cloth and not immune to the charms of the opposite sex, devoted himself to Anna's affairs. But now it was the king himself who postponed the Courland hearing. It was as important to His Majesty as it was to Peter that ducal authority and prestige be strengthened in Courland. King Stanislaus did not want to create a precedent in Mitau for any Polish nobles with similar aspirations. So in order to reinforce the grand duke's position, he authorized a special commission to examine conditions in Courland before the Sejm handed down any decision. This meant another delay.

This time, instead of returning home when the deputies adjourned for the summer, Anna-Dorothea accepted an invitation to attend the weddings of two of the king of Prussia's daughters.

A trail of broken hearts marked the grand duchess's path as the sisters meandered west, going leisurely by boat down the Elba and then on the Moldau to Prague. When she entered the chapel in Berlin for the double ceremony and was escorted to a seat alongside the royal family, Anna-Dorothea was certain there had been some mistake. She knew that only the tsarina or the empress of the Holy Roman Empire was entitled to sit there, had either one been present. Or else the place should be vacant. But His Majesty had decreed otherwise.

It did not take Anna-Dorothea long to discover why. When the mother of one of the bridegrooms, Friedrich-Wilhelm II's sister, the princess of Orange, indicated her interest in Wilhelmina as a wife for a third son, Anna at once wrote Peter:

> Of course, Wilhelmina is only ten but she is old enough
> to be betrothed. Friedrich-Wilhelm II is most enthusiastic
> about his sister's suggestion and welcomes the prospect of
> having our daughter in his family. But His Majesty wants to
> be sure that, in the absence of a male heir, the Courland
> throne will go to Wilhelmina and her husband.

Nevertheless, Anna-Dorothea had learned enough of practical foreign affairs to realize that even though the Courland throne could pass to Wilhelmina, there was little likelihood that either Poland or Russia would permit a Prussian-dominated Courland. So she was not unduly disappointed when she returned home to have Peter inform her that Catherine the Great had vetoed the proposal.

Duty called Anna-Dorothea back to Warsaw a third time. Winter had already laid its heavy hand on the city spread out along the Vistula. The days were short and dismal, with overcast skies that transformed the capital into a study in black and white. The Sejm was in session, the king had his commission's favorable report in hand, the Courland affair was inching toward the top of the agenda, and Abbé Piattoli was worried.

For still noticeably absent from the crowded Pod Blacha salons were the dissident younger deputies. They normally controlled the vote and yet they avoided Anna and Elisa as if the sisters were the devil's advocates. Because he was their leader, Count Olek (Alexander) Batowski held the key and was one of the most influential men in the Sejm. Batowski had acquired his liberal ideas and worldly manners in France—where he had served as captain in the famed mercenary regiment "Le Royal Suedois." Piattoli tried repeatedly to present the count to the grand duchess, but Batowski held aloof and sanctimoniously informed the abbé that he felt it highly improper for any member of the Sejm, which was, after all, to decide the suit between the grand duke and the Cour nobles, to frequent the salons of the grand duchess. The count was not easily manipulated, but the abbé was not a man to admit defeat. Piattoli won out—and produced the elusive lawmaker.

How the grand duchess wooed Batowski to her cause is not hard to surmise. Part of her art of being a woman was knowing when to act like one, and obviously a different approach was called for with the slender, attractive Pole. Almost Anna-Dorothea's age, he had glowing charcoal eyes, bushy black brows that accentuated his unusual pallor, and wore his jet-black hair shoulder length and unpowdered in a visual protest against the old customs and ways of thinking.

As a public gesture of support, the day the grand duke's case was brought onto the Sejm's floor, His Majesty accompanied Anna-Dorothea to the parliament. The fifes of the royal military band piped, the drums rolled, and His Majesty and the grand duchess entered the Sejm, with Elisa trailing a few steps behind—Anna was very fussy about protocol, even with her sister. And behind Elisa came a single lady-in-waiting, with a pillow for Anna's chair and a small bag containing various necessities for Her Excellency's comfort during what promised to be a long session. Slowly—and significantly—so every delegate might see them, the king ceremoniously escorted the grand duchess and her entourage up to the temporary tribune he had ordered constructed for her, directly opposite his own and overlooking the great hall where the deputies sat in semicircular rows.

Count Batowski was, by choice, the last to speak before the

vote, and he made an eloquent appeal on behalf of the grand duke. Even the surprise of finding the fiery patriot in the grand duke's corner was insufficient to sway the decision.

The trumpets blared, the Speaker pounded his gavel and announced in a stentorian voice, "The vote!" The lawmakers queued up to drop the telltale black and white balls in their respective urns, and the count's cohorts rallied in support of his stand. But the country deputies, who were still so old-fashioned they spoke only Latin and wore oriental-flavored clothes and had their heads shaved à la Turk, upset Piattoli's calculations. Instead of deciding in favor of the grand duke as the abbé had anticipated—and as the king had wished—they sided, to a man, with their cousins and peers across the border.

Anna-Dorothea, who had been peering over the balcony in expectation, fainted when the tally was announced. She was hustled off by two of His Majesty's aides-de-camp to the loge behind King Stanislaus's box. While the duchess's lady-in-waiting alternately wrung her hands and ineffectively fanned Anna-Dorothea with her hat, the Baroness Elisa, who was already provoked at Count Batowski for having played hard to get, kept muttering "I told you so" as she applied damp compresses to Anna's forehead.

But Batowski had not given up hope. Racing to the podium, he gave another impassioned plea. A skilled parliamentarian, he then demanded a second roll call as the lawmakers were streaming out for recess. And this time he won.

Whether the glamorous grand duchess was the handsome count's mistress before he won the decisive Sejm vote or whether she did not succumb until later is anybody's guess. But what is known is that the day following the Sejm triumph, King Stanislaus trotted over to the Pod Blacha to bid Anna-Dorothea farewell and to slip an emerald ring, carved on top with his profile, on her forefinger. *"Ma chère fille,* I feel as if joy and pleasure were leaving me," he murmured and brushed away a tear. Then he kissed her good-bye. and the sisters were off, traveling across the flat northern landscape at a brisk pace in the early summer sun.

The pair were welcomed by Grand Duke Peter as conquering heroines, and life at Würzau resumed for Anna as before her three glamorous visits to Poland. Peter puttered among his flower beds and kept switching the statuary about in the gardens. He was forever rehanging pictures in the gallery and had learned the joys of painting. And in spite of Anna-Dorothea's hard-won victory in the Sejm, he continued to devote the absolute minimum of time to ducal affairs.

Scarcely six weeks had elapsed when Batowski appeared in Mitau as the new Polish resident to the duchy. Since his predecessor had been there only a matter of months, the count must have had a hand in his own appointment.

To an outsider, the ducal couple appeared as congenial as ever. In their marriage of convenience, strict fidelity was not an obligation, but nevertheless proprieties must be observed.

Because of protocol, and dozens of prying eyes, it was not easy for Anna and Olek to be alone together. One day, a courtier reported having seen the pair on horseback dashing recklessly through the blazing red and gold birch forest abloom with thousands of fall wildflowers. Another time, a sharp-eyed Medem cousin commented, insinuatingly, "The Grand Duchess is positively blooming. Haven't you noticed? Ever since her return and the arrival of that Polish Apollo."

Elisa did her best to gloss over the triangle by pointing out that her sister was merely doing her duty. It was essential for the grand duke and duchess to remain on good terms, "for reasons of state," she emphasized, with Courland's feudal lord, the Polish king—and hence automatically with his resident.

Elisa was loyal in public, but in private she stormed at her sister. She regretted the day they had ever set foot in Warsaw, and every night she prayed that "Mr. No-Good" would be recalled. She never referred to the count by any other name, and in her voluminous correspondence she always stoutly refused to admit that a man named Batowski ever existed.

In the beginning, gratitude alone might have drawn Anna to the Polish aristocrat, but by winter 1792 when she found herself pregnant, her affections were also engaged. As their love grew deeper, the political skies of Courland grew heavy, and thunder in distant Poland warned of coming storms. With the culmination of the Russian-Turkish war at Jassy earlier in the same year, Catherine II was once more free to turn her attention westward. When she seized Warsaw, history was repeating itself. Two decades before, Russia, Prussia, and Austria had helped themselves to Poland's richest provinces—more than one-third of Poland. Now in the spring of 1793 the trio was again raping Olek's fatherland, while contesting one another's rights.

Peter had already publicly proclaimed that the grand duchess was carrying another Biron. He was not the first sixty-nine-year-old husband whose young wife was enceinte with someone else's child, but Peter was a proud man and he was determined not to let scandal taint his house. So in midsummer, when Cossacks were sighted near Courland's eastern frontier and the Cour Diet professed concern that if the grand duchess gave birth to an archduke in Mitau, the tsarina might seize him as hostage, Peter decided that Anna-Dorothea must leave. One could never be sure what the formidable tsarina had in mind, and recently it had been rumored that Catherine II was resolved to do away with any of Peter's male descendants. She would not be the first Russian ruler to kidnap the heir to a land she coveted. Or it is possible that Catherine believed Peter was a Romanoff and wanted no bastard male claimants to the Russian throne, no matter how far removed.

At his next cabinet meeting Peter announced that for the duchy's sake, the grand duchess was shortly departing for Friedrichsfeld, his estate outside Berlin. Under the circumstances Anna-Dorothea was happy to go, especially as she wanted Olek, not Peter, with her when their baby came.

The following morning Anna-Dorothea was soaking leisurely in her silver tub. She had her maid cover her from head to toe with a special soap imported from Vienna which the girl first whipped to a lather with a butter whisk. Then the grand duchess signaled her little blackamoor to go up the back stairs to the closet overhead and pour fresh water down. It was splashing over her when her outraged sister burst in. Elisa had just learned of Peter's decision and she was wild.

"If you think I'm going to accompany you wherever you go to give birth to Mr. No-Good's child, you're sadly mistaken. I want to get as far away from you as possible!"

"Elisa! We've never quarreled before. Please!" Anna beseeched, stepping out of the tub into the warm towel her maid was holding to wrap around her. "Besides, where will you go?"

There was no answer. Elisa had stormed out, slamming the door, and before the day was over, she was en route to the Augustenburg court, which she had an open-ended invitation to visit at any time.

Anna-Dorothea herself was off within another forty-eight hours, escorted as far as the frontier by scandal-conscious Peter, who put on a stellar performance. The Mitau-Berlin trip was arduous in the best of circumstances, especially the northern route, which Anna chose in order to avoid as much military activity as possible. Its rigors were compounded by the extremely hot weather and even more by Anna's overriding fear that she might fall into Russian hands as she crossed strife-torn Poland—and then be recognized. Once again, as at the time of her wedding, she must have felt the redoubtable tsarina breathing heavily over her shoulder. What might the terrible Catherine do to her and to her baby?

Anna was traveling lightly, for speed's sake, in a single carriage, with a lady-in-waiting and one of Peter's aides-de-camp. They glimpsed soldiers only once, a few scattered groups at a distance. The moment the frontier was crossed, the potholed, heavily rutted Polish roads were exchanged for excellent Prussian ones, with well-scrubbed post stations at regular intervals, and Anna was soon safe at her destination.

Olek arrived in time for the infant's birth. Not surprisingly, in the light of Anna-Dorothea's harrowing past weeks, the healthy, tiny girl arrived well ahead of schedule, in mid-August. Dorothea, as she was named after her mother, would have been hard to mistake for a Biron, given her coal-black hair and huge dark eyes—Wilhelmina, Paulina, and Joanna were the blondest of blondes—although Peter immediately claimed her. Anna kept the child with her, in the nursery of whatever residence she was living in, while Dorothea was growing up, and at one point openly referred to the youngest princess as her favorite.

To Anna's delight, Friedrich-Wilhelm II and his queen permitted the sovereign's niece, Princess Louisa of Prussia, to be godmother. The young Prussian princess, with whom Anna had become friendly during her previous Berlin stay, came out regularly—Friedrichsfeld was originally the princess's family seat—with the latest Berlin gossip and was their only visitor. Anna-Dorothea pled delicate health and did not go into the capital, no doubt to avoid any embarrassing questions about the infant's parentage. Twice weekly, a special courier arrived from Peter with family news, including a rundown on domestic affairs.

Nothing is known about the ensuing twenty months Anna

spent there leading a retired, bucolic life with Olek. But by the time anemones and violets again appeared under the beech and bluebells were in bud, the grand duchess, who had the constitution of a husky draft horse, claimed she was feeling poorly. With a little prompting, the doctor recommended a cure for her "stagnant juices," and she selected Karlsbad.

This is an interesting choice. While Karlsbad's waters had worked wonders for Anna-Dorothea when she was there before, that particular spa happened to be located in Bohemia, where Olek and other Polish patriots listed as potential troublemakers in Catherine the Great's black book were forbidden to set foot, on pain of death. This could have been the reason Anna selected it, on the theory that it would do both Olek and herself good to separate—briefly. It is more than possible that life far from court —the ducal court or any court—was no longer the other side of the rainbow, especially since she was cooped up with a moody, melancholy lover. For the brutal second partition of Poland, almost a month to the day after Dorothea's birth, and the subsequent tragic news trickling out of that unhappy land shattered Olek, and his despair, compounded by his inactivity and his inability to help his fatherland, had deepened with each passing month. Matters had not been helped by their second winter in the Prussian country-side, which set a record as one of the longest and coldest ever and kept them indoors, often for weeks at a spell.

To give Olek a project so he would not have time to brood over her absence or over wretched Poland, either, Anna-Dorothea set him to search for a permanent home they could call their own. Batowski accepted the inevitable. Although he was tormented by jealousy whenever he was away from her side, Olek was to spend the better part of the next two years obediently scouring the high-ways and byways of half the German states and most of Switzer-land looking for Anna's Garden of the Hesperides.

Anna-Dorothea was the success of the Karlsbad season. When-ever the Courland siren appeared—at the baths, on the promenade, in the casino—gentlemen were drawn to her like wasps to a dish of jam, and the other women, from Princess Esterhazy, the pampered darling of the Hapsburg court, on down, were soon complaining of their admirers' fickleness. Before she left, Anna gave an al fresco luncheon in a neighboring valley for her new friends and assorted beaux. Tables were set for eight. A brass band appeared, and the merry guests were soon following Anna-Dorothea in an improvised polonaise, winding their way among the trees on the edge of the clearing. Lively mazurkas followed. The men continuously changed partners, and the women's light, fluffy summer gowns dissolved in a pastel blur of rose and blue, yellow and violet against the green of the glade as they pirouetted ever faster. Some of the younger blades vowed to commemorate the gay affair by erecting a small marble temple of love dedicated to Anna-Dorothea. The temple was still standing, overgrown with climbing roses, at the end of the nineteenth century. Anna returned to Friedrichsfeld rejuvenated.

The smell of burning leaves and freshly turned sod was in the air when Anna-Dorothea and Olek learned further sinister news from the east. To consolidate her Polish holdings, Catherine the Great had treacherously spirited King Stanislaus-Augustus off to Russia—where he died in gilded imprisonment in 1798. Anna-Dorothea at once dispatched a messenger to Peter, fearful that the absorption of Courland must ultimately follow this tragedy. "Go to Saint Petersburg at once," she urged. She knew Peter's tendency to procrastinate. "If you don't waste a minute, you may be able to exchange Polish suzerainty for Russian, and still keep some measure of independence."

Anxiously she awaited a reply, but snow was on the ground before a special courier arrived from Würzau. As usual, Peter had delayed his departure, and when he finally arrived in Saint Peters-burg, he was too late. Catherine the Great's systematic bribery of Cour officialdom over the years paid off. The Courland Diet, meeting in an extraordinary session—behind Peter's back after he left for Russia—formally requested that Catherine annex the duchy. She was only too happy to comply. Peter was forced to abdicate, but he did manage to dictate the terms, and when it came to finances, he was his father's son and drove a hard bargain. The tsarina paid him a king's ransom—over two million rubles—for his Courland real estate. In addition, Catherine gave him a handsome income for life and—what was most unusual—allowed Peter to finagle a large pension for Anna-Dorothea after his death. The grand duke must still have been in love with his wayward duchess; she had bewitched Peter as she would every other male who crossed her path.

While Anna watched from afar, Peter returned to Mitau to supervise the stripping of Würzau and the River Aa palace and the packing of his various collections, his art, memorabilia, books, and furnishings, as well as his hyacinth and tulip bulbs imported from Turkey. Then he piled Wilhelmina, Paulina, and Joanna into his luxurious travel coach and the Biron flag was lowered on the palace's standard for the last time, to indicate he was no longer in residence. Unwilling to forgo an iota of his due, Peter rumbled off westward, the end of August 1795, with his vast household, his retainers, his resident troupe of actors and singers, and his chamber orchestra.

While it was not unusual, in the circles in which Anna-Dorothea now moved, for a married woman to have an acknowledged liaison, it was essential to retain superficial ties with hearth and home. Peter behaved handsomely, and by the time Dorothea was three, a new modus vivendi had evolved between the ducal pair. In exchange for Peter's buying Anna an estate of her own choosing and footing all the bills for the half year she was to live with Olek, Anna-Dorothea agreed to spend the other six months with Peter in Sagan, bringing Peter's putative daughter along so she could get acquainted with the other princesses.

Sagan was a duchy in Lower Silesia, about 140 kilometers southeast of Berlin, which Peter had bought years before. Its principal village, also called Sagan, was a typically dull German town, and except for the pine forest in the background, the countryside around could not, by any stretch of the imagination, be termed picturesque. Forbidding was a better word for the huge moated castle, with its hundreds of grimacing gargoyles, which towered above the edge of the small community. Contemporaries referred to it as spectacularly uncomfortable, although it was embellished with a Gothic extravagance which gave it a certain air of grandeur and solemnity. The raucous croaking of hundreds of ravens swooping about its time-blackened towers provided lugubrious background music, and little imagination was required to discern among them troubled ghosts from the castle's tumultuous past.

To please Peter, Anna-Dorothea always made it a point to

arrive before the opening hunt of the season. The high spot of the grand duke's calendar, this famous sporting event had attracted so many people to Courland that it resembled a migration rather than a private house party. The hunting was equally good around Sagan, as the many trophies of elk, boar, wolf, and bear lining the castle's great high-ceilinged entry hall bore witness.

Guests and their numerous retainers came from as far afield as Prague and Berlin and stayed for a week or longer. Evening entertainment—with at least one opera as the highlight—was provided in the new theater Peter had built when he restored the castle's destroyed left wing. Because the duchy was near the Central European concert circuit, Peter was able to persuade various Italian divas and Berlin musicians to winter in Sagan and perform with his resident troupe. The grand duke was surprisingly adventuresome in his musical tastes, and many were introduced there to *Don Giovanni* and other works of one of his favorite composers, Wolfgang Amadeus Mozart, a brilliant young Salzburg native who had recently died.

Anna-Dorothea kept Sagan's 130 rooms filled with an endless procession of visitors and exhausted her ingenuity devising ways to keep them busy. She made the cold impersonal castle spring to life, "like Sleeping Beauty at the kiss of the Fairy Prince," Peter complimented her, gratefully.

Anna's role as chatelaine left only bits and pieces of her time for the older Courland princesses, who were presently in their teens. But she was proud of their accomplishments—Wilhelmina liked to recite Vergil in the original; Paulina's voice was developing nicely; and Joanna played the piano rather well—and she had them perform as the occasion warranted. Dorothea, who was ten years younger than Joanna, had not yet developed any special talent.

Sagan's massive walls of native stone kept the huge structure too damp to remain there throughout the summer. But long before Peter left with the three older girls for his vast Bohemian domain, Nachod, the Piccolomino estate he had purchased between the Mountains of the Giants and the Mountains of Orlice. Anna and little Dorothea were off to Löbikau—and Olek.

This Saxon property which Batowski had located for Anna was conveniently situated southwest of Berlin and roughly equidistant from there and Sagan. It remained her favorite residence the rest of her life and the grand duchess was forever redecorating and adding on to it. Batowski supervised the initial remodeling of the schloss, which was far too large for its width and of a most impractical design, with bedrooms opening off one another instead of off a corridor; he also reduced the size of the ground-floor salons and lowered their ceilings to achieve the feeling of intimacy Anna desired.

Löbikau was Anna-Dorothea's dream come true. But as happy as the couple was here and as busy as Olek kept himself—he next restored numerous unused farm buildings in order to make the estate viable—this was only stopgap work for him. Barred from the political activity that was his lifeblood, the count was more and more embittered by his forced exile and his inability to help Poland. The cycle Anna established—six months in Saxony and six months in Silesia, with a Karlsbad cure thrown in for good measure—did not help matters, and he was increasingly depressed over lengthening periods of time. His melancholy wrung Anna's heart, and she tried everything to draw him out of himself.

One month he was interested in books. Using a trumped-up excuse, she slipped off to Leipzig and its celebrated bookdealers to purchase as a surprise for him the latest Didot edition of Racine from Paris. But Olek's pleasure was short-lived.

As the season approached for Anna-Dorothea's third visit to Sagan, Olek was off on another tangent. Perhaps he would not mind being alone so much if Löbikau were smaller. It was so large he rattled around in it when she was gone. A short time later, the postillion's horn announced the arrival of a guest, and Anna-Dorothea introduced Olek to the Milan architect she had summoned to design his new retreat. Daily the grand duchess and the two men tramped over the grounds in search of a suitable location; nightly Olek pored enthusiastically over scale drawings. After he selected a spot in the nearby woods, a half league distant, Anna gave a party to commemorate laying the cornerstone, and construction was under way before she left.

When the scent of budding wildflowers and flowing pine sap was in the breeze and the birds' song heralded spring, Anna-Dorothea was back from Silesia, and Olek took her over to see Tannenfeld. The small pavilion, designed in an italianate style to match the big manor house, was charming. There was only one thing wrong, Olek complained. "It looks so . . . naked . . . like a baked potato without its jacket." It was useless to point out that the heavily wooded area had been stripped bare at Batowski's specific request. Like Aladdin's djinn, Anna clapped her hands, and in a matter of days—financed by Peter's bottomless purse—several centuries-old oaks were transplanted there in time for the gay fête Anna planned to celebrate Tannenfeld's completion.

But the count's happiness was again fleeting, and the petulant Pole sulked once more. Like an Eastern potentate, Olek accepted Anna-Dorothea's bounty as homage due him. He had taken her and her bounty for granted too long. It was typical of Olek and his attitude toward life that he should realize how much he loved and needed Anna only when she was losing interest in him. Overly tender one minute, ferociously jealous the next, Olek was wearing her out with his moods.

CHAPTER THREE

The Grand Duchess & Baron d'Armfelt
1799-1803

BARON GUSTAV D'ARMFELT WAS ON HAND to greet Anna-Dorothea when she returned to Karlsbad that May 1799, and she was delighted to see him. From her point of view, a stranger was always a welcome addition to that closed society of handsome Hungarian bores, graceful, frivolous Viennese, and chivalrous, heroic Poles, and she had met the fabled adventurer toward the close of her previous stay there. He was suffering from some mysterious ailment which was very painful—and was also turning his skin yellow, as yellow as that of the Chinese man brought back from Cathay by the Jesuits, whom Anna had once seen in Warsaw. Probably d'Armfelt was suffering from a liver ailment, but his bizarre explanation for his strange hue—that the Swedish regent was having him poisoned—together with the fabled Don Juan's incredible past made him even more extraordinary and exciting in Anna's eyes. People whispered of this much-decorated Swedish war hero's strange, almost sinister fascination and how his magnetic personality imposed itself ruthlessly on any man, woman, or child who accepted him as a friend. Certainly the House of Biron would never be the same once his tall shadow crossed its path.

D'Armfelt's life was so interwoven with current events, political intrigue, and love affairs that it read like a play with a cast from *tout l'Europe* and a mise-en-scène that extended from Versailles' Hall of Mirrors to the gilded alcoves of Europe's loveliest—and most notorious—women. The baron had been the favorite of the late Gustave III of Sweden, who had been assassinated some years before at a masked ball in the royal palace. When the murdered sovereign's brother, who coveted d'Armfelt's mistress, was named regent, he sent the baron abroad as his Neapolitan ambassador, hoping to supersede him in the beauty's arms. When she scorned him in favor of her absent lover, the vindictive regent accused d'Armfelt of long-distance plotting against the Swedish throne. The regent sent a warship to Naples to arrest him and bring him home, but Lady Emma Hamilton, the wife of the British ambassador there, and Countess Skawronska, the niece of Catherine II's lover, Prince Potemkin, persuaded the Neapolitan queen, Maria-Carolina, to help spirit "their *cher petit*" to freedom. Whereupon the regent had him tried for treason, condemned to death in absentia, and solemnly burned in effigy in the Swedish capital. D'Armfelt's mistress, Madeleine de Rudenschold, paid a pretty krona for remaining faithful to the absent d'Armfelt. Wild with jealousy, the scorned regent had her convicted on a false charge. She spent half a day in the public pillory on Stockholm's main square before being exiled to a small Baltic island.

Four years Anna-Dorothea's senior, Gustav d'Armfelt was as big a man as Peter, but his poor proportions—his burly, broad-shouldered body was too big for his short legs—hardly comprised the heroic specifications for dreams. He was handsome, no doubt, when he was younger, but dissipation was already taking its toll of his rugged good looks. Yet Anna-Dorothea found the attentions of the famous philanderer flattering, and in no time, he was her favorite escort. D'Armfelt was excellent company, and his conversation, larded with what he knew and had seen firsthand and spiced with names of international repute, opened a welcome window onto Western Europe for Anna.

They were seen everywhere together, and gossip flew around the tiny town like a flock of starlings. Early each day, the ex-cavalry officer arrived on horseback at her inn, *Zum Pomeranzenbaum* (The Orange Trees), leading a second mare for the grand duchess for their morning canter. In the afternoon, they strolled along the banks of the Köpl and through the narrow main street—it was considered more healthy, and chic, to walk than to ride—to the fountain in the tree-lined principal square, where they drank the prescribed bumpers of the Stürdel's steaming, health-giving waters. Occasionally, d'Armfelt drove her himself in his smart little barouche—its top folded back and the grand duchess shading her face with a flowered parasol—out into the surrounding country-side to locate the destroyed monasteries and other haunted romantic ruins, which the late English writer Walpole described in his best-selling Gothic tale *The Castle of Otranto,* which was one of Anna's favorites. They also visited Egra, where Count Wallenstein, the famous Bohemian general who had built Grand Duke Peter's Sagan castle, had been murdered.

After one of the Kürhaus's twice-weekly concerts, a disgruntled Saxon count, who had squired Anna-Dorothea occasionally on previous visits, vented his spleen at her continued preference for the gay Swedish Lothario. "That scum of a Nordic Dragoon! Her Excellency should be told that it's her storied wealth, not her story-book charms, that attracts him."

Within the hour, some meddlesome fool repeated these offensive words to d'Armfelt. Though he was a man of modest means and not averse to accepting monetary favors from his mistresses, money was never his prime consideration. For a woman to interest him, she must first appeal to his senses. Not a man to brook disparaging remarks, he promptly challenged the officious noble to a duel and selected as the appropriate site Dorothea's Meadow —as the grassy stretch in front of the picturesque temple of love that had been erected years before by the grand duchess's admirers was now called. Fortunately, neither protagonist suffered more than superficial cuts before alerted authorities called a halt to the proceedings.

If Anna-Dorothea was not already d'Armfelt's mistress, it could not have been more than a hop, a skip, and a jump from the dueling field, where he had risked his life for a matter of honor, into her bed. Their affair might have been a typical vacation-time romance. The grand duchess's cure was almost finished, and shortly she and Gustav would go their separate ways. Then fate intervened.

A mutual Swedish friend passed away. The deceased Baron Taube was a man without a country because he had been involved in the assassination of the late king of Sweden—for patriotic motives. When he took fatally ill, he had worried so much about a final resting place that Anna, to set his mind at ease, promised him burial at Löbikau. This was easier said than accomplished, and when the ducal intendant threw up his hands in depsair, Gustav stepped into the breach and assumed the task. An opportunist par excellence, the baron had nothing to lose. The Karlsbad season was drawing to a close; he had no immediate plans and very little cash. In a few days he cut the governmental red tape and was en route to Löbikau with the coffin—and Anna-Dorothea.

At the outset, Anna's ménage à trois worked because Batowski accepted d'Armfelt at face value—as a Karlsbad acquaintance who had kindly offered his services at a difficult moment. Anna continued to smother Olek with affection and attention, and his suite still adjoined hers. But when she redecorated Gustav's spacious four-room apartment—in another wing—to suit the tastes of the Scandinavian gentleman, Batowski realized he had a serious rival. By sullenly withdrawing to Tannenfeld, Olek committed a cardinal error, for he left the field clear to Gustav. D'Armfelt recognized a vacuum when he saw one. He wrote his long-suffering wife, "Löbikau is like Calypso's Isle. Its enchantments are infinite"— and stayed on with the charming duchess.

Anna-Dorothea was getting ready to rejoin Peter at Sagan for the winter months when the grand duke sent word to delay her departure. Sixteen-year-old Joanna was pregnant and had eloped with her lover, an Italian musician.

The unfortunate girl was paying the price for her upbringing. The three older Courland sisters, Wilhelmina, Paulina, and Joanna, had been raised in the conventional fashion of contemporary princesses. Relegated to palace nurseries and relinquished to staff and governesses from birth, the trio rarely saw Anna-Dorothea while they were growing up, even when she lived with Peter, and the two younger ones lacked any sort of parental love and direction. Wilhelmina was the exception. As the firstborn, she was Peter's favorite and given preferential treatment, fussed over, and cosseted—when the grand duke felt in the mood. Peter intimidated Paulina and Joanna, who never knew the human side of him that their oldest sister did.

They never saw Peter do his imitation of the horribly ugly old Kalmuck Boujeninova, who used to stretch her face, as if it were made of rubber, to amuse Tsarina Anna. They never saw Peter sit cross-legged and cackle like a hen that had just laid an egg, demonstrating to Wilhelmina how the six court jesters lined up to greet the tsarina and the Biron family every Sunday after services in the imperial chapel. Instead, Joanna and Paulina considered their father a dour old curmudgeon to be avoided whenever possible, which was easy to do in the drafty corridors without end and empty, high-ceilinged rooms of the cavernous castles and residences that they called home.

Impatient to find out what life was about, Joanna indulged in a secret romance with the young singer-actor who directed the grand duke's resident troupe and gave the trio of princesses their music lessons on the side. When the innocent girl found herself pregnant, the couple fled Nachod. All they took with them was Joanna's trinket box of jewelry, which they planned to sell for passage to America, where they expected to go after they got married.

Peter alerted the Bohemian authorities and sent his own household officials and staff scouring the countryside for a trace of the runaways. The governor of Erfurt, a Biron family standby, located Joanna where her lover had left her with friends en route, while he continued to Hamburg to arrange for their trip overseas. Advising her father she was safe—"Joanna reminded me of a poor dove caught in a net, she was so frightened"—that dignitary sent her home with a suitable chaperon and a Prussian officer as escort.

Peter could not forgive Joanna for tarnishing the family image of respectability he was laboring to project and refused to see the fugitive when she was brought back. Joanna was not the first highborn girl to be seduced by someone beneath her. Generally, people laughed, and the unfortunate affair was quickly forgotten or furnished the plot for a second-rate novel. But it was different with the Courland princesses. Peter was painfully aware that aristocrats who partook gladly of his prodigal hospitality still winked behind his back and laughed at the parvenu grand duke.

In Mitau Peter had been unable to live down the past, but in Bohemia he had high hopes of success. There he had purchased palatial Nachod, an estate so vast it comprised an entire political unit and assured its owner an automatic seat in the Bohemian Senate. And recently he had acquired a suitable town house in Prague. Now what would the Bohemians say? What would people say at the Prussian court? And in Silesia? "Blood will tell." "The apple doesn't fall far from the tree." And other similar platitudes.

Peter did not want Anna-Dorothea to come to Sagan at present. Instead, to escape the tattling, and tittering, he dreaded, the grand duke slunk off alone. Heartbroken and sick—no doubt the aches and pains that befall most seventy-five-year-olds had been aggravated by the commotion provoked by Joanna's disappearance—Peter proceeded to Gellenaü, an out-of-the-way spot in the Bohemian countryside where he would not be recognized and where a health healer was highly recommended. The man proved to be a quack, and Peter suffered a stroke. Regular doctors were called, but Peter had lost the will to live and was slowly going downhill. Anna-Dorothea was notified.

She was shocked at the news, for she had no inkling he was in poor health. Before dashing off, she sent a courier posthaste to Sagan for Peter's resident physician. Surely he was best prepared to minister to Peter. Posting over slippery roads lined with trees already thick with hoarfrost, under overcast, snow-laden skies, Anna hurried south. She met the girls, coming from Nachod, en route, and together the grand duchess and her four daughters hastened on.

When they reached Gellenaü, Anna-Dorothea at first refused to get out. The grand duke of Courland could not be there, in that modest manor house in the middle of nowhere. But there was no mistake.

The family doctor, who had ridden day and night to get there from Sagan, hurried downstairs when he learned of the grand duchess's arrival. "Ah! Your Highness! Thank goodness you're here! There's little more anyone can do." Sanctimoniously, he clasped his hands in prayer and looked heavenward. "It is simply a question of time—and not much time at that. His Highness used up what little strength he had with the counsel of justice—"

"The counsel of justice?" Anna was surprised.

"He just left. Didn't you meet him? The grand duke insisted on sending to Prague for him—to put a codicil in his will." The troubled man lowered his voice so no one else might hear. "The grand duke has disinherited the Princess Joanna. Sheer willpower has kept him alive until the deed was done—signed, sealed, and witnessed." He shook his head disapprovingly and was silent for a moment. "His Highness will surely want to see you. I'll go ahead and tell him you're here."

With his finger to his lips for silence, he tiptoed back up the stairs and into the room at the top. Anna followed slowly. Seconds later he reappeared, wiping his glasses. "He's dead!"

Recovering his composure, the doctor escorted the grand duchess into the death chamber. "Everything's happened so fast! It's hard for me to believe," Anna murmured as she stared down at Peter's still, shrunken body. She would have liked him to know how she had rushed to get there.

The one member of the family sincerely to regret his passing was Wilhelmina. His spoiled pet, she dearly loved her father. As for Anna-Dorothea, it is hard to say what her emotions were. Love had never played any part in her marriage, as far as Anna was concerned—nor had she expected it to. But she and Peter had been married for more than twenty years. They had lived together a good part of that time, and she had repeatedly demonstrated to him the respect and kindly feelings that derive from a long and on the whole pleasant intimacy. So she must have felt some sense of loss—and perhaps gratitude.

The duke died on January 13, 1800, and a few days later a simple funeral was held in the neighboring parish church with only the grand duchess and her daughters and the ducal households in attendance. Wilhelmina sobbed throughout the service. At one point Paulina, too, burst into tears. Pathetic Joanna, visibly pregnant, was seated in the back row with her governess—out of respect for the dead man's feelings—and nervous little Dorothea, Batowski's big black eyes peering from her thin, pale face, was shepherded out for some fresh air as the pastor droned on.

That afternoon a medical bulletin was issued, attributing the grand duke's death to a misapplied mercury cure, and the next morning the carriage bearing Peter Biron's mortal remains rattled off in the swirling fog toward the burial ground in Silesia.

Courland princesses Wilhelmina, Paulina, and Dorothea now ranked among Europe's richest uncrowned heiresses—wayward Joanna had not received a ruble—and their mother, the celebrated Grand Duchess Anna-Dorothea, was a widow possessed of fabulous wealth.

Since custom dictated a year of mourning and Anna had to arrange Peter's affairs, mother and daughters settled in Prague, in the spacious Czernin palace that had been Peter's last purchase. She summoned Gustav—not Olek—to join her. It was the level-headed Swede, not the excitable Pole, whom she missed; besides, the baron's vast practical experience and firsthand knowledge of the Continent would make him an invaluable financial adviser and general mentor in the days immediately ahead.

But with Peter dead, Olek was not content to stay put, and he kept writing Anna that his place was by her side. So it was. For at the height of their affair, the pair had signed a marriage contract in which Anna promised to marry Count Batowski within a year after the grand duke's death, or pay a repentance sum. Olek had not wanted her to forfeit anything, and when the lawyer argued that it was customary to do so, Batowski suggested that Anna name only a token sum. But she had purposely set the figure high, very high—150,000 rubles—to convince Olek that she loved him for all eternity.

"A marriage contract? You never mentioned that before!" D'Armfelt whistled with amazement, although similar documents were not uncommon in the Baltic countries. He and Anna were still at the table in her small upstairs salon. He had finished the out-of-season berries sent as a gift by the governor of the city and was skillfully extracting some of the seeds with a gold toothpick. So that was what had been bothering the grand duchess. That was why she had not eaten a mouthful of food. With an imperious wave of his hand, the baron dismissed the flunkies who came to clear the table so he might talk to Anna undisturbed.

"What shall I do?" Anna queried. "Olek's letters sound so urgent that I expect him to walk in at any moment." She twisted around nervously at a sound at the door.

"What do you mean, what should you do?" D'Armfelt shifted the large bouquet of variegated tulips in front of him to see her better. "Write and tell him that you'll see him in Löbikau in the spring when we're en route to Sagan on estate matters." The baron got up and began pacing to and fro. "Tell him anything. But don't have him come here." He stopped and brushed the top of Anna's head with an absentminded kiss. Confident that he was now number one in Anna's affection—and had the added advantage of being on the spot—he proceeded to dispose of his tiresome rival by making it easy for Anna to reconcile inclination with duty. "You must concentrate on your daughters for the moment and not compromise their future. A Courland princess can marry a prince, if she wishes, but not if she has . . ." D'Armfelt paused a moment to underline what he was about to say.

"Yes?" Anna's voice was almost inaudible.

". . . but not if she has an insignificant Polish count as a stepfather." He walked over to her and gently propelled her to the cluttered writing table standing in a corner. "If you marry the count, you will lose your rank and privileges as a Serene Highness—your due as the widow of the late grand duke." He assumed a stern air and carefully emphasized each word. "Remember Batowski is a Pole. And he was in Catherine the Great's bad graces. If you marry him, who knows? Her son, Tsar Paul, might even withhold every ruble of your pension."

Anna knew the wisdom of what the baron was saying. Since it was a foregone conclusion that the temperamental Pole would not take the breakup of their long affair lightly, and because the matter must be resolved discreetly for the girls' sake, it was essential that Olek not come to Prague. With Gustav standing over her as she wrote, Anna informed Olek she was coming to Löbikau. Now.

Whether d'Armfelt accompanied her at her own request—because she was afraid she might weaken when she found herself alone with Olek—or whether Gustav went along because he wanted no slipup is not known. But go he did. The unsuspecting Olek was so happy to learn that Anna was returning to the schloss that he rushed to meet her at the Meissen Inn, which was her last overnight stop on the way. He surprised her, all right—but not as much as the sight of the baron exiting from the great Courland berlin surprised him.

"Olek, we're two adults," Anna began the next morning, when the pair were alone in her suite. "Let's discuss the family obligations which prevent our marriage. . . ."

"Prevent our marriage?" Batowski could not believe his ears.

"I'll pay the full compensation we agreed upon," Anna hurriedly continued, drawing the marriage agreement from her travel sack.

"Do you think a price tag can be put on my love?" Horrified at the realization of what Anna was saying, Olek jumped to his feet, angrily punctuating his remarks by punching one clenched fist into the open palm of the other hand. Mercurially, his anger yielded to supplication. "What has happened to the eternal love we swore each other?" he pleaded, kneeling before Anna, who was seated on the divan. "The memories of those enchanted months at Friedrichsfeld? And at Löbikau? Don't they mean anything to you anymore? What about little Dorothea?" He clasped his arms around her legs and laid his head on her lap.

The emotional Pole gave a virtuoso performance that ran the gamut from threats of suicide to exalted protestations of love. After three long hours, Olek himself wrote finis to the maudlin melodrama. With a dramatic gesture, he snatched the marriage promise from the table where it lay, tore it to shreds, and fed it piecemeal into the flames of the small fireplace, sobbing "Anna, Anna!" convulsively. Then he turned around and, for good measure, proceeded to shred and toss in, one at a time, the duchess's love letters—a bulky packet neatly tied with pink ribbons that he carried with him everywhere, to read whenever his longing for Anna-Dorothea became unbearable. Bits and pieces of mutilated paper floated to the floor in silent testimony to the shattered affair.

Completely exhausted, physically and emotionally, Anna flung her arms around his neck; her tears mingled with his. "Olek! I'll never forget your sacrifice! Never! I swear it!"

The following day, Anna-Dorothea, Olek, and Gustav break-fasted together amicably, like civilized human beings, and continued on in Anna's coach to Löbikau. Anna and Gustav settled down in the schloss, while Olek was once more in Tannenfeld. But the count knew it was time to move on.

Anna had loved Olek so long that she found it harder to let him go than she anticipated. She knew he did not have a ruble to his name, and when she thought about the huge sum he had chivalrously relinquished, her conscience troubled her. It was not as hard as Anna expected to persuade Olek to accept a pension—a kingly one. And he was off.

With her personal life disentangled, Anna returned to Prague and her daughters. Wilhelmina was nineteen and Paulina a year younger. They were of an age to be married off.

The previous summer, Peter had sent Wilhelmina to join Anna at Karlsbad so that she could be presented at the elegant spa where the Holy Roman Empire's peerage traditionally gave a preview of their nubile daughters. And after she came home, several interested families made preliminary overtures to Peter for her hand on their sons' behalf.

Now a half year later, drawn by the astronomical size of Wilhelmina's and Paulina's inheritance, and the princesses' blonde loveliness, suitors were converging on the Czernin palace from the four points of the compass. Of every size, shape, and description, they shared two common denominators: lengthy paragraphs in the *Almanach de Gotha,* the aristocracy's *Who's Who,* and staggering debts—as practical d'Armfelt was quick to ferret out. Anna promised her daughters they should have the final say in selecting their husbands. She wanted them happy and, of course, married to someone who would bring credit to the house of Biron. She owed that much to Peter, who had tried so hard to overcome his family's taint of parvenu. Surely with so many candidates there must be several qualified to suit each one.

The most enterprising of the lot was Prince Friedrich-Hermann-Otto von Hohenzollern-Hechingen, heir presumptive of the oldest branch of the house of Brandenbourg. More enterprising and practical than his rivals, he had come prepared to wed whichever of the girls would have him, although he preferred Wilhelmina because she had inherited the lion's share of the grand duke's vast holdings, as well as both Nachod and Sagan, the two largest estates. He himself was a conceited ass who could talk only about his impressive lineage, but Hermann-Otto's wife would one day be ruling duchess of his tiny country.

When Wilhelmina turned him down, Paulina accepted with alacrity—even though she was second best. She was so anxious for a life of her own that she was happy to accept any qualified man who appeared. Besides, it would be nice to be first for a change—the first Courland princess to be married—and not always be tagging along behind, or between, her sisters. But Paulina was independent enough to have ideas of her own. On the eve of her marriage, she insisted that her guardian draw up a tight financial agreement denying her husband-to-be any power over her huge fortune, which included the Silesian duchy of Holstein and other assorted real estate.

The nuptial service was held in the nearby Church Maria Schnee, which Anna-Dorothea had had decorated with white hothouse lilacs. Because they were officially in mourning, the guest list was limited to the family. The bridal night was passed at home at the Czernin palace, and the next morning the carriage of the new princess of Hohenzollern-Hechingen and her groom clattered noisily over the cobbled stones of the ancient Maltese Square, then crossed the great arched Charles Bridge spanning the Moldav and headed toward Swabia.

One Courland princess wed, and one to go right now. For Dorothea, not quite seven, was too young for even a tentative childhood engagement. And Joanna was secreted away in the countryside awaiting her illegitimate baby.

When a letter arrived from Princess Louisa of Prussia, little Dorothea's godmother, saying that her brother, Prince Louis-Ferdinand, wanted to meet the oldest Courland princess, Anna was delighted. She already had a warm spot in her heart for this young prince, who had written charming poems about her beauty when they were introduced some years back. Since Anna and the family—d'Armfelt, Wilhelmina, and Dorothea—were about to leave for Sagan on estate matters, a rendezvous was arranged at Leipzig.

But though Anna might be thrilled at the possibility of having a nephew of Frederick the Great as a son-in-law, the prospect of marriage into the royal house of Prussia did not overwhelm Wilhelmina. So the whole way north, as the big berlin swayed and bumped across Saxony, Anna sang Louis-Ferdinand's praises in an attempt to kindle some spark of enthusiasm in her daughter. The twenty-six-year-old prince was so handsome that women were forever throwing themselves at him, but Anna carefully omitted any mention of his notorious string of mistresses or his mountain of debts. Anna was no prude. Men would be men, as the saying goes—especially spoiled royal ones—and Wilhelmina had enough money to provide for them both. Like every Prussian youth, Louis-Ferdinand had entered service early, before he was twenty, and to his credit had a record of bravery under enemy fire which had made him the idol of the army. There was even a popular poem about him:

> Six feet tall, he stands
> An image of a War God,
> The Hero of his comrades,
> The noble women's idol,
> With blue eyes, blond and bold.
> And in his strong young hand
> The old sword of the Prussians,
> Prince Louis-Ferdinand.

But Wilhelmina remained unimpressed, and Anna-Dorothea wondered if there was a man alive who could satisfy her.

Louis-Ferdinand arrived at Leipzig the same time as the Courland entourage and sat up late that night, until the candles in his suite were guttering, plotting the morrow's strategy with his brother-in-law. The latter young man, the husband of Dorothea's godmother, had been commandeered to accompany the prince to Leipzig in order to be able to keep Berlin posted on developments. Straitlaced Friedrich-Wilhelm II was tired of his high-spirited first cousin's never-ending peccadillos and hoped Wilhelmina would provide the solution.

As early next morning as convention allowed, Prince Louis-Ferdinand and his brother-in-law appeared in the grand duchess's suite. The grand duchess, too, had left nothing to chance or improvisation. Mother and daughter's introductory remarks, moves, gestures, had been carefully choreographed. Afterwards the young couple were left alone, discreetly chaperoned by Dorothea, who was proud to have so important a role. In the evening, Louis-Ferdinand, an accomplished clavichordist, played a number of his own compositions and one of Frederick the Great's sonatas, with his brother-in-law accompanying him on the cello.

The prince found that Wilhemina's beauty and fine figure had not been exaggerated. He wrote home enthusiastically, "Advise the King that the Princess exceeds my expectations," and the second evening, he requested an interview with the grand duchess in the morning before she departed. Anna-Dorothea knew what this meant, and so did Wilhelmina. When the girl protested to her mother that she did not think she could ever love Louis-Ferdinand, Anna was astonished. What did love have to do with marriage for a Courland princess? Especially in the case of one of the most eligible bachelors of the day?

Anna decided to let Gustav try to talk some sense into Wilhelmina. Her daughter was forever running to the baron for advice, but this time, whatever Gustav counseled Wilhelmina made no evident impression. The grand duchess learned the reason for her daughter's lack of interest a scant month later.

At 5:00 P.M. as usual the family ate their one substantial meal of the day in the first-floor parlor Anna had temporarily converted for that purpose; so they would not feel lost in the Sagan castle, she had opened only one wing. Afterwards, they moved into the high-ceilinged salon, with its gilt-highlighted carved woodwork and faded green silk walls, overlooking the rose gardens. Because it was hot, Anna lingered on after the others retired, finishing a piece of needlework for a sofa bolster and listening to the night sounds. Somewhere an owl uttered its lonely, eerie cry, a solo voice raised high above the chorus of croaking frogs. The grand duchess took her last stitch and cut her thread.

Going out into the great shadow-filled hall where the moonlight spilled in broken cascades across the marble steps, she stooped to pick up a silver candlestick from the console to light her way to her room, and noticed that two holders still remained. That was strange. Wilhelmina and d'Armfelt had said good-night some time ago. Anna lit her candle from one of the candles burning in the large candelabrum alongside, then started toward the stairs. Suddenly she heard the sound of low voices and Wilhelmina's laugh. Picking up her skirts in one hand, Anna walked swiftly to the adjacent darkened gallery. As she rounded the opened door, she caught sight of a couple locked in a tight embrace.

"What is the meaning of this?" she gasped. D'Armfelt and her oldest daughter were as startled as the grand duchess. "Go to your room, Wilhelmina. I'll attend to you in the morning."

"No, Maman, I'm staying." The girl stepped defiantly forward, unselfconsciously smoothing her crumpled taffeta gown.

"Wilhelmina, what are you up to?" Anna-Dorothea demanded angrily. Too astonished to think, the grand duchess forgot herself and, reacting instinctively, slapped her daughter. The sound reverberated in the duchess's pounding ears.

"Run along, Wilhelmina," the baron said authoritatively, "I'll join you presently," and started to follow Anna back into the salon.

"No! We were planning to tell Maman in a short time." Wilhelmina rubbed her smarting cheek where her mother's large sapphire ring had cut the surface. "We'll do it together, this minute." Wilhelmina possessively grasped d'Armfelt's arm. And the salon's great double doors shut on the three of them.

In retrospect, Anna-Dorothea may have wondered why she had not been suspicious about what had been transpiring, literally under her nose, especially since their arrival at Sagan. For Wilhelmina—the new duchess of Sagan—had shown an unexpected interest in her inheritance. D'Armfelt, in his capacity as the family's business consultant, spent most of his days in the saddle, riding over the enormous estate, visiting its hundreds of tenant farms, talking to the authorities in the numerous towns and villages belonging to the duchy, attending to the myriad details that had arisen since the grand duke's death. No wonder Wilhelmina went along, returning late each afternoon, as tired and dusty as he.

Once the grand duchess got over the initial shock—and the later knowledge that Wilhelmina was pregnant—she wasted few tears. An experienced woman of the world, she had known that in time the notorious rake would move on, but she had expected to choose the moment for his going. It hurt to have Gustav leave her, and it was shallow comfort to know that Wilhelmina had done the pursuing.

Nevertheless, Anna did not dwell on the past. It was the immediate future that counted. She was concerned only that Wilhelmina's life not be ruined because Gustav chose to go from mother to daughter. It was up to him to save Wilhelmina from the consequences of his folly, and this could be done only by finding a complaisant husband—someone the equal of a prince of the royal house of Prussia.

D'Armfelt might have been a rascal, but he was a clever one. How Prince Louis-Ferdinand was discouraged as Wilhelmina's suitor is not known. But it is altogether likely that Gustav already had a salvage operation in mind when he invited Prince Louis de Rohan-Guéméné to Sagan. For by then, the baron knew Wilhelmina was with child.

The roly-poly, blond Prince Louis de Rohan was a candidate par excellence to replace the Prussian suitor. The blood that flowed in his veins, though French, was every bit as royal as Louis-Ferdinand's. For the prince, who had been forced to flee Paris to escape the Revolution's guillotine, was a cousin of the late Louis XVI. As the princess de Rohan-Guéméné, Wilhelmina need yield precedence to few, anywhere. When d'Armfelt approached him with the facts, the impoverished Rohan had no objection to second-hand goods, provided the price was right. Wilhelmina was sensible enough to go along—the prince was pleasantly inoffensive —with a single condition. She was perfectly willing to share his name—and pay handsomely for the privilege—but not her bed. She loved Gustav too much for that.

A marriage contract was hastily drawn up, similar to Paulina's, to protect her estate, should Rohan prove a spendthrift mate, and the prince de Rohan and Wilhelmina were married before July was out, in an intimate ceremony in the castle's chapel with the local Catholic priest officiating. No one was present except those directly involved—Wilhelmina, Prince Louis, the grand duchess, d'Armfelt. Afterwards, the four proceeded in a char-à-banc to a clearing in the nearby woods, where servants had already laid out a festive picnic. Bottles of fine Rhine wine were set to cool in the fast-flowing water of the Bober, and peasants appeared from one of Sagan's villages to entertain with native songs and dancing.

The whole affair was as low-key as Paulina's wedding had been—"because we're still in mourning" was Anna-Dorothea's official explanation. When word trickled out from the Silesian countryside that Wilhelmina was married to a French Prince of the Blood, not the rumored Prussian one, international society was only briefly surprised. They had learned to expect just about anything of those Courland women. They were right. A few months later they learned that Joanna was married to the swarthy Italian duke of Acerenza.

At the time Joanna's illegitimate baby was born, either just before or just after Wilhelmina's wedding, the governor of Prague, one of the princesses' guardians, successfully baited a trap for Joanna's lover and had him thrown in prison and beheaded. In Central Europe, punishment for seduction was in inverse relationship to one's rank in society. With the culprit disposed of, and knowing how anxious the grand duchess was to get Joanna married off before she got into more trouble, d'Armfelt helped ingratiate himself back into Anna's good graces by purchasing—with a generous dowry provided by Anna—the favorite protégé of Queen Maria-Carolina of Naples for the disinherited princess.

"What a clod!" was Joanna's sisters' only recorded comment when they met their new brother-in-law the day of the ceremony. "His tongue runs faster than a galloping horse, I agree," the grand duchess retorted, "but he is cheerful and pleasant." Of course, nobody bothered to consult Joanna. She made her feelings painfully clear by feigning a migraine on her nuptial night and marching off to bed without the groom.

Each member of the quartet—Anna-Dorothea, Wilhelmina, Gustav, and Prince Louis—knew the importance of keeping up appearances, and there was nothing to indicate to the rare visitor the tangled skeins of their lives. A quiet life together in the country-side was mandatory until after Wilhelmina's confinement. Fortu-nately, the huge Sagan castle afforded adequate space so they were not on top of one another, for it is hard to believe there were no acrimonious exchanges. Still, d'Armfelt had long before demon-strated a knack for turning discarded mistresses into adoring friends, and in time Anna-Dorothea joined this list. Her relations with her daughter were little changed. Since there had never been much mother-daughter warmth between them, the grand duchess did not have the acute sense of betrayal by a loved child.

When heavy northerly winds announced the changing of the seasons, the family moved to Löbikau. As the end of Wilhelmina's term neared, Anna sent her off with a trusted lady-in-waiting to Hamburg, presumably to visit relatives. D'Armfelt joined her, and on the anniversary of her father's death, Wilhelmina gave birth to Adelaide Gustava Aspasia, who was to be known as Vava.

To pass the baby off as a premature Rohan was not even con-sidered. Instead, in accordance with time-honored convention, Wilhelmina was named "Vava's godmother"—that she might settle a sizable estate upon the infant—and Vava was whisked off to distant Finland to be raised by a d'Armfelt cousin who had a daughter of similar age. Later the customary letter disclosing her true parentage was written by Wilhelmina and d'Armfelt for Vava to open on her fifteenth birthday:

Know, dearly beloved child, that you are the testimony of the truest love that joins the hearts of the undersigned. They have taken care of your fortune and if they have not been able to guide your education according to their desire, their wishes and their blessings will serve as a shield for you in the life you will live. We both sign this act with our own hands, placing thereon our seals, and our hearts pressed one against the other are an eternal pledge to you of our love for you. . . .

   [Signed] Gustav Baron d'Armfelt
   [and] Cathérine Frédérique Wilhelmina Benigna,
   Princess of Courland,
   Duchess of Sagan—
   Sagan, 19 October, 1801

Meanwhile, so well kept was the secret of Vava's existence that at the Congress of Vienna in 1814–15, when Wilhelmina was under the closest scrutiny by the imperial secret police and her name appeared over and over again in its daily reports, there was never a hint about her only child, who was by then almost fourteen.

Wilhelmina's confinement had been a difficult one, and because of the midwife's clumsy ministrations, it was impossible for her ever again to conceive. She returned home, weak and wan, to spend weeks stretched out on the chaise longue in her boudoir, listlessly trying to regain her strength. Young Dorothea was told that Wilhelmina had been in a bad carriage accident, and each afternoon the child was allowed to pay her sister a brief visit.

Seeing the youngest princess daily for the first time—Dorothea usually was off with her nanny and not around grown-ups—d'Armfelt took an interest in the frail, peaked child, whose huge black eyes dwarfed the other features of her small face. He was fond of youngsters—he was as good with them as he was with the ladies—and missed his own tribe.

The little princess had learned some English from her nanny. She also had a smattering of French, picked up by listening to people talk in the salon, and a little Polish, garnered haphazardly from Olek and the servants in the anteroom. But she could not read. The baron was dumbfounded. He decided to find out whether the child was stubborn or stupid.

When he discovered that Dorothea's nanny had not even taught her the alphabet, he took on the challenge. Without a word to a soul—albeit with time hanging heavily on his hands—Gustav arranged to work with the girl an hour each day. In short order, Dorothea was doing exceptionally well, and it was clear she had outgrown the nurse her mother had imported from London. A firm believer in cold baths, a stout birch rod, and little else, that stern old spinster sometimes whipped the slight princess, who already had a mind of her own, until she was bloody. These beatings made Dorothea's servants pity her—an added humiliation for the proud youngster that only made her more rebellious and nervous.

D'Armfelt was proud of the small princess's achievements with him, and he convinced Anna that Dorothea was a potential wunderkind. A child of Dorothea's age was normally too young to merit serious attention from any mother of the grand duchess's rank, but a prodigy who might reflect glory on the family was another matter. Anna gave Dorothea's education top priority. A brilliant curriculum was in order. To teach it, a suitable preceptor was called for, in addition to the conventional governess.

While Anna sent letters of inquiry east, west, north, and south, Dorothea continued reading with d'Armfelt, Wilhelmina's health was slowly mending, and Anna's family circle was enlarging. She now had three grandchildren: Paulina's Constantine, the newly arrived, first sprout on the right side of her genealogical tree, and Wilhelmina's Vava and Joanna's Fritz on the left.

April's showers, that 1802, were shot through with sunshine when Gustav claimed a recurrence of whatever ailments had originally taken him to Karlsbad and expressed a desire to consult specialists in Paris. Whether because the baron was truly ill or because the tensions that lay beneath the surface in the great schloss were slowly rising—and threatening to engulf them all—his suggestion was snapped up with alacrity by Wilhelmina. With a little-known officer, General Bonaparte, as France's First Consul, and the Continent reasonably quiet since the French-Austrian treaty at Lunéville the previous year, travel was easier. And the oldest Courland princess, who was feeling more like herself, was anxious to be on her own. Taking Prince Louis de Rohan along to introduce her to her illustrious new in-laws, she and d'Armfelt set off, the trio traveling, naturally, at Wilhelmina's expense.

Succeeding letters to Anna-Dorothea catalogued arguments, misunderstandings, and quarrels between the mismatched pair of lovers—Gustav was twenty-four years older—as they wandered about, from Paris to London, back to Paris, to Prague, to Dresden, and to other intermediate points. Ultimately the spell binding them wore thin, and Wilhelmina cast herself free, although the baron's letters show he was more in love with her than ever.

As Anna confided to her sister, "The rupture was inevitable. Even in good health, Gustav lacks the patience that a long relationship with a younger woman requires. And strong-willed Wilhelmina is used to having her own way."

Anna-Dorothea must have seen them leave the schloss with relief. To live under the same roof, given the existing circumstances, could not have been easy. Whether the grand duchess missed the aristocratic philanderer is anybody's guess. As for d'Armfelt, as soon as he was reinstated in Swedish good graces and appointed ambassador to Vienna the following year, he worked to promote a marriage between Anna and the duke of Östergotland, the elderly uncle of the Swedish king.

Anna had little desire to settle in Sweden, and the Courland princesses' guardians, who were already displeased with the three older girls' marriages, were adamantly against transplanting delicate Dorothea to that rigorous climate. Peter's will provided Anna with a larger income than that of most reigning duchesses. She was enjoying her independence and saw no reason to remarry and sacrifice her title with its attendant privileges. Instead, she decided to follow her sister Elisa's pioneering footsteps and lead an independent life.

Elisa was now established in a minor way on the literary scene by the recent publication of a book of poems, but she was well ahead of her time and the road there had been a rocky one. Though she had become reconciled with Anna at the time of Peter's death, she was shocked by her sister's decision. To her, it was one thing for Elisa von der Recke, the divorced wife of an obscure baron, to flaunt the conventions of the day which limited a woman's actions and which refused to admit that a single woman might prefer that status and have a useful or happy existence. But for anyone as prominent as the grand duchess of Courland to throw off the traces in similar fashion was an altogether different matter.

Anna-Dorothea was adamant. She would continue to summer at Löbikau, and since she needed the resources of a large city for Dorothea's multifaceted education, Berlin would be her winter headquarters. Dorothea's godmother and King Friedrich-Wilhelm III wanted to see the Courland princess raised as a friend of the royal children. His Majesty considered himself a protector of the widowed Anna and her daughters because of their sizable holdings in his realm; the bulk of Dorothea's inheritance was there, and the king wanted to be sure that when the time came for the girl to marry, it was to one of his subjects. The royal family would make Anna's Berlin stay a pleasant one. And the grand duchess had already ordered that the great palace Dorothea had inherited there be aired of mothballs.

CHAPTER FOUR

The Grand Duchess & Dorothea
1803-1808

THE VAST BAROQUE PALACE at number seven, which Frederick the Great had built long ago for his sister, was one of the most magnificent of the many private residences lining Unter den Linden, Berlin's finest public promenade. It was located so near the Brandenburg Gate that on a sleepless night, Anna-Dorothea could hear the shouts of the guards posted there mingling with the voice of the watch padding past, underneath her window, crying the hour: "God give you good morrow, my masters! Past three o'clock and a fair morning."

Prince Louis-Ferdinand, whom she had once coveted as a husband for Wilhelmina, was soon a devoted escort, and Anna's reputation as a femme fatale did the rest. The Swedish ambassador, Baron C. G. von Brinckmann, who claimed to know everything, whispered to anyone who cared to listen, "The Grand Duchess, purring like a cat, confided to me that Louis-Ferdinand is the strongest man on earth. She's in a good position to judge. She's always gotten what she wants. No vine has grapes too high for the Grand Duchess of Courland." But contrary to what that busybody might think, she was not the prince's mistress.

Anna had arrived during a low point in Louis-Ferdinand's torrid affair with the titian-haired daughter of a local innkeeper. The grand duchess thoroughly enjoyed Louis-Ferdinand's company, but as she got to know the young prince better, she decided she much preferred to be with him in the daytime, before his tongue thickened with drink, and she elected to be the prince's confidante rather than his surrogate mistress. Anna-Dorothea did not lack other admirers, however: There was a never-ending queue of carriages in number seven's great courtyard, headed by the smart coupe of the ardent Russian ambassador.

The grand duchess was far more sophisticated and cosmopolitan than she had been when she lived in Berlin with Peter, and she now considered the court there stultifying. She found dreary the gaunt, white-haired queen mother, who always received wrapped in layers of sweaters, flannels, and shawls in her damp, plant-filled solarium; the thin peppermint tea with stone-hard cookies left over from the previous Christmas and the conversation matched the setting. Queen Louisa was equally dull and, to make matters worse, was forever expounding on the godlessness of the French. The grand duchess had recently enjoyed a stimulating trip through parts of French-occupied territory and still had stars in her eyes from the preferential treatment accorded her: a thirty-man honor guard to shadow her every move and official banquets in her honor every time she turned around.

The day Queen Louisa focused on Napoleon, now France's consul for life and titular ruler in all but name, and carped, "Why, he comes from the humblest origins. He cannot possess any real ability. No man of genius could possibly spring from so modest a background," Anna, who greatly admired Bonaparte, had her fill. She found the Prussian aristocracy no more stimulating, obsessed as it was with antiquated ceremonials. She also objected to the capital's extreme social stratification, which made it impossible to meet other, more interesting personalities. She enjoyed stimulating people, with or without pedigrees, and the bluest of blue blood with nothing else to recommend it failed to impress her.

The adventuresome grand duchess was curious to visit one of the several Jewish homes where intellectual salons were flourishing and sample for herself this recent Berlin innovation, encouraged by Frederick the Great, who had released the Jews from a ghetto of prejudices reaching back to the Middle Ages. His nephew, Prince Louis-Ferdinand, who was no snob where arts and letters were concerned, took her to a Jewish hostess's "aesthetic tea," and she discovered there the creative, talented minds she sought. She also met the cream of the German theater—actors and actresses who were considered beyond the pale and never invited into respectable Prussian homes. Fired with enthusiasm, Anna-Dorothea determined to establish her own circle.

With her status as a former sovereign, her wealth, and her important connections—and her own radiant charm and personality—Anna was in a unique position to compete for the same coterie. Neither Friedrich-Wilhelm III or Queen Louisa made any pretense of being scholarly, and they disliked the trend of a handful of the more daring elite to socialize in what Their Majesties considered obscure, unsuitable places with unknown riffraff. But for the elite to mingle at the grand duchess of Courland's was a different story. Royal acceptance of Anna's burgeoning salon—although Their Majesties disapproved of its increasingly French orientation—gave it an added aura. Number seven was soon the place to see—and the place in which to be seen.

To guarantee the presence of the literary lions of Weimar on their rare visits to the capital, Anna-Dorothea prevailed upon Elisa to join her. The frail, asthmatic Baroness von der Recke, with her watery blue eyes and perpetually runny nose, had none of the beauty of her younger sister, but she had as sharp a mind, and had lately established a significant relationship with Christopher-Auguste Tiedge, a member in good standing at the German Athens. "Ours is a platonic friendship," Elisa was careful to explain when she arrived at the Unter den Linden palace with the author of several popular ballads in tow. The two moved into an apartment on one of the sprawling residence's several inside courts. There, Elisa, who had little money of her own, happily shared everything, from the food on her plate to the fruit in her hand, with her odd little gnome with a clubfoot and frayed, spotted clothes. To Anna's amusement, number seven's new seraphic poet-in-residence referred to Elisa, who towered over him, as "She," as though he were speaking of God.

In addition to meeting celebrities from Weimar—including Wieland, Schiller, and Goethe—the grand duchess's guests could hear Louis-Ferdinand improvise, almost nightly, at the clavichord. The Swedish ambassador and other diplomats also appeared regularly, for the great palace was an ideal listening post for Central and Eastern European news because of its hostess's Russian connections.

Anna-Dorothea's salon quickly became the center of all that was gayest and most provocative in Berlin. When Mme. de Staël reached Berlin early in the spring of 1804 to study contemporary German philosophy and culture for a book in progress, the famous

French woman of letters made number seven her temporary head-quarters until she could settle in her own apartments at the Stadt Paris, on the River Sprée quai.

Anna felt sorry for the lonely Albertine, Mme. de Staël's eight-year-old daughter who was tagging along in her mother's wake, and sent the girl off with Dorothea to a children's ball the queen was giving. Suitably chaperoned, the pair departed in the required long dresses and with the powdered hair the occasion demanded, in one of the great Courland carriages, with two footmen riding behind and a runner preceding them to clear a path through the crowded thoroughfares with his traditional ball-headed staff.

Later, following the theaters' final 8:30 P.M. curtain, friends started gathering, as usual, at number seven. They were already seated for supper when the Swedish ambassador bustled in and hurried over to where Mme. de Staël was holding court.

"Has anyone told you, Madame," he demanded in a loud voice —to be sure he'd be overheard—"that your daughter slapped the Crown Prince?"

"The Crown Prince?" Mme. de Staël was shocked. *"Mon Dieu!* When Albertine returned I asked her if she had had a good time. She replied that some boy whom she called 'a snotty brat' had pulled her hair. She didn't say another word."

Hearing Mme. de Staël's horrified exclamation, Anna had hurried over. She was relieved to discover it was nothing serious. "The Crown Prince can be a holy terror. If it's any comfort to you, Madame," she soothed her guest, "Dorothea slapped His Highness so hard last week when he came to play that he was taken home with a bloody nose and earache. When I asked Dorothea what he had done, she told me he spat at her." Anna laughed. "Her Majesty refused to believe it. She was so outraged she forbade her children to play any more with that 'rabid Courland beast.' But a day or two afterwards, the incident was forgotten, and the Queen invited Dorothea again."

Anna's salon, as celebrated as it was, would not be the only one in the Unter den Linden palace. Within a year after Mme. de Staël's visit, Dorothea had her own. Composed of her governess's circle of talented friends, the princess's was completely bourgeois in orientation, not mixed like her mother's, and it was tailored by the governess to polish her brilliant charge. More than one guest to number seven visited both the grand duchess's and the princess's apartments.

For while Anna had been busy establishing the reputation of her drawing room, she also continued the great talent hunt for the proper team to handle her daughter's accelerated studies. It took far longer than anticipated. By a stroke of luck, the grand duchess discovered Fräulein Regina Hoffman through a Karlsbad acquaintance. Of indeterminate age, the governess looked like a sad-faced nag, with her buck teeth, mousey hair, and perpetual pouches under her small beady eyes. When her fiancé died, she had taken refuge in a convent, only to flee on the eve of her vows, a confirmed freethinker.

To locate a preceptor was more difficult. While she was searching, Anna learned that the Abbé Piattoli, King Stanislaus-Augustus's private secretary, had been thrown into prison when Catherine the Great seized the Polish capital. Remembering the abbé's help with Grand Duke Peter's suit in the Sejm, Anna tracked him down and, through an elaborate system of bribes, managed his release. To her agreeable surprise, Piattoli was so grateful to be out of his dreary dungeon that he accepted Dorothea as his pupil.

A love affair flourished briefly between the laicized Florentine monk and the renegade nun. When they came to a stormy parting of the ways, the lonely little abbé was so devastated that Anna despaired of ever comforting him. In an inspired moment, the grand duchess introduced him to her favorite lady-in-waiting, who had recently been jilted herself. Finding solace in each other's arms, the middle-aged pair married. Anna set them up in their own suite in the vast Unter den Linden complex and persuaded them to adopt her daughter Joanna's illegitimate three-year-old son, Fritz. Anna was delighted that the little boy would be properly provided for. As her letters to him in later years showed, he was to be her favorite grandchild.

The abbé and Fräulein were jealous of each other's hold on Dorothea and were forever jockeying for their pupil's affections. If Dorothea chose to follow the advice of Piattoli, Fräulein was seized with a horrible attack of indigestion and blamed her charge for her acute discomfort; if Dorothea listened to Fräulein, the abbé afterwards subjected the girl to an unending tirade. The quick-witted princess learned to play one off against the other, and to do and study whatever she wished. Her excellent but lopsided education reflected this pleasant game.

The willful princess led Fräulein a merry chase and rarely came when she was called. A favorite trick was to scamper, an apple in her right hand, a book she wanted to read in her left, from one bust-filled niche to another, high up in the library's spacious shelves—from Aristotle to Homer to Plato—tantalizingly out of reach, while red-faced Fräulein, her heavy black skirts and cumbersome petticoats draped over one arm, huffed and puffed up the creaking, ladderlike steps in futile pursuit. For princess or no, Dorothea must learn to obey.

Fräulein was a devotee of Jean-Jacques Rousseau and adhered to the health program outlined in his *Emile*. Daily—rain, sleet, or snow—the pair went walking in the great Thiergarten nearby. Anna's avant-garde stepmother had also been a Rousseau disciple, but Frau von Medem had never made Anna and her sister, Elisa, wear the sacklike dresses Fräulein put on Dorothea. "The pressure of tight clothing might lead to an accumulation of stagnant juices," Fräulein quoted the French philosopher by way of explanation. He also advocated that the child go hatless, "so the bones of her head might grow hard and less porous."

To ensure peace and quiet for Dorothea's heavy work schedule, the grand duchess set her daughter up, at the princess's personal expense, in a far wing of the huge palace with her own staff, carriage, and horses, to allow her to come and go as her studies dictated. Anna saw her daughter only when Fräulein brought her over to greet her each morning and when the girl dined with her once a week.

With Dorothea, to wish was to command. She desired declamation lessons? She got them from Iffland, the prime mover of the Berlin theatrical scene. Berlin's leading tragedienne directed her in several skits. The princess and Fräulein regularly attended the Royal Theater, where she had a year-round loge alongside her mother's, and, as befitted a wunderkind, Dorothea also went twice weekly to the Berlin Observatory to study the stars with the royal astronomer.

Warmed by Fräulein's and the abbés love, Dorothea's potential blossomed. Not surprisingly, the youngster, who a few years before had suffered from the fears and suspicions of a young child brought up alone in the cold indifference common to palace nurseries, now developed into an insufferable little prig who never let anyone forget that the enormous Unter den Linden palace belonged to her.

Fräulein, in her eagerness to have the girl exclusively to herself, fostered the precocious princess's tendency to be bored with children of her own age—with a single exception. The governess dared not refuse to let her play with those of the Prussian royal family, which treated Dorothea as one of its own. The queen mother spoiled her outrageously and arranged for Dorothea and the crown prince, a year her junior, to share the same art teacher on the off chance a little competition might incite both sheltered darlings to better efforts.

Time passed, but the tug-of-war over their pupil continued unabated between governess and preceptor. Piattoli was so worn out by the constant struggle that when Anna requested that because of his close ties to the Russian foreign minister, he go to Saint Petersburg on the last matter pending in the final closing of the grand duke's estate, he was glad to get away. But he left with grave misgivings. He was reluctant to entrust Dorothea, who was now almost eleven, completely to the designing governess. Although he wrote Dorothea regularly, directing her studies from afar and repeatedly counseling her to take any problems and questions to Madame, her mother, his efforts were futile. As Piattoli had foreseen, the love-starved spinster seized the opportunity afforded by his extended absence to consolidate her hold on Dorothea at Anna's expense—which was not hard to do, given the customary remote-control system of bringing up princesses.

Almost two years passed, during which Wilhelmina established residence in Dresden. Berlin was out of the question after her aborted engagement to Prince Louis-Ferdinand, but Wilhelmina was hardly the loser. For the Saxon capital, which was the number-two city of the German states, was gayer than the stodgy Prussian one, as the exuberantly rococo, decorative frivolity of its architecture bore witness. In Dresden the ancient regime still ruled supreme, crinolines remained de rigueur and Wilhelmina, the princess de Rohan—aided and abetted by her enormous inheritance—enjoyed the prominent role that was her due as the consort of a Prince of the Blood. There she fell in love with Prince Wassily Troubetzkoi, who was an important cog in the anti-French spy network in Central Europe. Since she did not share the grand duchess's pro-Napoleonic bias, Wilhelmina divorced Prince Rohan and married the tall, melancholy Russian—counter to the advice of her two sisters, Paulina and Joanna, her only intimates, who wrote her frantically from Prague, where they were then sharing a palace.

Meanwhile, Piattoli was still unable to negotiate the disputed ownership of the River Aa palace in Mitau. If the palace belonged to the duchy, it was already paid for in the package sale arranged by the tsar's predecessor, Catherine the Great; if it was Peter's personal property, which was Anna-Dorothea's thoroughly documented contention, it remained to be purchased.

Should Anna go to Saint Petersburg herself? Her sister, who was full of common sense, despite her naiveté where her soul mate was concerned—Herr Tiedge, when he was not reciting his latest masterpiece while holding Elisa's hand in the moonlight was carrying on a lusty affair behind her back with one of the grand duchess's buxom chambermaids—always proved a good sounding board for Anna. The best time to talk uninterrupted with Baroness von der Recke was early in the morning. At that hour the baroness, who was forced by certain physical problems to spend a half hour answering nature's call and did not care to waste time, received while sitting on her *chaise percée;* the French Bourbons used to do likewise, though Their Most Christian Majesties did not bother to camouflage the seat on which they perched with a floor-length, artfully draped plaid shawl, as Elisa did. After she finished going over the previous day's accounts with her chef, she was always available to discuss her sister's problems before she settled down at her writing desk.

The two held lengthy consultations over Piattoli's latest dispatches, and Elisa told Anna what she knew her sister wanted to hear. The grand duchess should go to Russia. The only way to resolve the River Aa palace dispute was by a direct appeal to the tsar. Piattoli could not do this. Anna-Dorothea could. And since Austria's defeats at Ulm and Austerlitz that winter of 1805 and the subsequent peace treaty dictated by the French emperor

—Anna's hero, Napoleon, had been crowned the previous year— travel was no longer circumscribed by troop movements.

It was as unusual for a woman to journey alone to distant Saint Petersburg as it had been for Anna to return from Berlin to Mitau without Peter years before, and for a woman to do so solely to pit herself against the omnipotent Tsar of All the Russias was unheard of—especially for a grand duchess. Anna accepted the challenge.

She hoped the tsar, who had a reputation for dalliance, would prove as susceptible to her charms as the late King Stanislaus. It would certainly make her task a lot simpler. The duchess considered her beauty a prime resource to be assiduously tended, and a proper wardrope was an essential. No trousseau was chosen with more consideration than were the grand duchess's new outfits to bewitch the tsar. The fashions displayed in the latest *Journal des Modes Parisiennes* to reach Berlin were enchanting: The high waistlines, square necklines, and short, puff sleeves favored by the Empress Josephine were equally flattering to the grand duchess, two years her senior.

It was spring by the time everything was set. The trunks of court robes and ball gowns and street dresses, and coats and furs— in case it turned cold en route—the trunks for the laces, ribbons, fans, furbelows, and other innumerable accessories of a lady of high fashion were in order; the latest books and reviews so that her reader might help her pass the tedious hours rumbling eastward —all were packed away. Because she liked her comfort and was fussy about cleanliness, Anna was also transporting some of her furniture and day-to-day necessities.

The Cours were genuinely glad to see their former grand duchess and she, them. Each town Anna passed through—she was making only overnight stops now and would visit with her family on her return west—tried to outdo the others in receiving her. In one village, a group of peasant women gathered, their leader sang a verse of greeting, then the rest repeated it and danced in a gently swaying circle around her coach. Elsewhere, natives dressed in white recited short poems under bough-bedecked welcome arches and then presented her with the white ribbons on which the verses were inscribed.

Anna-Dorothea's long train of vehicles, with ladies-in-waiting, staff, servants, and baggage, stretched endlessly, with a repair wagon bringing up the rear. Escorted along the way at times by local gentry whose mounts were gaudily decorated for the occasion, her cortege presented a picturesque spectacle that attracted peasants from far and near. Entire families lined her route so they might tell their grandchildren they had seen the grand duchess of Courland and she had waved graciously at them as she passed. Each evening when her bed, curtained *à la française,* with bed steps in the form of a small chair, was reassembled in a different inn, one or two superstitious peasants' wives managed to slip their little ones between the ducal sheets to assure their offspring a lifetime of good luck.

The road in from Riga was a nightmare. Boulders lying along the way mercilessly jostled Anna's berlin until she was afraid it might fall apart. Every bone in her body protested, and she marveled at the imperial *feldjägers* darting past, bouncing high in the air from the wooden seats of their small two-horse buggies like rubber balls.

From the moment she approached Saint Petersburg, everything augured well for a successful trip. On the capital's outskirts, one of the tsar's aides-de-camp cantered up, the sun striking fire from his chestful of medals, to advise Her Excellency that Alexander I had placed at her disposal the identical apartments that Peter's family had lived in during Tsarina Anna's reign, a delicate gesture that Anna appreciated. When the duchess reached the sumptuous Winter Palace sprawled along the Neva River's granite quais, where great Italian baroque residences lay glistening in the soft light, another aide waited upon her and introduced himself as her newest son-in-law, Wilhelmina's husband. He brought word that Alexander intended to call the following day and announced that he had been attached to the grand duchess's household for the duration of her stay. Anna was delighted to meet him and construed his assignment to her suite as another indication of special imperial concern on her behalf.

Glad to be at the end of her long journey, Anna slept late the next morning and kept Piattoli waiting while she leisurely followed her customary beauty routine—one maid rinsing her face with crushed cream of cucumbers, then brushing her still glossy auburn hair the requisite two hundred strokes, while another applied lemon halves to her elbows to bleach them and keep them satin smooth. Belatedly, she had Piattoli ushered in. He welcomed the grand duchess with relief, for he was anxious to return home and had great faith in her ability to wind up the Courland matter. From personal experience, the little, black-cassocked abbé knew that Anna, for all her vaunted femininity, could have outwitted Attila the Hun and ridden roughshod over Genghis Khan, had either one crossed her. He was in the midst of his briefing when suddenly he pushed back his chair and sprang to his feet, letting the pile of documents on his lap tumble to the marble floor in wild disarray. Anna turned round, frostily, to discover the cause of the inexplicable interruption—she had left specific instructions not to be disturbed—and was dumbfounded to discover standing in the doorway a good-looking blond officer in a white dress uniform, unadorned except for the Order of Saint Andrew on a wide green ribbon round his neck. It was Alexander I! Finding no one in the entry to announce him, His Imperial Majesty had walked in.

Startled, Anna rose, but before she had time to drop in a curtsey, the tall twenty-nine-year-old tsar leaned down and kissed the petite grand duchess's cheek in accordance with Russian court custom. By so doing—and by his flatteringly informal arrival—Alexander indicated his intention to treat Anna, who was sixteen years his senior, as family—the ultimate compliment.

The tsar was handsome in an exotic way, with high cheekbones, a Kalmuck nose set in a chubby, round face, sideburns as bushy as a squirrel's tail, and a fresh complexion that resulted, supposedly, from washing his face daily with a block of ice. The imperial shoulders were heavily padded—gossips claimed one was lower than the other—and his cinched-in, wasp waist had to be seen to be believed. Since even a sovereign's buckskin breeches had to be wetted down before they were donned, His Imperial Majesty must have been hoisted into his, for he wore them so skintight that no woman was ever left in doubt concerning the imperial desire.

Because Alexander was deaf in the left ear—his father, the late Paul I, had been overly anxious to accustom his son to the noise of battle and had placed him, as a youngster, too near firing cannons —Anna turned to converse with him head on. For, unlike ordinary mortals, the Tsar of All the Russias could admit to no imperfections.

"We must get business out of the way at once," Alexander insisted, as the distraught little abbé scrambled to collect his scattered sheets and disappear. "Then we can devote the rest of your visit to more pleasant matters. Have Piattoli give the necessary papers to my finance minister this afternoon. I promise action shall be taken."

That evening, to offset Alexander's impromptu initial glimpse of her, Anna took infinite pains with her toilette. When she swept into the imperial ballroom, the entire room hushed and the most blasé courtier's eyes boggled. Every inch the glamorous grand duchess, she shimmered from head to toe in cloth of silver heavily interwoven with gold thread, cabochon emeralds the size of pigeons' eggs glowing at her throat, on her slender wrists, and atop each diamond spoke of the tiara nestled in her upswept hair. A Biron heirloom, the spectacular parure recalled to everyone present the days when Grand Duke Ernest was at the height of his power in Russia. Alexander hastened to her side, and the entire court followed suit, crudely shouldering one another out of the way in an unseemly rush to be among the first to be introduced to the dazzling visitor.

Anna-Dorothea accepted the tsar's frank appraisal of her charms and maintained a graceful badinage, a sophisticated game of eyes and words, with him. The tsar loved to dance and ordered the music to begin. Anna hitched up her court train, leaned back gracefully against his arm, and glided off. The music quickened, and Alexander held her close. What the tsar wanted was self-evident. Without promising anything, Anna-Dorothea did not discourage His Imperial Majesty.

Later the tsar astounded his household when he insisted on helping the grand duchess to her coach himself, an extraordinary compliment. Holding Anna's arm far longer than was necessary, he mounted the carriage steps with her to see her comfortably settled—and to make an assignation for afterwards. But with a smile the grand duchess skillfully extricated herself from Alexander's embrace. With a light tap of her fan on his shoulder and a low "Tsk! Tsk!" that was scarcely audible to eavesdroppers, she got in, signaled her coachman, and was off before the amazed tsar could recover from his surprise.

In the days ahead, Anna-Dorothea afforded the spoiled tsar, who was used to having a woman swoon with delight if he raised an eyebrow in her direction, the hitherto unknown excitement of the chase. Anything the grand duchess desired, any place she wanted to see, wherever she wished to go, in or around Saint

Petersburg, she had only to express herself. The tsar placed at her disposal the imperial household, carriages, and residences. Anna did the same thorough job of sightseeing she had done elsewhere in Europe. First, she crisscrossed the capital in a barouche with the little abbé to get an overall view. Next, she visited the imperial institutions for deaf-mutes and the blind, the Summer Gardens with their rare, imported vegetation, and the endless art collections at the Hermitage. Then one day, to the tsar's amusement and to the horror of the local aristocracy—no one on record had ever seen a Russian noblewoman indulge in any sort of exercise—she traversed on foot, with the faithful Piattoli, the entire length of Nevski Prospect, the capital's Unter den Linden. Many places and sights were so familiar to her from stories Grand Duke Peter had told her that they must have seemed like old friends, especially Peter's father's riding academy where Tsarina Anna, dressed always in a costume she herself designed—a yellow buffalo-skin skirt embroidered with silver galloons, topped by a blue vest trimmed to match—used to exercise her favorite horses daily under Grand Duke Ernest's watchful eye. Whatever she did, wherever she was, the grand duchess was never out of earshot of the booming in the citadel to announce the close of day, an essential function at this season with its one hour of darkness. As the days grew warmer, and the flowers in the imperial gardens became a riot of color and scent, a feast for the droning bumblebees, the tsar moved out to Kamenoï-Ostrow and Anna went with him. The grand duchess was proud to have Alexander so attentive, but she never neglected an opportunity to remind him, discreetly, why she was in Russia. The question is, was she still thinking of him as the autocratic ruler whose goodwill she must curry and did she calculatedly withhold her favors until she got what she wanted? Or, as some historians intimate, did she weaken and yield impetuously—before she achieved her goal? Perhaps she never did surrender. As might be expected, there was never a hint in her travelogue letters to proper Elisa:

> My weeks here in the countryside have been happy. I have dined, alone, with Tsarina Elizabeth, who is living a secluded life while awaiting another child. And I have gone to Tsarkoë-Tselo to see the dowager empress, who plied me with sherbets and rose-petal candies until I was too stuffed to move.

Last night there was one of those concerts for which the imperial court is famous—with twenty horn players, each assigned a single, but different, note to play throughout the performance. Tuesday, there was a special fête in a temporary ballroom out-of-doors that had for its highlight a mixed Ukrainian choir. . . .

Much as the grand duchess relished her success at court, eventually the boating, the bowling, the swings in the daytime, the fireworks and other elaborate evening entertainments palled. Hour after hour, the courtiers lolled around on long Asiatic divans, gossiping amid clouds of incense and nibbling pistachio-filled dates, clapping their hands for a servant to bring more tea from the samovar, or crouched silently over the ever-present gambling tables. It was impossible to find stimulating conversation—few of the aristocracy could read yet, and under their Western veneer the nobles were raw and uncultured. Anna grew impatient to leave, but even she dared not importune the tsar.

The vivacious grand duchess was so enchanting an addition to his court that His Imperial Majesty was loath to see her go. But he was also a gallant man, and ultimately his finance minister appeared with the long-awaited documents—detailing a generous settlement. Anna was thrilled, and even the skeptical Piattoli was impressed. For the grand duchess had succeeded in two months in negotiating what he had been vainly attempting to do for the past two years.

The day for departure arrived. Anna watched from her window while Alexander's farewell gift, a magnificent porcelain dinner service for forty-eight, made locally but in the French style, and a hexagonal table of blue cut glass, a specialty of the imperial factory, were carefully unloaded, already packed in innumerable wicker hampers, and transferred to several of the ducal baggage wagons. Then, with the two aides-de-camp the tsar had ordered to accompany her as far as the Russian-Cour border trotting on either side of her great berlin, their gold epaulets and braid glittering in the hot summer sun, Anna-Dorothea headed west to visit her family.

That fall, while Anna was still reliving childhood memories at Alt-Aültz with the Medems, the scene changed drastically in Berlin. In early October 1806, Prussia, nudged by Alexander I, declared war against France, and the queen was accompanying the king into battle.

The royal departure was a stirring, flag-waving spectacle not to be missed. So Dorothea and Fräulein went with the royal children—Dorothea's playmate, the crown prince, proudly wearing the sword and helmet his father had given him on his last birthday—to witness Friedrich-Wilhelm III and Queen Louisa parade on horseback through the Potsdam Gate at the head of their troops. A scant week later, patriotic exaltation turned to panic when an exhausted, sweat-drenched messenger galloped into the city with word of their crushing defeat at Iéna. While the crown jewels and treasures were carted off for safekeeping in one direction, from the opposite the queen's coach-and-six hurtled back to the palace. Her Majesty, who had narrowly missed capture in the earlier fighting, ordered the immediate departure of the royal children, spent an hour burning government records, then sped off to rejoin the king at the front.

That same afternoon, Dorothea and Fräulein returned from their daily walk in the Thiergarten to find a member of the royal household impatiently awaiting them. She brought word from Dorothea's godmother of her brother Prince Louis-Ferdinand's heroic death at Saälfeld, charging against vastly superior forces, and instructions to leave immediately for Danzig as she and her children were doing.

Dorothea and Fräulein quickly joined the general exodus. Since every post horse had been commandeered for the royal family, they had no alternative but to use Dorothea's city ones, ill-suited as those handsome beasts were for either heavy duty or the long journey that lay ahead. The road east was so crowded with refugees that traffic barely crawled. Dorothea was afraid to look out the window, lest she discover French soldiers in hot pursuit. As their carriage ground on through swamps and morasses and over the pitted roads of Pomerania, they were often held up for hours, even days. During the interminable delays, deserters and plunderers, ransacking freely, terrorized the occupants of the many vehicles stalled along the way.

At a halt near Starzard, the governess asked the innkeeper for the latest news.

"Napoleon's entered Berlin!"

"Already?" Fräulein was incredulous.

Her informant nodded. "And made straight for Potsdam, he did."

"What for?" Dorothea demanded. She was amazed to find, staring at her from behind the reception desk, a picture of the French emperor.

"He wanted Frederick the Great's sword, he did. He's taken it from his tomb and sent it as a trophy to the French veterans hospitalized at Les Invalides in Paris, he has."

"H-how can you stand the sight of that m-man?" Dorothea cried, stuttering slightly—a speech impediment that was evident only when she was overwrought. Her face was white with emotion and tears rolled down her cheeks. She walked around, tore down the picture of Napoleon, and shredded it. Then, without another word, she mounted the stairs to her room.

When the weary pair reached Danzig, at the mouth of the Vistula, everything was lacking. The city was being readied to withstand an expected French assault, and the king had already ordered the court further east to Königsberg. Fräulein and Dorothea had had no word from Anna in weeks—she, in turn, was frantically trying to locate her missing daughter—and since they were near Courland, they decided to push on in the hope of finding her there.

The cold was biting; snow fell. Dorothea and Fräulein were numb to the bone, and the somber sadness of the desolate landscape chilled them further.

Proceeding along the Strand, they traveled on the beach to avoid the deep ruts in the freezing roads, and when the overladen vehicle sank to its wheel hubs, the coachman prudently moved to the water's edge where the wet sand provided a firmer base. Wave after wave rolled in from the Baltic, penetrating the coach's interior and drenching the occupants with spray, until Dorothea was sure they would be washed away. The second night out of Königsberg, the travelers reached a cluster of weather-beaten shacks, too few to be dignified by a name. Only the Kürische Haff separated them from Memel, which was almost at the Cour frontier, but the wind was howling and its whitecapped water was so rough that no boatman dared set forth.

"It's so cold it's impossible to spend another night in this carriage. We must go inside," Fräulein insisted.

"In that ramshackle little tavern? I'd rather die," Dorothea protested.

"You very well might, if I let you stay here. Come along, Your Highness, and tomorrow we'll be in Memel." When the governess opened the flimsy door, the overpowering stench and the crowd of dirty, carousing fishermen in its one public room gave the prim spinster second thoughts. But Dorothea, taking Fräulein at her word, had mastered her fear and was already walking, head held high, through the group to the huge tiled stove in the center. People were huddled around its warmth, disputing places with several scrawny dogs and a chicken or two, but someone moved aside to give the soggy girl room on the bench. When Fräulein, horrified, forbade the princess to accept—the spot was still warm from that creature's bottom—Dorothea gave the governess an angry look and sat down without reply. A well-meaning, shabby sailor in dirty, much-patched clothes passed her a mug of hot punch, and she was soon fast asleep on Fräulein's shoulder.

An equerry, one of many sent out by the grand duchess to search for the missing pair, discovered them there the next morning. Bundled in welcome, warm furs that Anna had prudently sent along—the governess, in her haste, had forgotten to include any—the bedraggled pair continued on. A few days later, Dorothea set foot on Courland soil for the first time. Wherever she stopped, peasants sang improvised hymns in her honor and threw themselves on their knees in the snow to kiss the feet of their former grand duke's daughter. Dorothea was touched; she gestured to show her appreciation—she did not speak Courish—and tossed them coins. But the most welcome sight of all, after the past weeks' harrowing hardships, was to see Maman framed in the great doorway of Alt-Aültz, waiting to greet her with outstretched arms.

Since Anna had planned a long visit in Courland on her way back from Russia, she had not been perturbed at the unexpected turn of military events which made a return west impossible. She was enjoying a family reunion. But her daughter could not adjust to life in the Medem family's isolated manor house.

The princess hesitated to consider her new-found relatives acceptable. She was aghast to see her aunt by marriage, rich as she was, forever knitting sox and trotting in and out of the kitchen, supervising the meals being prepared by a battery of servants, tasting and seasoning the vast simmering kettles and casseroles herself. Nor was she amused at one of Anna's favorite family anecdotes—how the first time her maternal grandfather came to call on his bride-to-be, he tumbled out of his carriage stark naked, because his valet had forgotten to awaken the *starosta,* who was sleeping off the effects of a gay Saint Jean's Eve party, in time to dress. This incident, which sophisticated Anna viewed from the vantage point of her years with amused affection, epitomized uncivilized Courland for her haughty daughter. As Dorothea was to comment years later in her memoirs, "Never in all my life have I seen so much eaten so often. They eat if they are hungry, they eat if they are tired, they eat if they are cold . . . they never stop eating." But what else was there to do in the long, cold, endless nights of the rude Baltic winters except eat—and make love?

The unacceptable financial situation in which uprooted Dorothea found herself made her outlook even more jaundiced. With her vast Prussian properties being laid waste by French soldiers, the independent princess was totally reliant on her mother's bounty for the first time. To the average adolescent, this would scarcely constitute a hardship, but for the proud Dorothea it was the crowning indignity.

When the bleak weather intensified, smothering the landscape with fog and heavy blankets of snow, Anna and Dorothea moved to Mitau. Although the Cour capital was one hundred leagues from the nearest fighting, it was touched by the war, for Cossacks rode through on their way to the front and returned with convoys of prisoners. The Russians were not noted for taking care of their captives, and the piteous condition of these sick and wounded Frenchmen deeply touched Anna. With authorization from the local governor, she set up at personal expense an infirmary which she administered herself and where she worked long hours, even assisting fearlessly in the typhoid wards.

This makeshift hospital was located in a wing of Anna's former home, the ducal palace whose disputed ownership had originally brought her east. Normally, Anna would have expected that residence to have been placed at her disposal. However, kings outranked grand duchesses, and the tsar had already placed it at the disposition of the exiled Louis XVIII of France and his tiny court.

Because of her sympathy for Napoleon, Anna showed little interest in the exiled monarch, who reciprocated with a chilly reception for the same reason.

But Fräulein established a close friendship with the refugee monarch's swarthy favorite, Comte d'Avaray, so Dorothea was often at the palace, even if Maman was not. Perching her on his knee, the king called the child *"ma petite Italienne"* because of her dark eyes, and plied her with questions about her studies. If Fräulein was to be believed, His Majesty was most receptive when the governess and her new suitor concocted a brilliant scenario. Since the childless king was searching for a wealthy bride for one of his two absent nephews, the pair of incorrigible schemers proposed the youngest Courland princess. She was approaching marriageable age, and there were few richer heiresses on the Continent.

Anna did not take the matter any more seriously than she did the talk of her daughter's possible engagement to Prince Adam Czartoryski, Piattoli's former pupil, in whose Saint Petersburg palace the abbé was now staying. But this match had both the worthy abbé and Dorothea living in the clouds.

It was natural for Piattoli to talk to Prince Adam of his Dorothea whenever they were together in the evening, and for the abbé's letters to the girl to be full of stories about Czartoryski. In his daydreams the abbé, who loved them both, envisioned the pair marrying and the three of them sailing away into the sunset to spend the rest of their lives together on some enchanted island —preferably in his native Italy.

While Anna had not yet given any serious thought to a husband for her fourth daughter, Dorothea was already convinced that only an older man could furnish the security and stability she craved. Prince Czartoryski might easily be her father—he was twenty-three years her senior—but had there not been an even bigger difference between the grand duke and Maman? Dorothea knew by heart the story of how this famous Polish patriot, King Stanislaus's first cousin, was taken hostage by Russia for his country's good behavior after its final partition. When his friend, Grand Duke Alexander, mounted the throne as Alexander I, Prince Czartoryski became his foreign minister.

Dorothea's idealism was fired by Czartoryski's unrelenting efforts to reunite the scattered Polish kingdom under the Romanoff aegis; her imagination lingered over the ill-starred prince's broken romance with the beautiful Tsarina Elizabeth, Alexander I's consort. When Piattoli arranged for the pair to exchange portraits, Dorothea was struck by the Pole's grave features, and encouraged by the abbé's glowing letters, she saw herself as Princess Czartoryska, playing a supporting role in important events of the future.

When the little black-cassocked abbé wound up the grand duchess's affairs and rejoined the family in Mitau, Dorothea pestered him for more specific details about Prince Adam. To make herself worthier of so distinguished a man, Dorothea was concentrating on more serious studies and had added several additional hours of algebra—this was no hardship, since it was her favorite subject—to her work schedule.

Meanwhile, the dramatic 180-degree swing of Alexander I's foreign policy toward Napoleon, from enmity to friendship, had destroyed Czartoryski's hopes for Poland, and he resigned from the Russian cabinet. With his country still in the grasp of foreigners and with no political future, the prince was thinking seriously about marriage as a source of solace and financial reinforcement, and he decided to take a long look at the girl about whom the abbé had talked so much.

By timing his stay in Mitau to coincide with the July 1807 meeting of the tsar and Napoleon at Tilsit, Prince Czartoryski would accomplish two things simultaneously. He could become acquainted with Dorothea and could also learn more quickly the decisions being taken at the conference site and how they affected Poland. When Anna heard that Prince Czartoryski was contemplating a trip to Mitau, she extended an invitation to stay with her. Prince Adam had been away when she was in Saint Petersburg, but she felt indebted to him for the benevolent interest he had taken in her affairs when the abbé lived with hm.

When Dorothea met Prince Czartoryski in the drawing room the afternoon of his arrival, her memoirs relate that "for the first time in my life I felt embarrassment and extreme shyness." The solemn, dark-haired Czartoryski, in an unadorned somber frock coat with breeches to match, could have stepped out of the portrait Piattoli had sent her of him, imperious expression and all. Dorothea found him perfection personified and hoped he was as delighted with her as she was with him.

He was. Czartoryski's good friend, the abbé, had spoken the truth when he described Dorothea as not pretty and on the thin side. Thin? She was like a reed—and with the largest eyes the prince had ever seen. But Czartoryski did not expect beauty in a wife. More important, Dorothea was of an age for him to mold as he saw fit, and Piattoli had high praise for her intelligence, the one attribute Czartoryski prized more than any other.

Whenever the princess was permitted to be in the same room with him—carefully chaperoned—Prince Adam never did more than pass the time of day. Dorothea decided that he was the strong, silent type and was more enthralled than ever. The prince was not given to small talk under the best of circumstances, but he was quieter than was his wont for his thoughts, twenty-four hours a day, were riveted on Tilsit and on what was transpiring there.

He was not the only person in the Bachstrasse house who was focusing on that small town. Anna's enthusiasm for Napoleon soared as she envisaged the two young autocrats, the thirty-eight-year-old French emperor and the thirty-year-old Alexander, meeting unattended in a gold-fringed pavilion on a barge in the middle of the Niemen River, redesigning the face of Europe to suit their pleasure. While another of Anna's friends, defeated Friedrich-Wilhelm III, sat on horseback in the rain watching silently from the shore, and Russian and French troops lined either bank, Prussia was reduced to a third-rate power consisting of four provinces, and poor Poland disappeared from the map.

Homeward bound from Tilsit, the tsar paid his respects briefly to Anna. On the spur of the moment, Prince Adam decided to accompany Alexander when he continued on; the prince was anxious to profit from the uninterrupted tête-à-tête which the journey from Mitau to Saint Petersburg in the tsar's carriage would afford, to salvage what he might for his unfortunate fatherland. As he bid Dorothea good-bye, Czartoryski remarked, cryptically, that he hoped when she returned home she would go by way of Warsaw and pay a call on his mother. Dorothea took these words as the prince intended she should. He was sincerely interested in her. But the indomitable hero of the Polish resistance was indecisive in private life and under his mother's thumb. Because he would never get engaged without the aged Princess Czartoryska's approval—

she was presently grooming a distant cousin to be his wife—and since Dorothea was still too young for anything formal to be arranged regarding her future, the girl must, next, meet his mother.

Czartoryski's suggestion that she stop over in Warsaw made Dorothea even more impatient to be on her way back—to civilization. But the rich, leaf-scented air and the smell of turned earth bespoke autumn's end before civilian travel west was feasible. Poland's post-Tilsit status made Dorothea's desired detour to its capital impossible for Fräulein to organize unassisted; nor was the governess qualified to help with anything as delicate as the proposed encounter with Prince Czartoryski's prickly mother. Unfortunately, Piattoli had to return to Saint Petersburg on the grand duchess's affairs. Otherwise the worldly abbé could have accompanied the girl and resolved her problems. Dorothea had no alternative. Although relations wih her mother had been ruffled by her dissatisfaction and unhappiness in Courland, if Dorothea wanted to go to Warsaw, she must ask Maman for assistance.

But Prince Adam had been so inattentive to Dorothea, both while he was in Mitau and since—he had not written her a line— that the grand duchess found it hard to consider him a serious suitor. Nor did she consider the prince a suitable one. She had too many reservations about the family. The Czartoryskis might be distinguished, but their disdain for anyone and anything not Polish was notorious; furthermore, the elderly princess was famous for her churlishness and ruled her son. Anna could see no possible basis for a happy marriage under those circumstances, and it was a pity she did not have her daughter's trust so she could convince the girl that it was solely because she cared about her and her well-being that she was against the match. Maman's valid arguments failed because the princess was so thoroughly programmed by Fräulein that she refused to credit Anna's opinion. Her mother was just being difficult, she thought. She was also positive that once she was married to the prince, she could wean him from his difficult mother.

Since Prince Czartoryski had suggested Dorothea go to Warsaw, Anna did not forbid it. But opposed as she was to him for a son-in-law, the grand duchess was determined to do nothing to help. And she did not. Accordingly, Dorothea was forced to bypass Warsaw, but she stopped in Memel to see the disconsolate Prussian royal family, who were awaiting Napoleon's good pleasure to return to Berlin.

Everything the princess saw reinforced her dislike of the French. The once flourishing land they were passing through had been ravaged by war; famine and epidemic raged. As they neared Berlin, she ordered the coachman to slow down until it was dark. Dorothea, who had been born at Friedrichsfeld, considered herself Prussian—technically she and the rest of the Birons had been Russian subjects ever since Catherine the Great bought their duchy —and she could not bear to see Napoleon's soldiers strutting along the Unter den Linden as conquerors. Her Francophobe feelings did not improve when she discovered the French commandant of occupied Berlin had appropriated her palace, number seven Unter den Linden, for himself and his staff, and allocated a single, wretched inside room for her and Fräulein to share. After many complaints, Dorothea and Fräulein were upgraded to two tiny rooms which were formerly Dorothea's chambermaids'.

Six weeks later, Anna arrived in broad daylight with her customary fanfare. Duly impressed by the unending column of carriages and enormous ducal household, the commandant hastened to restore the grand duchess's personal quarters. Maman's preferential treatment in the Princess's own palace rankled and, coming on the heels of Anna's refusal to facilitate the girl's desired Warsaw visit, nudged Dorothea's indifference to her mother toward veiled animosity. Her resentment increased when she found the cosmopolitan grand duchess, with her penchant for all things French, welcoming occupation officers as an agreeable addition to her soirées. However, Anna permitted no ugly scenes with any of the Prussians present and insisted that her multinational guests park their resentments in the antechamber along with their wraps.

Like Fräulein and other patriotic Berliners, Dorothea adopted mourning for the duration of the French stay in the capital. Maundy Thursday, when she made her mandatory weekly appearance in her mother's salon, the sight of her diminutive black-clad figure, glowering like a prophet of doom, effectively dampened the spirits of those present. Her scowl deepened when she saw someone in a French uniform approach, and she looked pointedly in the opposite direction. When he drew abreast, the nearsighted Dorothea recognized the commandant in person. That horrible man! She wanted none of him and dashed frantically from the room. As she disappeared from sight, the general turned good-naturedly to the grand duchess. "Is the princess afraid one of us is going to rape her? I only wished to congratulate her on her confirmation tomorrow." Anna was mortified.

Although as a Cour, Dorothea was born a Lutheran, she had had no religious upbringing; Piattoli furnished her only with worldly moral guidance. Since the girl's confirmation was an important milestone in the eyes of aristocratic Berlin and constituted her debut in society, Fräulein had scurried around and found a pastor willing to undertake an accelerated program, twice a week for one hour, to teach Dorothea she was a Christian. The service was held in the great fourteenth-century Church of Saint Nicholas on Poststrasse, and Anna arranged to have the Courland princess confirmed alone rather than in a group—as befitted her importance. With characteristic independence, Dorothea provided her own profession of faith rather than the conventional answers to the catechism. At the end of the long ceremony, the impressionable girl was so overcome when she took communion that she fainted.

Normally a girl was not considered ready for the matrimonial sweepstakes until after her confirmation, but because Dorothea was one of the Continent's richest heiresses, the situation was reversed, and an impressive string of suitors had been queuing up ever since her return from Mitau. There was an unlimited choice of candidates, for few families would not welcome her in their midst. It was up to Dorothea to select the husband she desired, and the day after Dorothea's confirmation, Anna sent for the girl to discuss her wishes.

The last time mother and daughter had had a serious talk had been in Mitau. Czartoryski had dominated the conversation then—and he did again. If the atmosphere between the young princess and the grand duchess had earlier been so supercharged it crackled, it is not hard to imagine what the scene must have been like now, almost seven months later, when their positions had appreciably crystallized. Dorothea's heart was set on Prince Adam. She was building her whole future around him. Anna, on the other hand, was more persuaded than ever that he was not the right man. With Poland transformed from an independent kingdom under the late King Stanislaus into the duchy of Warsaw under the Saxon king, Anna no longer considered the Czartoryskis in any position to aspire to a match with a Courland princess. Dorothea could do better. The grand duchess took personal offense at old Princess Czartoryska's stalling tactics—her last-minute change of plans had forced the prince to cancel a recently proposed visit to Dorothea— and she was incensed at Prince Adam's continuing silence. Dorothea was equally hurt at the prince's neglect, but she would never admit this to Maman.

When the family moved to the Saxon countryside for the warm weather, Dorothea remained secluded at Tannenfeld, her father's little pavilion in the woods, which the grand duchess had given her. There she continued those studies designed to make her worthy of the enigmatic Pole, while Anna was left to entertain the more persistent of Dorothea's suitors, who had enterprisingly followed the family to Löbikau.

Both Dorothea's self-improvement program and Anna's efforts to keep her daughter's prestigious suitors from despair were exercises in futility. For that fall of 1808, the tsar and Napoleon's vice-grand-elector, Talleyrand, a man whom Dorothea knew only by reputation, held a series of meetings at not-too-distant Erfurt and cold-bloodedly selected a husband for her—for reasons of state that had nothing to do with personal feelings.

Anna-Dorothea von Medem, the grand duchess of Courland, and her youngest daughter, Dorothea (Bibliothèque Nationale, Paris)

Peter Biron, the grand duke of Courland (Musée Talleyrand au Marais)

Anna-Dorothea (center) and her daughters (clockwise from upper left) Wilhelmina, Paulina, Dorothea, and Joanna. Miniatures by Cecile Duchène. (Collection of Wava von Essen and the National Museum of Finland, Helsinki)

Wilhelmina, the duchess of Sagan.
Lithograph by J. Kriehuber,
from a miniature by Moritz
Michael Daffinger. (Bildarchiv
der Österreichischen
Nationalbibliothek, Vienna)

Metternich. Engraving
by J. Kriehuber, from
portrait by Sir Thomas
Lawrence. Bibliothèqu
Nationale, Paris)

Vava (Adelaide Gustava Aspasia Armfelt), left, with her foster
sister, Minna. Portrait by Jean Baptiste Greuze. (Collection of Wava
von Essen and the National Museum of Finland, Helsinki)

CHAPTER FIVE

The Grand Duchess & Dorothea
1808-1809

ALMOST TWO YEARS BEFORE, the winter of 1806–1807, when Talleyrand was governor of occupied Warsaw, Count Batowski, Anna's former lover and Dorothea's father, served as a member of his staff because he considered Talleyrand to be in an excellent position to help downtrodden Poland. Like most Europeans, Olek knew by heart the life story of the extraordinary exbishop of Autun. A priest against his will, Talleyrand had been consigned to the cloth by his blue-blooded family because of his crippled right foot. When the French Revolution leveled his prison as effectively as any earthquake, he took advantage to flee into public life and served Napoleon from the period when Bonaparte was First Consul. By the time Batowski met Talleyrand in Paris, the wily statesman was the number-three man—preceded only by the arch-chancellor and the arch-treasurer—in the imperial hierarchy, exclusive of the Bonapartes themselves.

Batowski quickly became one of Talleyrand's most trusted aides and was billeted with him in Warsaw's magnificent Radziwell palace. The pair spent many a night in the high-ceilinged library before a roaring fire, while the wind howled outside and storms blowing down from the north deposited yet more snow, discussing Napoleon's whirlwind courtship of beautiful eighteen-year-old Countess Walewska, which had the local aristocracy gasping. The conversation automatically led to the need for imperial offspring —then to Talleyrand's preoccupation with the continuation of his own bloodline, since he, too, had no legitimate children.

His nephew and heir, Comte Edmond de Talleyrand-Périgord, had lately come of age. As head of the family and possessed, personally, of a vast fortune and numerous titles, it was Talleyrand's obligation to find Edmond a suitable—i.e., rich and aristocratic —wife. Batowski tried to be helpful. In the course of conversation, Batowski mentioned Dorothea, whom he described as a "Peruvian gold mine." He did not disclose that he was her father.

Talleyrand filed this nugget away, but he was in no position to take action until he accompanied Napoleon to Erfurt to meet with Alexander I for eighteen days in September of 1808. The action Talleyrand took then constituted treason to France and treachery to Napoleon. Talleyrand's determination to do everything possible to thwart the emperor's ambitions and put a stop to his never-ending wars, for the good of France as Talleyrand interpreted it— echoing Corneille's famous line, "Perfidy is noble against tyranny" —marked a watershed in the history of the First Empire.

Talleyrand was a firm believer in the European balance of power, and Napoleon's disastrous recent intervention in the Iberian peninsula proved this thesis: Napoleon's ambition was insatiable, but the Grande Armée was not invincible. Napoleon's great minister was convinced that Alexander I was the instrument to break the Napoleonic stranglehold on the Continent and demanded, "Sire, why have you come here?" the first time he and the tsar were alone. "It is for you to save Europe, and you can only do so by standing up to Napoleon."

Nightly thereafter when official business and entertainments were over, Talleyrand joined the tsar in the luxurious salons of Alexander's cousin who was acting as his hostess. Although the Russian ruler was not yet ready to make a break with his seemingly omnipotent French ally, Talleyrand's revelations did not fall on disinterested ears. As a result of them, Alexander made his final Erfurt commitments deliberately vague, and he was anxious to keep his line of communications open with Talleyrand. Talleyrand took the opportunity during his final off-the-record conversation with the tsar to discreetly broach the possibility of Edmond's marrying the youngest Courland princess. The tsar was delighted at the idea and agreed to Talleyrand's request that he ask Anna-Dorothea, a Russian subject, for her daughter's hand. To do so cost him nothing and assured him not only of the French minister's gratitude but of his continued valued services. Furthermore, it was not much of a detour for Alexander to return home by way of Saxony, and it would be a pleasure to see the delectable grand duchess again.

Since Talleyrand's nephew, Comte Edmond, was at Erfurt in his uncle's suite, he must accompany the tsar.

The excitement at Löbikau when the imperial aide-de-camp arrived with word that Alexander was passing that way and would stop to dine the next afternoon was immense. Two visits from the Tsar of All the Russias in so short a span of time was a distinction for even the grand duchess. The schloss was put through a maelstrom of activity but presented a calm, well-ordered facade by the time Alexander cantered up with a small entourage. Resplendent in his white uniform, with his cinched-in wasp waist, padded shoulders, and skintight breeches, chubby-faced Alexander was in a mood to please. A captivating smile softened his haughty expression, and he had a pleasant word for everyone he met.

At dinner all ears were attuned to catch each pearl of imperial wisdom. Unexpectedly, the tsar turned and asked, "Princess Dorothea, don't you see a remarkable resemblance between M. de Périgord and Prince Czartoryski?" At Talleyrand's request, Batowski had done some last-minute investigating about Dorothea and had told the tsar of her interest in Prince Adam.

"Of whom does Your Imperial Highness deign to speak?" The girl was puzzled.

"Of that young man I introduced you to earlier. He's sitting over there." The tsar pointed to Comte Edmond, a few places away across the table. "As I sit here, I am struck by how much the two look alike."

"Sire, you must excuse me," Dorothea answered truthfully. "I did not take a good look at him before. I am very nearsighted and I cannot see far enough to decide from here."

When they left the dining room, Alexander told the grand duchess he wished a few words with her. Before joining the tsar in the library, she beckoned Dorothea to her side. "Be polite to the French Ambassador," Anna whispered. "Talk to him. You know the Emperor considers him his friend. I've been unable to get your sisters to say a single word to him. And your Aunt Elisa harbors the most ridiculous prejudices against anyone connected with Napoleon. She can't even be polite. You're too young to show your political opinions. I expect you to take care of His Excellency, for I do not want him to leave here dissatisfied with us and our hospitality." It would not hurt, either, if her daughter kept an eye on M. de Talleyrand's nephew. Anna herself had not had a chance to say more than two words to the handsome French officer. Dorothea should see that he was amused, for his uncle was one of Napoleon's most prominent officials. These instructions given, Anna hastened after the tsar. It would be several months before Dorothea learned that she was the subject of their two-hour tête-à-tête.

Alexander wasted no time in preliminaries. "I must tell you, Madame, that I have certain important obligations to M. de Talleyrand, and I want to acknowledge them. I have found a way in which you can help me do so."

"Yes, Sire?"

"M. de Talleyrand has asked for the hand of Princess Dorothea for his nephew and heir, Comte Edmond de Talleyrand-Périgord. I have affirmed that this marriage will take place. You had proof of my friendship when you came to Saint Petersburg. I count too much on your *friendship*"—the tsar repeated the word and stressed it—"not to be confident that you will enable me to give M. de Talleyrand the sole proof that he wants of my *friendship*." Again the word was significantly accented.

Anna replied that anxious as she was to show her devotion, she was afraid that this time Alexander had asked for something she was unable to give. By her position in the world, Dorothea had a great deal of independence, and she was very anti-French. Anna had very little influence over her. "There's another problem, Your Imperial Majesty. I have always promised Dorothea she would be free to marry whomever she chooses."

"Has she any preference?"

"Yes. She prefers Prince Czartoryski."

"Are you in favor of this?"

"No, Sire," Anna answered candidly. "Their age difference and especially the problems posed by his difficult mother, who has shown such bad grace over the whole affair, convince me that Prince Czartoryski could never make Dorothea happy."

"Then I don't see why she shouldn't marry M. de Périgord. To avoid any unnecessary trouble from the Prussian court and others who might be opposed to the Princess marrying a Frenchman, you must tell no one about the marriage I wish until the last moment. I believe your daughter is too well brought up not to accede to your decision. My dear Duchess, I refuse to accept any excuse. I have given my word. I ask for yours."

Anna hesitated.

"Yes?"

The imperious tone of voice reminded Anna that the Tsar of All the Russias was used to getting his own way. He had not hesitated to point out she was indebted to him for her successful sale of the River Aa palace. Anna was dependent on imperial goodwill for her enormous pension, so she must be realistic. "Very well, Sire. I will do what is necessary to persuade Dorothea."

"Good. I will keep you advised." Alexander opened the door. His mission accomplished, he was anxious to depart.

Next morning, Anna sent for Piattoli. Since the little abbé was responsible for Dorothea's romantic fixation on Czartoryski, he must come to Anna's aid. Once that tie was dissolved, Anna hoped it would be easier to get Dorothea's consent to this brilliant match.

Piattoli had his own sense of integrity, and to the grand duchess's amazement, he refused to comply. He loved Princess Dorothea and he loved the prince. He knew them both and was convinced they would be happy together. Silently the little figure withdrew, his head with its halo of white hair around the bald center shaking like a dandelion gone to seed. Piattoli was devoted to Dorothea and heartbroken over the untenable situation in which he found himself. The pleasant hours he spent daily working with the princess—when she always asked for advice and comfort about the uncommunicative Czartoryski—would turn agonizing. Using his poor health as an excuse—it had been deteriorating since his wife's death—he retired to the nearby village of Altenburg, where there was a good doctor, to live out his few remaining years in seclusion.

Dorothea was miserable at her beloved mentor's unexpected decision. In complete ignorance of the true reason for Piattoli's departure and for the tsar's visit—she had no reason to connect them—the girl returned heavyhearted to Berlin for a winter of study. She would miss the little abbé and promised to visit him when she was in Löbikau in February for Maman's birthday.

Unbeknown to Dorothea, the intervening months before she came back were filled with a dizzying number of trips for Comte Edmond and various couriers, racing to and fro in the worst weather between Paris, Löbikau, and Saint Petersburg, to conclude the desired nuptial agreements. When the tsar left Löbikau, the

French ambassador to Saint Petersburg, who had promised his old friend Talleyrand to act as intermediary, continued on in the imperial coach as far as Leipzig. There the diplomat wrote a glowing report on the Courland family, which he entrusted to Comte Edmond to take to his uncle in Paris, together with Alexander's encouraging account of the grand duchess's initial reception of the marriage proposal. Within thirty-six hours of his nephew's arrival, Talleyrand got the mandatory authorization from Napoleon to proceed with the preliminaries.

The first the startled Edmond knew of his uncle's plans for his future was when he was ordered to turn around and proceed to Löbikau at once with Count Batowski. Talleyrand had asked Olek, as a former intimate of the grand duchess, to handle the financial stipulations, which were necessarily complex considering the size of the fortunes involved. Edmond brought with him a letter from Talleyrand formally asking the grand duchess for Dorothea's hand—in which that man of the world, with characteristic shrewdness, flatteringly stressed his nephew's good luck at the prospect of gaining so congenial a mother-in-law. Although Edmond knew that as heir of the great house of Talleyrand he would have little say about his bride, the dashing comte could not have been pleased with his uncle's selection. Ten years Dorothea's senior, and already a confirmed boulevardier with a love of the military, Edmond would have been better off, and probably a lot happier, never married—at least not to someone as studious as the Courland princess. But he had no choice. Edmond remained at Löbikau only overnight before continuing on to the French embassy in Saint Petersburg, where he was temporarily posted to be readily available as the matrimonial scenario unfolded.

His traveling companion, Count Batowski, stayed at the schloss. Nobody could have been more welcome. Aside from her genuine pleasure at seeing that once dearly beloved face again—the grand duchess had not seen Olek since their rupture after the grand duke's death eight and a half years before—Anna was delighted to have an unexpected guest. Anna's openly avowed admiration of Napoleon, whom she considered a man of destiny come to benefit mankind, had understandably strained her close ties with the Prussian royal family. Since a stay in Berlin without easy entrée to the court was unthinkable, she intended to remain at Löbikau until Dorothea was wed. Then with her final family obligations behind her, the grand duchess planned to visit Paris. Meanwhile, the gay, gregarious duchess was finding life in the country a trial at this dreary season, despite numerous forays to the neighboring Dresden court of her newest admirer, the elderly Saxon king.

Anna's continued misgivings over her role in the weeks ahead, coupled with her desire to keep Olek with her as long as possible, dragged out the drafting of the dowry arrangements. When Olek was at last able to send these documents to Paris, he enclosed the grand duchess's reply to Talleyrand's official request for her daughter, which emphasized that Dorothea's consent had yet to be won. Reading between the lines, Talleyrand decided additional pressure was needed. He advised Batowski to stay put to guarantee that Anna did not vacillate further, and wrote his friend the French ambassador in Saint Petersburg requesting that Edmond return to Löbikau for a third time—for the grand duchess's birthday in February—and bring with him a letter from the tsar pushing the marriage. Next, he subtly completed the destruction of Prince Czartoryski's suit for Dorothea by advising Anna that as a respectful son, Talleyrand had requested and received his eighty-one-year-old mother's blessing of the proposed match. How could the grand duchess know that this was deliberate window dressing and that Talleyrand was not close to the elderly Comtesse de Talleyrand? Since it had been impossible for the senior Talleyrands to admit publicly that their oldest child and the future head of one of France's first families, Charles-Maurice, was crippled, Edmond's uncle—the famous diplomat—had been farmed out while growing up and had not once slept under the parental roof. This Talleyrand could neither forgive nor forget.

Dorothea, the unsuspecting bride-to-be, arrived at Löbikau in the midst of a blinding blizzard, and after greeting her mother and Count Batowski, whom she had almost forgotten—it had been so long since she had seen him—she prepared to continue on to her own little pavilion in the nearby woods. Anna would not hear of it. Tannenfeld was fine for summer use, but not at this time of year. Dorothea must stay in the schloss. The blue suite was already prepared. Too tired to argue, Dorothea yielded.

The next morning, she learned from Wilhelmina and Paulina that Joanna and Aunt Elisa were not coming for the celebration.

That was strange, for attendance at Maman's birthdays was a family "must"—for the princesses, if not for their families. Dorothea would miss Joanna, the princess nearest her own age. Joanna was the only one of the three older girls Dorothea could talk to. The more Dorothea thought about her absence—and her aunt's —the uneasier she became. She knew they had never before dared fail to appear. There was no one to tell her that Joanna and Elisa refused to be present for what they termed Dorothea's "betrayal." And what was the cosmopolitan Count Batowski doing in the remote Saxon countryside, far from Paris, at this season? Why had Maman been so insistent that she stay in the schloss? Dorothea was unpleasantly mystified.

The situation was clarified that afternoon. When Dorothea came downstairs, the others were still off finishing letters for the departing courier, so she settled herself with a book to wait. Unexpectedly she heard the postillion's horn announce the arrival of a guest. A lackey entered.

"Where is the grand duchess?"

"In her cabinet. She does not want to be disturbed."

"But she asked to be told when the French officer returned."

"The F-french officer?"

"Yes, Monsieur, the comte de Périgord. The gentleman who accompanied the tsar here in the fall, and then came back later with Count Batowski."

"The comte de Périgord? Back later with Count Batowski?" Like magic, the missing pieces slipped into the puzzle. Once more Dorothea heard the tsar's voice when he had dined with her, asking, "Don't you see a remarkable resemblance between M. de Périgord and Prince Czartoryski?" Petrified that she might find herself alone with the comte—she could not even remember what he looked like—Dorothea bolted up the stairs two at a time and hurtled into the safety of her rooms.

Fräulein, who was toasting herself in front of the blue-and-white Nuremburg porcelain stove, looked up, astonished.

"H-he's here!"

"Prince Czartoryski?"

"N-no! That French officer! I'm sure he's come to marry me!" Dorothea burst into tears and flung herself blindly onto Fräulein's ample bosom.

"Well, you will refuse him."

"B-but Maman?" Dorothea raised her head to look into Fräulein's face in search of some ray of hope.

"She's never forced you to do anything you didn't want to do."

"Y-you know of her love of France and how she wants to go there."

"She can't make you marry anyone you don't want to." Fräulein tried to reassure the sobbing girl. "Remember, she's promised that you shall marry the man of your choice. I heard her. Calm yourself, or you won't be in a fit state for dinner. Nothing could be worse than to show your feelings in public. That won't help a thing."

Dorothea lay down, but the dinner gong sounded before she was in sufficient control of herself. Nevertheless, she got up, washed her face, and joined the family. She found Maman, her cheeks flushed with pleasure, unwrapping a birthday present from the tsar—a gold bowl on a tripod—with the help of Count Batowski and the young Frenchman who had brought it. The grand duchess introduced Dorothea, and she took her first good look at the man she was destined to wed. Wavy chestnut hair crowned a narrow, well-shaped head; he had an oval face with light brown eyes, regular but elongated features, and a weak mouth. His build was trim and showed to advantage in his well-fitting lieutenant's uniform, whose fashionable cut—together with the precise manner in which Edmond's valet had trimmed his mustache and sideburns—proclaimed the dandy. Dorothea found his regard evasive, and when she did manage to catch his eye, his expression was so lifeless that she could decipher neither character nor intelligence in it. Deeply disturbed, Dorothea escaped as soon as decency permitted.

Early the following morning, the grand duchess summoned Fräulein. A long time elapsed before the governess returned, with a woebegone expression—and sealed lips. Then it was Dorothea's turn. She found Maman sitting up in bed amid myriad lace pillows with the bed curtains tied back. Two slices of lemon were bound to her temples—the current cure for wrinkles according to the latest edition of the *Journal des Modes*. Correspondence lay scattered over the flounced taffeta cover, an unfinished breakfast tray was alongside, and one of her poodles was curled up asleep in a ball at the foot. "The time has come," Anna-Dorothea announced, motioning her nervous daughter to a nearby chair, "to tell you the real reason for the tsar's visit to Löbikau."

Anna gave a bowdlerized version of their long conversation.

"The tsar is greatly obligated to M. de Talleyrand and has given his word that this marriage will take place," she concluded. "Although I owe His Imperial Majesty an immense debt of gratitude, I have told him that I cannot—and will not—force you to marry against your wishes." Anna paused dramatically. "The tsar has refused to accept any excuses. You know, of course, that as the tsar's subject—and pensioner—it is of prime importance that I retain His Imperial Majesty's goodwill. I therefore beg you not to refuse without weighing the advantages that can result for your entire family from this alliance." Anna did not hesitate to present the choice facing Dorothea in a way that would, the mother hoped, leave her daughter no alternative but acquiescence.

Fishing among the mail spread every which way on top of her bed, the grand duchess handed her daughter an envelope importantly encrusted with massive red and black seals. "Comte Edmond brought this for the tsar. It's for you, too."

Dorothea read it—and was outraged. The imperial communication was sheer blackmail, an outright ukase.

"Next, I want you to read this." Her mother gave her Talleyrand's letter, which was designed to reduce in advance any possible objection to the marriage. Dorothea was impressed, and filled with curiosity about the writer. She reversed the single sheet, studied the signature, then returned it to Maman without a word. In her memoirs, written long after the event, in which Dorothea captured with almost total recall how she was tricked into marriage, she commented, "I do not think M. de Talleyrand ever drafted the most important diplomatic note with greater care than he gave this letter."

"Don't you have anything to say?" Anna hoped her daughter was not going to make things harder.

"Dear Maman, if I did not feel already pledged to Prince Adam, if, from the age of twelve, I did not consider him the only man I could ever marry, I would do what you so desire. I don't believe Prince Adam's delay in coming here is his fault. I've made promises to him that I feel bound to keep." Dorothea had a hard time explaining herself, and must have felt like a small girl again, plodding through wet sand on the beach. For something of a youngster still remained within the rebellious, strong-willed princess and made her reach forward, apologetically, to try to kiss her mother's hand.

Anna had had trouble enough persuading herself she was doing the right thing for everyone concerned. She had steeled herself for their encounter, anticipating that Dorothea would be difficult, but this unexpected, childish gesture apparently snapped her self-control. She snatched her hand away, and in a terrible scene that Dorothea never forgot, Anna's imagination ran riot. The princess was sacrificing her mother's tranquillity. Dorothea was going to draw down on the grand duchess's head the rancor of the powerful M. de Talleyrand. Emperor Napoleon would believe Dorothea's refusal emanated from her hatred of the French, and every single member of the family would suffer as a result. Carried away, Anna lashed out, "You, my favorite, are very ungrateful!"

Dorothea stuck obstinately to her point. She was engaged to Prince Czartoryski.

"Very well," Maman terminated the conversation, bitterly disappointed. "You must at least show M. de Périgord some courtesy. I will let several days elapse before I send M. de Talleyrand an answer, in order not to make you appear ridiculous and to have it seem that you have thought the matter over."

The complex mother and equally complex daughter might have had their agonizing differences in the past, but never before with such a harsh exchange of words. The sight of her normally calm, dignified mother so upset greatly disturbed Dorothea, but she refused to yield. Despair was a disease to which long exposure at Prince Adam's hands had made Dorothea immune, and she retreated to her rooms to try to justify, in her own mind, her right to happiness.

In the afternoon, Anna prevailed on Olek to try to talk some sense into their obstinate daughter. But Batowski got no further than Anna had. Dorothea's stubborn resistance spoiled Anna's birthday. She was too upset to be effervescent, the dinner celebration fizzled out dismally, and everyone retired earlier than usual.

Anna slept badly. Awakening early, she tried the usual panacea, a brisk walk outdoors, but even the cold February air failed to resolve her dilemma: how to persuade Dorothea to acquiesce to the match so the grand duchess might fulfill her commitment to the tsar. Suddenly she had an idea. Hurrying inside, where the lackeys were waxing the parquet floors by skating around them with their stocking feet encased in special sheepskins, Anna stopped one and sent him to Batowski's suite with word she wanted to see the count as soon as he was awake. When Olek appeared, she dispatched him posthaste to Altenburg. Piattoli was responsible for Dorothea's fixation with Czartoryski. It was up to him to bring the girl back from her dreamworld into reality.

Fate handed Piattoli the unsympathetic role of the family mentor who, at death's door, betrays the confidence his beloved pupil has placed in him. The abbé had been tormented these many past months by personal misgivings over Prince Adam's shabby performance. When Count Batowski appeared, Piattoli was too sick to think clearly or again refuse the grand duchess's request as he once so courageously had. With the greatest difficulty, he barely managed to scrawl the few lines the count dictated.

It was dark before Olek returned and gave them to Dorothea. There was no reason for the girl to think twice about what Batowski might have been doing at Altenburg, and it was years before she learned the real reason for his trip there. She was delighted to hear from her beloved mentor and hastened to read the note in the privacy of her room. Perhaps it might shed some light on Czartoryski's inexplicable silence.

Despite the abbé's quavering handwriting, his stark message leapt off the page:

> My Young Friend,
> All our hopes are destroyed. I have received word from
> Poland telling me that the marriage of Prince Czartoryski is
> finally arranged to the old Princess's protégée. Warsaw can
> talk of nothing else. *Voilà!* This is the explanation of his
> long silence. I am in such pain, I cannot write more.

Dorothea could not believe her eyes. There had to be some mistake. She must see Piattoli and talk to him. She rang for the steward to order a carriage and raced off in the blustery night to Altenburg.

The abbé's cubicle was dimly lit by a single flickering candle, and Dorothea hardly recognized the haggard wraith lying there. Kneeling alongside his bed, she clasped his scrawny hand and tried to control her convulsive sobs.

In a voice so indistinct she had to lean over to understand him, Piattoli mumbled, "Be happy. You have been the great concern of my last years. Forgive me for having tried to guide your future." He stopped to catch his breath. "Henceforth entrust it to

Madame, your mother." Sheer force of will had given Piattoli the strength to talk, but emotion, coupled with physical exertion, proved too much. The little abbé turned his head to the wall, and without giving Dorothea a chance to open her mouth, he motioned feebly for her to leave. It was almost dawn—and still snowing—when she got home.

Batowski reported their daughter's rash expedition to Anna before she was out of bed. She was horrified. The girl had gone to Altenburg? Alone? In the middle of the night? Dorothea must be desperate.

Afraid Anna might repent or renege, and determined to please his powerful patron, Talleyrand, by keeping the marriage on track, Olek reminded her of recurrent rumors of bad blood between Prince Czartoryski and Alexander since Poland had been wiped off the map. There was no need to elaborate. The grand duchess understood. In the light of the two men's present hostility, it would be one thing if Dorothea flouted the tsar by flatly refusing to wed Comte Edmond. But to do so expressly to run off with Prince Czartoryski might easily prove the grand duchess's undoing. And as last night's escapade vividly illustrated, Dorothea had her mother's courage and might do exactly that.

To dissipate any lingering doubts that Dorothea might still cherish, a scene written and directed by Batowski—with Anna's obvious concurrence—was performed that evening when the schloss's great bronze dinner gong sounded. The courier had come shortly before, and as was customary, each member of the household brought to the table the most recent tidings from abroad. An elderly Polish countess who was a pensioner of Anna's arose from a sickbed to be coached in her lines. The last to assemble, she rushed in, out of breath, her wig slightly askew, with wisps of dyed black hair flying in every direction, clutching a handful of mail exultantly.

"Excuse me! Excuse me! I had so many letters from Warsaw I could not get through them quickly. *Ma chère,*" she turned wide-eyed to the duchess. "Can you believe it! After so many years as a bachelor, Prince Czartoryski is finally engaged! I have every detail!" To emphasize her scoop, she raised an envelope triumphantly in her shaky hand.

So it was true. Convinced at last of the prince's defection, and bitterly indignant, Dorothea pushed back her chair so abruptly it toppled over with a crash. The noise riveted all eyes on her. "M-maman! May I speak to you a moment—alone?" she begged, and disappeared into the adjacent salon. The grand duchess was at her heels.

"S-since Prince Adam has seen fit to break his promise," Dorothea's voice choked, "I c-consider myself no longer bound by mine. I will m-marry whom you wish. You c-can tell M. de Périgord."

"Oh, my dear! My dear!" Anna flung her arms about the crushed girl delightedly, ignoring her tears. "You are doing the right thing. Absolutely. I must tell M. de Périgord at once." Afraid to give her daughter a chance to change her mind, Anna hurried back into the dining room with the good news. And Dorothea crept upstairs to sob herself to sleep.

The deceptive measures the grand duchess resorted to in the end to force her sixteen-year-old daughter into another's arms must have troubled her, for the following morning, Anna did an un-heard-of thing. She reversed procedure and went to her daughter's bedroom. "I want to congratulate you again on your common sense and thank you, on the family's behalf," she said, kissing the sacrificial lamb. "Now," she coaxed, "you must be gracious to M. de Périgord." Dorothea followed Maman downstairs, crestfallen and sad-eyed. "He's in there." Anna pointed to the library and smiled encouragement.

The two young people who were fated to be husband and wife sat face to face and stared self-consciously past each other in silence. Gathering her courage, Dorothea was the first to speak. "I hope, Monsieur, that you will be happy in the marriage that has been arranged for us." Her voice was pitched so low that Edmond had to strain to hear. "I esteem you but I cannot love you. I am yielding to my mother's wishes. Perhaps I will be happy. I hope so." Dorothea looked him solemnly in the eyes. Her voice was stronger. "You will find, I think, my regrets at leaving my country and my friends simple to understand."

Mon Dieu!" Edmond jumped to his feet. "What you say seems quite natural. I, too, am not marrying from choice. I am doing so only to please my uncle. At my age, I'd prefer a bachelor's life."

When Piattoli died a short time later, Dorothea placed in his coffin the portrait of Prince Czartoryski that the abbé had had made in Saint Petersburg and sent her some years before—burying her first expectations with her illusions. But she could not inter her dreams. The apathetic bride-to-be, who had agreed to marry Edmond from a sense of rejection and pique, lived in a landscape of gray dejection. Any animosity she felt toward her mother for pushing the match was buried by the avalanche of Czartoryski's supposed betrayal.

Anna was thankful the unpleasant decision making was behind her and looked to the future. For Dorothea's marriage held an unexpected dividend for the grand duchess—she would be accompanying her daughter west as the guest of M. de Talleyrand.

Although Paris was the fashion center of the Continent, it would never do for a Courland princess to arrive without a suitable trousseau, and Anna fluttered over these preparations—and her own new wardrobe—with the vivacity of the early awakened birds chirping in the vines outside her bedroom windows. Every morning promptly at ten, Dorothea was in Maman's bedroom for endless hours of fittings under the watchful eye of Berlin's finest dressmaker, a French émigrée who had eagerly rushed her troop of minions to Löbikau for this prestigious commission. Then the princess sat silently, like a dummy, while countless hats, bonnets, and toques, to match each costume, were pinned on her listless head and their veils adjusted by the Prague dictator in these matters. Dresden, which had only recently abandoned hoopskirts, was too old-fashioned to be consulted about gowns. But no one could equal its seamstresses when it came to the finest undergarments. Since time was short, three of the Saxon capital's best were installed in the green suite, stitching away at meters and meters of filmy cambric, cobweb-thin lawn, linen, and sheerest lace. Stockings, gloves, and shoes were ordered by the dozen.

To be on the safe side, Anna sent word to Altenburg that any mail from Poland addressed to the late abbé should be referred to her. This was a wise precaution, for a letter did arrive from Prince Adam. His mother, the old princess, had finally consented to his marriage with Dorothea, and the prince was winding up his affairs so he could come and claim her. Anna had been afraid of some last-minute intervention by those unpredictable Poles, and without a word to Dorothea, who did not learn of this exchange until she and Czartoryski met at the Congress of Vienna, five years later, the grand duchess hurriedly sent Prince Adam an announcement of her daughter's impending marriage.

Another potential hitch developed at the other end of the rainbow—the groom's—and was as quickly averted. Edmond returned to Paris to find his uncle Talleyrand in Napoleon's bad graces for supposedly conspiring against the imperial regime. In a violent scene that quickly made the capital's rounds in gory detail, the emperor hurled at Talleyrand a steady flow of Corsican invective. "You are nothing but shit in a silk stocking!" His Imperial Majesty concluded, and stripped the brilliant statesman of his most important offices, leaving him only the lofty but powerless ceremonial role of vice-grand-elector. Napoleon was in no mood to grant final authorization for Edmond's brilliant marriage. But he also had no wish to offend the tsar, who had acted as matchmaker and whose subject Dorothea was. So imperial approval was granted—circuitously—to Edmond's father.

Nothing but a Lutheran ceremony was possible at Löbikau. Since Edmond was a Catholic and religion was no issue with Dorothea, Anna selected Frankfurt as the site for the service. The city was on their route west, and the prince primate there, who was a long-standing intimate of both the Biron and Talleyrand families, agreed to officiate.

Edmond's sister was unable to be present, and his mother was dead. (She had been in the last tumbril to go to the guillotine. She had courageously refused to lie and declare herself pregnant, as did other of her friends, in order to escape that terrible fate.) In protest against the marriage, the Francophobe members of Dorothea's family—the three older princesses and Elisa—refused to attend. Only dour-faced Fräulein, Edmond's complacent father, and a beaming Anna flanked the solemn groom and the downcast bride as they knelt, April 22, 1809, before the altar in the candle-lit chapel in the Cathedral of Saint Bartholomew, which overlooked the River Main. Afterwards, the prince primate gave Dorothea a wondrously wrought little bird that chirped and beat its wings inside a golden cage, an appropriate gift for the woebegone bride, pitchforked out of girlhood at sixteen.

The guns were barking once more. Forty-eight hours later, the groom, who was only a pawn in his uncle's chess game, left to join the Grande Armée's general staff while the bride, face to face with a terrifying plunge into the unknown, set off westward at Maman's side.

CHAPTER SIX

The Grand Duchess & Talleyrand
1809-1810

THEY TRAVELED LEISURELY—Anna took a number of side trips to show places of interest to Dorothea—and several weeks later the spacious berlin drove through the gates of Paris by way of the Place de la Bastille. Napoleon had recently embarked on a massive building program to remake the dark, walled, medieval city into the most beautiful, modern capital in the world. There were so many slabs of sandstone lying in the middle of the boulevards that the coachman had to slow the horses to a walk and pick his way carefully around them. Soon they were lumbering across the Seine on the crowded Pont Neuf, one of the newer bridges, whose sides were not lined with four- or five-story buildings and shops. They continued along the Left Bank, turned right down still another narrow, unpaved street, muddy like the rest from the open sewer in its middle, and pulled up in the gathering dusk at 57, rue de Varenne, in the great inner courtyard of the hôtel Matignon.

The entry heralded the magnificence to come. When Talleyrand had recently purchased it, the Matignon was already one of the most spacious and beautiful residences in the aristocratic Faubourg Saint-Germain. Determined to have a home befitting his exalted position in the imperial hierarchy, Talleyrand remodeled and added on to the mansion and bought the adjacent property, to create the largest private park in the city. The hôtel—as the French called a large private mansion—was located between the court and the gardens in the classic French manner, with the separate buildings housing the servants' quarters, stables, kitchens, and carriage house attached on either side but hidden behind a one-story arcaded facade.

Liveried footmen rushed to help the grand duchess and Dorothea descend. Fräulein and Anna's chief lady-in-waiting followed
from the second carriage, and the rest of the enormous ducal
staff were shepherded elsewhere. Crossing the formal entrance hall,
mother and daughter ascended the broad marble Staircase of
Honor. The light from the three-branched candelabra held by
lackeys preceding them fluttered fitfully over the many paintings
and tapestries lining the walls and landings, picking out here the
diamond in a cavalier's toque, there the white ruffles of a Talleyrand ancestor and the alabaster skin of a girl.

On the second floor, the two parted company. Talleyrand,
with his customary attention to detail, had selected for the bride
the only suite decorated in modern style. The younger generation,
he had observed, liked the look of the furniture that came into
vogue after Napoleon's Egyptian expedition: straight-limbed mahogany lines with a glittering ormolu decoration. He assigned
Anna one of the master apartments, which represented the ultimate
in traditional French interior decorating—splendor without vulgar-
ity. The tastefully displayed eighteenth-century cabinetmakers'
chefs d'oeuvre were a joy to behold, but a special pleasure to
lovers of fine china like Anna were the extravagant bunches of
porcelain flowers. These bouquets, copies of those Louis XV had
ordered for his country houses, came from the royal factory at
Vincennes. They overflowed squat, ormolu-decorated tubs reposing
on a pair of elaborate consoles, which were fitted between the tall
french doors and surmounted by matching gilt mirrors to reflect the
eternal beauty of the pale petals. There was also a built-in bathtub
—the latest luxury, which only a few of the great Parisian mansions
possessed.

Anna-Dorothea was looking forward to meeting her host. What
was it her friend Mme. de Staël had said about him? "What a pity
M. de Talleyrand's conversation can't be bought. I'd go into debt
to have it." The fabled force of his intellect, his legendary power
of fascination, his high rank, and the esteem in which the tsar
held him added to the fifty-five-year-old vice-grand-elector's appeal.

As the grand duchess entered the salon before dinner, she heard
a cadenced limp and was conscious of the pervasive odor of
amber—a sound and a fragrance to be linked with her memory
of Charles-Maurice de Talleyrand until the day she died. Even
his hobbled gait appeared elegant as he slowly dragged himself for-

ward to meet her. A broad-shouldered man of medium height, Talleyrand was attired in a bottle green velvet long-tailed coat and culotte, with a dress sword at his side, his chest ablaze with those jeweled orders and colorful ribbons his faithful valet—with protocol at his fingertips—deemed essential for the evening's events. Very little gray showed in his blond hair, which was only lightly coated with rice powder in the latest fashion. He had a pale, expressionless face with an arrogant mouth, too-long lids hooding blue eyes hard as sapphires, and a surprisingly insolent turned-up nose.

He sat down as quickly as she did—she had been warned it was hard for him to stand for any length of time—and rested his crippled foot, the right one, on a needlepoint stool. It was encased in a special high-laced shoe with a cumbersome, heavy metal bar attached. But Talleyrand managed to wear this cruel brace as if it were the last word in sartorial splendor—a fitting mate for the other leg, which was encased, like any gentleman's, in a black silk stocking and a handsome pump with a diamond buckle. He did not move a muscle of his face when he talked, and his slow, deliberate manner of speech was of a piece with his polished appearance. While they chatted about her trip, Talleyrand slowly outlined a pink Aubusson rose with the tip of his gold-handled cane, and his connoisseur's eye appreciatively appraised his fair visitor.

Anna's graceful beauty, which was only slightly faded at forty-eight—successive attempts to hide the increasing number of gray strands had turned her auburn hair black—appealed to his discriminating palate. So did her sovereign airs and seven hundred years of blue blood, even if her ancestors had been crude Teutonic Knights in the savage hinterlands when his were already riding at the French kings' right hand. Time and distance had magnified her career and achievements in Courland, Warsaw, Prague, Berlin, Saint Petersburg, and Dresden—transforming her into a glamorous political personality on terms of intimacy with everyone worth knowing in Central and Eastern Europe, and her affair with Tsar Alexander had titillated European court circles for years. Talleyrand pronounced the petite, vivacious grand duchess "delightful," the greatest compliment in his vocabulary.

Dorothea came in and was introduced. Talleyrand greeted her warmly but was disappointed that his new niece should be an underdeveloped, sallow prune. He had no taste for unripe fruit.

Every night Talleyrand held open house, and at this period

he had dinners four times a week for never less than forty; his guest list was largely dictated by the emperor. Napoleon was essentially a man of work, and fashionable diversions were not for him. But he insisted that Talleyrand and other high dignitaries entertain regularly and lavishly, not only to impress natives and foreigners with the prestige and wealth of his empire, but also to enable the police to keep tabs on what Parisians were saying and thinking.

Since tonight was family night, Catherine de Talleyrand, the statesman's wife, soon appeared, then the others: Edmond's father and sister, Melanie.

Meals at the hôtel Matignon were a celebrated Parisian ritual, and Talleyrand offered Anna-Dorothea his arm and slowly led the way into the dining room. In the center of the table reposed a welcome arch, modeled after the plans for the Arc de Triomphe which was being built to crown the slight hill at the end of the Champs-Elysées. This particular culinary masterpiece—there was a different one nightly to serve as the mainstay of the decorations —was intended as a tribute to M. Edmond's bride and her mother by its creator, Talleyrand's famous chef, Boucher, who had made his table the envy of Paris. A chubby man, with a large carving knife tucked into the belt of his starched white uniform like a Turk's scimitar and a tall, fluted bonnet set at a rakish angle atop his jet black hair, Boucher normally presided over the serving of each meal with as much aplomb as Napoleon watched a cavalry charge led by one of his swashbuckling marshals. Because the guests were late sitting down, his sauces might curdle; he was glowering and his cap was quivering, two telltale signs. Moving quickly to avert a drama of potentially earth-shaking magnitude, Talleyrand beckoned his temperamental "Cher Mâitre" to his side and deftly smoothed his ego.

An array of soups was ladled out and served by the footmen standing behind each guest's chair; an assortment of fish followed. Next, small pâtés, melon, and roast meat in pastries. Then Talleyrand, with the prerogative of a grand seigneur but contrary to custom, selected a succulent rack of lamb *pré-salé* to carve himself. Starting with the grand duchess, he offered the slices around the table in order of the guests' importance, ending with Dorothea because she was the youngest.

Among the melodies floating down from the trio of musicians

lodged in the small gallery above, the sound of voices mingled with the tinkle of glass and silverware. Suddenly Catherine de Talleyrand's high-pitched voice drowned out the others, ". . . suggested I get bigger drops for these pearl earrings. I replied, 'Whom do you think I married, the Pope?' "—an incredibly tactless remark for a woman whose husband was the ex-bishop of Autun. But that was Mme. de Talleyrand.

Vestiges of the breathtaking beauty she once possessed were still visible in the features of the blowsy, plump blonde. For a man of Talleyrand's flawless taste and fastidiousness, this French ex-courtesan, born in India, seemed a strange choice for a wife. But in the chaotic period following the French Revolution, mores and tradition had lost all significance. When Napoleon, as First Consul, insisted on the proprieties within his intimate circle and set an example by marrying Josephine, Talleyrand married his mistress as casually as he had doffed his bishop's miter. Little intimacy existed between the mismatched couple any longer, and society, with tittering enjoyment, laid every gaffe that went the rounds to the scatterbrained Catherine. It was too delicious for Talleyrand of all people to have Mme. Malàprop for a wife.

After platters of tiny sweet soufflés and jellied fruits were passed, the maître d'hôtel with a great flourish removed the pièce de résistance from the middle of the table, and the chef sliced his welcome arch, a mouth-watering concoction of nougat, biscuit, spun sugar, and whipped cream. Anna took only a taste. "It's delicious. But it's so rich, it would be a sin to take more," she was heard to remark with a dazzling smile that showed her still perfect teeth.

"Surely, my dear Duchess, you know that every sin is negotiable, eh?" Talleyrand's overly long lids opened for the briefest of seconds and that rarest of phenomena, the glimpse of a twinkle, was discernible.

The days whirled past like leaves in the breeze that came soughing through the Bois de Boulogne, the half wild royal hunting preserve out near the Abbaye de Longchamps where Talleyrand frequently took his guests for an afternoon drive. It was up to him, as the head of the family, to look after Dorothea, since Edmond was off in the service, and to arrange that she saw everything worthwhile. And it was every bit as important—although he did not say so—for Talleyrand to look after the captivating grand duchess with her important Central European and Russian connections. In this case, the duty came under the heading of pleasure.

Paris was everything Anna expected it to be—and more. Here was the Louvre, where the great masterpieces of the conquered and occupied Continent were on view. The Lion of Saint Mark stood in the fountain in the tree-lined esplanade before Les Invalides. The quartet of famous Venetian bronze horses was perched atop the Arc de Carrousel in the Tuileries' great courtyard. They were hitched to a huge empty chariot which was awaiting, as occupant, a golden statue of Napoleon I. Irreverent Parisians gawked below and punned, *"Le char l'attend"* (literally, "The chariot awaits him," but phonetically *"le charlatan,"* some people's name for Napoleon).

People were sitting in the Tuileries' gardens enjoying the flowering chestnuts and the late spring, reading rented newspapers affixed to long poles. Individual papers were too expensive to buy. Jugglers and acrobats, dancing bears, and goats climbing ladders performed in the streets. At Franconi's popular circus, a trained stag starred, and at many corners donkeys carried baskets of flowers for sale.

Little escaped Anna's eager attention. She visited the Musée des Petits Augustins, cluttered with statues and artifacts rescued during the Revolution from the churches that had been transformed overnight into stables or barracks. She bought barley sugar in the popular candy shop Le Fidèle Berger on the rue des Lombards and went to Le Petit Dunkerque on the rue de Richelieu for fantasy jewelry and other luxury items—umbrellas with mother-of-pearl handles, elaborate beaded reticules, and amusing gold vinaigrettes like the one in the shape of an articulated fish that had belonged to Empress Josephine.

Dorothea accompanied Anna and Talleyrand everywhere. She had become reconciled to marriage and life amid the French and responded with the natural buoyancy of youth to the sights, sounds, and splendors of the French capital. Mother and daughter were equally exhausted by the time Talleyrand brought them to Rosny to recuperate on his way south for his annual cure for his bad right foot. This rosy brick château, some sixty kilometers from Paris, was a maternal inheritance of Edmond's and had been built by Henri IV's famous minister, Sully. Sitting down at the handsome pearwood *bonheur du jour* in her bedroom to write Elisa and bring her up to date on the mother and daughter's activities, Anna's eyes swept over the verdant Seine valley spread out below, and she began: "It's as peaceful here as at Löbikau."

Anna returned to Paris alone—Dorothea was to remain in the countryside until Edmond came back from the battlefront—and by fall she was in her own apartment in a mansion at 103, rue Saint Dominque. There her life settled into a happy pattern—with Talleyrand. She was not far from his hôtel Matignon, and one morning began like the next in the best possible way—with a billet for his *Chère Ange* while she was still abed, sipping her café au lait and fondling her two poodles. Talleyrand's tiny, illegible handwriting raced at a slant off the blue, heavily crested sheet that smelled of amber, and always detailed plans for their day together.

Then the emperor returned to the capital. His court might be a parvenu one, but imperial protocol could not be waived, even for the grand duchess of Courland. Since she must be formally presented to both the emperor and empress before she could appear at the Tuileries, Talleyrand arranged for this necessary preliminary for the coming Sunday so that Anna-Dorothea would not miss any functions of what promised to be a particularly brilliant season. This did not leave her much time to get ready to meet the emperor, for of course she must have a new costume.

Leroy, Josephine's frizzy-haired protégé from Directoire days, who was the capital's dictator of feminine fashion and knew all the haut monde's secrets worth knowing, went into a state of shock at the grand duchess's preposterous request. He spluttered and stamped his high red heels sharply on the parquet at the very notion of producing an original creation in five days, but in the end he was only too happy to oblige, even though it meant keeping his midinettes working round the clock.

The rest of the week passed in a frenzy of shopping trips to the exclusive boutiques clustered in the Palais Royal arcades for the necessary accessories—sheer silk stockings at Meyer's, shoulder-length white kid gloves at Mme. Annette's, and white satin slippers at Janssen's, shoemakers to the imperial family. Strollers gawked at the colorful procession as Anna passed by, eager for a close-up of the legendary Slav who had all Paris in a turmoil. The grand duchess's uniformed chasseur cleared the way, succeeded by two liveried, peruked footmen. Anna followed, with her walking stick and quizzing glass. Her *demoiselles d'honneur* minced along the prescribed several steps behind dictated by the grand duchess's rank, with the two poodles in tow. Then came a secretary with a purse, lest Her Excellency soil her hands with money. And bringing up the rear was her little elaborately costumed blackamoor, staggering under an ever increasing burden of packages.

On the great day, Anna was dressed before the skies turned a faint gray. Her white mousseline gown, with its extravagant insets of embroidered pineapples down the front and around the bottom exquisitely worked in silver and gold à la Reine Mathilde, had the de rigueur décolletage and long court train; her hair had been restyled to the tyrannical couturier's specifications in order to show off better the mandatory feathered toque. She even omitted her customary *mouche*. "Mouches," M. Leroy explained disdainfully, "went out with the Ice Age." They remained in style only in one or two outlandish outposts in the hinterlands—like Courland.

When Anna arrived at the Château promptly at 8:00 A.M., the empress's lady of the bedchamber regretfully informed her and several Genevans who had preceded the grand duchess that because His Imperial Majesty had been away so long, he would hold no presentations until after he reviewed the troops. To help them pass the time, a member of the imperial household ushered them to ringside seats in a window overlooking the Tuileries' courtyard for the famous spectacle of the reviewing, which occurred weekly if the emperor was in residence and attracted Parisians and foreigners alike. By high noon, there still seemed to be no end in sight—the emperor reviewed 14,000 troops that day, far more than usual—and Anna was grateful for the individually wrapped chocolates, the latest novelty, that Talleyrand had thoughtfully sent over the night before. He was accustomed to the vagaries of the imperial schedule and also knew that no refreshments would be available at the Château, except for members of the imperial family. "The Courtier's Delight," as the candies' name implied, was intended for such emergencies and could be stowed in reticules or pockets without danger of squashing.

The great inner court lay deserted except for the imperial guards on regular sentry duty, and the sun was low in the sky before the grand master of ceremonies appeared in full regalia and, with an air of grave importance, bade the duchess follow him—without the Genevans. To be received alone was an exceptional honor and almost unheard of for a woman. Furthermore the hussars, standing at attention with their halberds before the entrance to the Throne Room, threw open not one but both doors as they announced her, a courtesy extended only to sovereigns.

These were the halcyon days of Anna-Dorothea's relationship with the French emperor—before disillusionment set in—and it is unfortunate the grand duchess left no record of her initial impressions of the magnetic little figure at the far end of the room, seated on a gilded chair with a large *N* encircled by a laurel wreath on its high back. The palatial hall swarming with bees (golden bees on the walls, carpets, and curtains) dissolved into a blur as she walked the immense distance from the door to the foot of the throne to make the required three curtsies. The grand duchess knew that the emperor was too stout and was prepared for his pallor, but she was not prepared to find his nostrils stained from snuff—or to see close up that the famous curl was plastered on his forehead with pomade.

Napoleon's gray blue eyes were friendly, and he was smiling. "We are honored, Madame, to welcome an intimate friend of our dear cousin and ally, Tsar Alexander. We shall do everything to make your stay a pleasant and long one." The emperor indulged in more pleasantries than was his wont—Napoleon was famous for his curtness to women, whom he considered largely as broodmares for his armies—before abruptly glancing at the grand master of ceremonies to indicate that the audience was terminated. That official approached and stood respectfully by while Anna withdrew backwards, gracefully kicking her train out of the way with the skill that comes from long practice.

Relaxed morals and uncompromising manners were the order of the day; the only unforgivable sin was to provoke public scandal. And this Catherine de Talleyrand did by embarking on a brazen affair with the handsome Spanish duke of San Carlos. Years younger than herself, he was an equerry on the captive Spanish princes whom Napoleon had billeted at Talleyrand's magnificent Berry estate, Valençay, after making his brother Joseph Bonaparte king of Spain. The emperor was so outraged by the affair that he ordered the dallying pair into exile—temporarily and separately—and forbade Catherine any future appearance in court.

If Napoleon administered a slap to Talleyrand when he stripped him of his grand chamberlain's key at the beginning of the year, Catherine slapped the other cheek of this inordinately proud man by her poor taste in flaunting the liaison. Of the two insults, his wife's was the greater, reflecting as it did on Talleyrand's private life. Any gossamer bonds still clinging between the mismated pair disintegrated, and the grand duchess seized her opportunity, as much the pursuer as the pursued. Anna was everything that Catherine was not. One of those women whose charm is overwhelming, she was a worthy companion for Talleyrand, who throughout his life loved to bed down beautiful women, preferably clever ones with whom he might discuss sensibly his favorite topics—the affairs of the world and books—afterwards.

While Anna was securing her place in Charles-Maurice's affections, Dorothea set to work to create her place as a young bride in the French capital. For Edmond finally returned from the wars, the recipient of numerous imperial citations for bravery, and purchased a Louis XV town house at 2, rue Grange Batelière with part of his wife's dowry. Dorothea promptly joined him, happy to move in from Rosny and experience life alone with her husband in Paris. Talleyrand's unique position in Paris assured the young couple of a select circle from the start, even though he was living on the margin of power.

Talleyrand's remaining high-ranking title of vice-grand-elector was, of course, an empty one. Reduced as he was to limited appearances at court and rare contact with the emperor, he went unfailingly to Sunday mass in the Château chapel because that was one of the best places to pick up the latest rumors. During these trying times a handful of his former mistresses from France's first families had closed ranks around their *ami*. Nicknamed his "seraglio" by salon-circuit fashionables, the fragrance of their former passion was preserved by the potpourri of memory. Determined to keep dear Charles-Maurice amused, they spent each morning tuning up the instruments of their small talk; they also constituted the best possible news-gathering agency, without arousing the suspicion of the imperial secret police, and vied with one another to present the vice-grand-elector invaluable snippets of information. For it was of paramount importance that Talleyrand remain as well informed as if he were still the emperor's right hand.

The grand duchess was the celebrity of the season. Like other Slavs who had visited Paris, she represented to the insular French the fascination of barbaric far-away places. Her elegant gowns and jewels fit to ransom a king were noted, admired, copied. Still, Talleyrand's seraglio was unimpressed, despite the fact that Anna's brilliant salon was a witty, intelligent ragout of disparate groups over which she presided with a multilingual fluency that was rare for the day—most educated French women spoke only French; Anna spoke five languages, with only the slightest accent to make her near-perfect French a joy to the ear. The seraglio did not care. Jealous of Anna's magnetic appeal for Talleyrand, its members remained aloof and admitted among themselves, when Talleyrand was not present, that they found the fabulous duchess boring with her regal airs. To address her as "Your Highness" because of some lost pinpoint of a duchy that they had trouble locating on any map was more than they could endure. Besides, wasn't one foreigner enough to satisfy their *cher ami?*

Not too long before, they had grudgingly opened their ranks to Polish Princess Marie-Thérèse Tyskiewicz because her extensive, impressive family connections in Austria as well as in Poland provided a made-to-order Continental listening service. No beauty—Marie-Thérèse had lost one eye in a childhood accident and affected dangling curls to hide the glass substitute—she was one of a bevy of high-born Poles who had fallen madly in love with the suave Talleyrand several years before, when he was governor of French-occupied Warsaw. Marie-Thérèse became his mistress pro tempore, and was so afraid Charles-Maurice might forget her when he returned to Paris that she followed him home, grateful for any crumb of affection he might toss her way.

Though the seraglio had trouble swallowing their pride and opening their ranks to admit Anna, Marie-Thérèse, who was an old friend from the grand duchess's Warsaw days, had no similar qualms. Thursday was the princess's regular evening at home, and her tiny apartment was so jammed that it was impossible to move without stepping on a countess by the time Anna arrived one night in early winter, her usual late self. She had been to the theater—copying the haut monde, Anna no longer did anything so bourgeois as to sit through an entire play or opera—and then had gone on to several other affairs before coming here. She paused in the doorway after she was announced to be sure that everyone present saw her in her newest Leroy creation. Then she swept in, ever the gracious sovereign—nodding to this one, smiling to that one, reveling in the sudden lull she caused, the murmurs that followed her as she threaded her way amid the guests throwing dice and gambling for high stakes, past the impassive professional croupiers required by law to keep the banks, around the tables of *tric trac*, écarté, and *biribi* to where Talleyrand sat at whist with his regular cronies.

"I never saw anyone take more pleasure in showing off a gown," one of the seraglio whispered, consumed with envy at the open adoration on Talleyrand's notoriously impassive countenance.

"The Grand Duchess requires adulation as a sick man wants leeches. She lives on it," another replied drily.

When Anna and Talleyrand got up to leave, the princess accompanied them to the door. Once she was out of earshot of the others, Marie-Thérèse reported with an air of importance that she had received confirmation from her most reliable Warsaw sources that Countess Walewska, Napoleon's Polish mistress, was carrying an imperial bastard. This irrefutable proof that the emperor was not sterile but that the empress had become barren was invaluable grist for Talleyrand's mill.

Because the emperor was contemplating divorce and remarriage —to a Romanoff—this was his "Be Kind to Russians" period. In short, his exceptional cordiality to Anna was politically motivated, as were most things Napoleon did, even though he kept repeating, "It is your due because the Tsar took a personal hand in the marriage of your daughter to one of my subjects."

One day an aide-de-camp appeared with a basket of fresh melons from the greenhouses at the palace of Saint Cloud; another time, an official arrived with an invitation for Anna to sit at Napoleon's table at a dinner for a visiting Central European dignitary. Each passing week saw Anna overwhelmed with similar imperial attentions, which were flatteringly extended on a family basis— that is to say, as a member of the European family of rulers—and which Charles-Maurice encouraged her to accept. An extra pair of ears at the Château was invaluable to him at the moment.

When His Imperial Majesty consulted Talleyrand, as the empire's ranking elder stateman, concerning Continental ramifications should he select the tsar's sister as his bride, Anna saw a way to be helpful to Charles-Maurice. She alerted friends at the Saint Petersburg court to keep her informed of what transpired by special courier. The minute tentative feelers were made by the French ambassador there—he had served his apprenticeship as matchmaker earlier, for Dorothea and Edmond—Anna was alerted. And she learned, well ahead of the French foreign office, that the tsar was favorably inclined, but that the tsar's mother, the dowager tsarina, Maria Feodorovna, was unalterably opposed.

"Don't forget another daughter died in childbirth because she was married off too young," Anna reminded Talleyrand. "My correspondents say no final decision has been reached but that Napoleon's request for the Tsar's sister has touched off a family storm. Naturally, Alexander will have the final say. The only trouble"—Anna considered herself an authority on all things Russian—"is that dear Alexander never really knows what he wants."

The imperial crisis hurtled to a climax. Two weeks before Christmas, Talleyrand and Anna were in the small Tuileries' theater to see Corneille's *Nicomède*. But the drama offstage took the spotlight from Talma, the great Comédie Française star playing the title role. Josephine, her eyes red from weeping, was not in her usual seat but in a box to one side, alone except for a single lady-in-waiting standing behind her. Just before the curtain went up, Napoleon appeared with his suite and took his place facing her in the imperial loge. Afterward, the court assembled in one of the galleries, and this time the emperor and empress entered together. Followed by their respective suites, they slowly made their way around, engaging some guests in conversation, making others miserable by ignoring them. Josephine did not try to hide her unhappiness. She started to cry and hurriedly left the room before she reached Anna and Talleyrand. Napoleon swiftly followed. The imperial households did likewise, and the room emptied unseasonably early.

If Anna did not count her personal blessings as she left on Charles-Maurice's arm, she should have. Unlike the about to be discarded Josephine, the grand duchess had her man—the only man Anna ever loved who was worthy of her. Theirs was a tender autumnal affair, late flowering and as special as the autumn crocuses in the high Alpine meadows.

Talleyrand's billet the next morning cryptically informed Anna that he was ordered to appear at court that evening. It was well past midnight before he arrived at the rue Saint Dominique, still in his red velvet gold-encrusted vice-grand-elector's uniform, to describe the painful Throne Room scene in which Napoleon divorced Josephine—the woman he still loved—with Talleyrand playing an official role.

Napoleon was free to remarry. Anna was confident that he would choose the tsar's sister, Anna Pavlovna, and already envisaged herself with an important post in the empress's household. Then, unexpectedly, word was bruited that feelers were also being made at Vienna's Hofburg. And Anna heard Napoleon comment at a masquerade at the arch-chancellor's that he did not care whom he married. "I am only marrying a womb," he announced in his peculiarly flat voice. The Austrian candidate ultimately won out.

On All Fools' Day, April 1, 1810, Talleyrand participated as vice-grand-elector in the civil ceremony at Saint Cloud uniting Napoleon and Marie-Louise. And the following day, he procured tickets for Anna and the Princess Tyskiewicz to sit on the temporary platform constructed for prominent government figures at the top of the Champs-Elysées, alongside the unfinished Arc de Triomphe (which had been disguised by boards and painted canvas to simulate the completed structure), to witness the pageantry of the imperial couple's noon entry into Paris.

Traffic was so heavy by dusk that the two women would never have reached their assigned places in time for the subsequent religious ceremony if Anna did not have access, as the grand duchess of Courland, to the special entrance to the Tuileries and the Louvre —Henri IV had united the two palaces—that was reserved for royalty.

Anna got her first close look at Marie-Louise in the Louvre's great salon, which had been converted into a temporary chapel. She was taller than Napoleon, with plenty of bosom squeezed into a tight-fitting pink gown, and not at all pretty, with bulging, porcelain blue eyes and the pouting Hapsburg underlip. For a young girl who had never owned more than a braided-hair bracelet and a single coral necklace, she was making up for lost time, aglitter with diamonds like a Christmas tree. Her Imperial Majesty looked pale—and tired. But who would not after being bedded down two nights running by an impatient husband-to-be anxious to provide his insatiable virility although he was twice her age. What a shock that must have been for the young Austrian archduchess who had been so carefully reared that she had never been allowed anything but female pets.

At first, Marie-Louise was not permitted to hold any big receptions because Napoleon was convinced that women conceived more readily when they did not exert themselves—"that is to say," Anna wrote her sister, Elisa, "outside the four walls of the imperial bedchamber."

When Talleyrand returned from a late May meeting at the Château, he disclosed that the emperor was convinced the empress was pregnant. "That's quick work, eh?" he chuckled. Some court wit lost no time punning that Her Imperial Majesty's looks would be improved once she had a *nouveau né* (literally, a newborn infant, but phonetically, a *nouveau nez,* a new nose). But this proved to be wishful imperial thinking. Marie-Louise had developed a passion for French cooking, especially French pastry, and her stomach upsets were caused by overindulgence.

Napoleon could not keep his bride to himself forever, and distinguished foreigners crowded into Paris for the spectacular festivities given by the Senate, the imperial guard, and the Hotel de Ville in honor of the imperial newlyweds. Talleyrand's hôtel Matignon, which was the one place of importance in the imperial capital with its parvenu court where the ancien régime Continental aristocracy felt at home, was more crowded than usual, and Anna, too, did her share of entertaining at the rue Saint Dominique. For many old friends were among those flocking to the city.

The grand duchess was exhausted by the time she headed east, leaving Dorothea behind with Edmond. Her annual Karlsbad cure rejuvenated her, and she continued on to Löbikau for a long, quiet summer with the family. She arrived laden with gifts—fine white sand for Elisa to use as a blotter when she sat writing, a magnificent watch fob, the latest rage, for Tiedge, and Paris gowns for Wilhelmina, Paulina and Joanna, who hastened there for a visit.

Political discussions might be taboo, but there was no dearth of subjects for conversation. For Anna-Dorothea had a lot of catching up to do where her older daughters—especially Wilhelmina—were concerned. Wilhelmina had already divorced Prince Troubetzkoi. The prince's duties as aide-de-camp to Alexander I had recalled him to Saint Petersburg permanently, and Wilhelmina had refused to follow. As she explained to her mother, she preferred to live in the west rather than at the imperial court where she would be at the tsar's beck and call. So she had paid Troubetzkoi off as handsomely as she had Rohan when she divorced him and had moved to Prague. There her sisters, Paulina and Joanna, dubbed "the Guardian Angels" because they took such good care of each other, were sharing a palace. Paulina had stayed with her husband, Hermann-Otto, until after the birth of her first child. Her duty done—she had a boy—she was busy consoling Wilhelmina's jettisoned first spouse, Prince Louis de Rohan—by whom she had already had a daughter. And pert Joanna did not want for her share of admirers.

The ancient capital of Bohemia was a prominent asylum for those who were working for Napoleon's downfall, and the Francophobe Courland princesses joined the aristocratic "Lodge of Roman Ladies," a stronghold of sworn anti-Bonapartists. Wilhelmina also loaned her great Bohemian estate, Nachod, to the Commander of the Death's Head Hussars, to be used by that German resistance organization as a training ground for its fight against the French occupation troops. When rumors reached her that the French emperor was considering confiscating her vast duchy of Sagan in retaliation, the plucky duchess of Sagan—Wilhelmina chose to use her inherited title—conscripted and outfitted five hundred men from that Silesian property as an on-the-spot defense measure.

About the time of Dorothea's wedding the preceding spring, the trio moved permanently to Vienna. Paulina and Joanna took an apartment in the Annagasse while Wilhelmina set up her own establishment nearby in the Palm palace, 54 Schenkenstrasse, under the old city ramparts. These quarters were sufficiently spacious to accommodate the three foster girls Wilhelmina was raising as substitutes for her own little Vava, who was being brought up in far-off Finland with her father's cousins. Two were illegitimate nieces; the younger, aged four, was Paulina's child by Prince Rohan; the older, aged eight, was the child of a natural son of her father, Grand Duke Peter. The other eight-year-old was the child of impoverished friends.

Wilhelmina, the prettiest of the grand duchess's daughters, was at twenty-eight one of the loveliest in that city of beauties. Unlike her mother, Anna, who charmed only when she made the effort to do so, the duchess of Sagan charmed twenty-four hours a day, without trying. One of those women who because she was attracted to men, attracted them, Wilhelmina's sensuality was immediately apparent; she wore it like a gleaming ornament and saw no reason to curb her desire. Her two marriages had left no more trace on her life than the dying foam from the ebb tide did on the Baltic sands, and she was still searching for her heart's desire.

When young Prince Windischgratz was grievously wounded in the battle of Wagram in July of 1809, Paulina and Joanna undertook to nurse him back to health. They were both half in love with him, and their older sister, too, was greatly taken with this scion of one of Austria's most distinguished families. Ruggedly good-looking, with prominent cheekbones, a firmly fleshed jaw, and deep-set smoky blue eyes, Alfred had unruly black hair that had a tendency to fall forward over his brow, and Wilhelmina always wanted to smooth it back for him.

One fall day, when it was so hot even the birds were silent in the shimmering air, Wilhelmina and Alfred climbed through the wooded slopes of the Köhlenberg in the prince's small barouche to a tiny picturesque inn he knew. They ordered *jause* (afternoon tea) served to them outdoors, in a narrow flower-carpeted meadow overlooking Vienna—its tan and gray roofs and green church domes—and the winding Danube, which was barely visible below through the leafy boughs peppered with dust. While Wilhelmina lazily coated the rich linzer torte with the jelly that was oozing through the traditional three holes in its flaky top, Alfred leaned back and lit a long, elegant cigar, a Belgian habit he was introducing into Austrian society.

As Wilhelmina lifted her glass to sip some Tokay, an intricately carved ruby on one finger sparkled, reflecting the same rays of golden sunshine as did the amber wine. Noticing it, Alfred leaned over and demanded peremptorily to know where she had gotten her ring. He had not seen her wear it before.

Wilhelmina was amused at his query. She had seen the offending piece in the window of a jeweler on the Köernerstrasse the other day and impulsively bought it—herself. But now that Alfred was making so much fuss about it, she would not dream of divulging the truth. The more steadfastly Wilhelmina declined to answer, the more jealous Alfred got.

In depair, he unexpectedly lunged across the table and, taking her by surprise, pulled the bauble off. When he refused to hand the stone back, Wilhelmina rushed around the table to get it. They grappled for a moment in silence, and Wilhelmina bit his arm. Startled, Alfred tightened his hold on her with one hand, and with the other, he stuck the offending piece between his teeth—to tease her. Wilhelmina slipped from his grasp. They scuffled again and Alfred swallowed the jewel. The war hero started to choke and turn blue.

Wilhelmina thought he was going to suffocate. "Help! Help!" she screamed. A startled waiter appeared. He took the situation in at a glance, but before he could summon assistance, the obstruction slid down Alfred's throat and he was able to breathe again.

"Oh, *mein Gott!*" he groaned, holding his stomach, his serious wounds from Wagram momentarily forgotten. Wilhelmina helped the young officer crawl into his carriage, drove him home herself, and summoned a doctor.

Fortunately, nature lent a hand, and a shaken Alfred returned the ruby forty-eight hours later. Wilhelmina took it without a word and replaced it on her finger, and the subject was never mentioned again. However, Wilhelmina had not been as calm as she pretended. Her deep concern over the foolish young man—Alfred was six years her junior—after the accident made her realize how much she cared for the dark, curly-haired officer, and by the time the duchess of Sagan came to Löbikau in the summer of 1810 with Paulina and Joanna, she was embarked on what was destined to be the longest and most tumultuous of her many liaisons.

CHAPTER SEVEN

The Grand Duchess, Talleyrand, & Dorothea
1810-1812

DOROTHEA SELDOM SAW TALLEYRAND and his wife, Catherine, but she quickly blossomed into one of the stars of the younger set. She also conquered the Faubourg Saint-Germain, that stronghold of names from the golden era of Louis XIV that were familiar to Dorothea from schoolgirl recollections of Saint-Simon's *Memoirs* and Mme. de Sévigné's *Letters*.

The emperor's marriage to the unsophisticated nineteen-year-old archduchess transformed the atmosphere of his parvenu court. The Tuileries assumed the cloak of sober respectability befitting a sovereign whose father-in-law was the venerable Austrian emperor and who was intent on establishing his own dynasty. When Napoleon selected a number of Marie-Louise's contemporaries from Paris's aristocratic foreign colony for her newly enlarged household and included Dorothea, Talleyrand wrote Anna the good news. He interpreted Dorothea's appointment as recognition of his support for the Austrian, rather than Russian, marriage when the imperial council had debated between the two, and concluded, "I am delighted with anything that provides a tie between members of my family and the Emperor."

Talleyrand's correspondence with Anna at Löbikau was deliberately harmless, written with the knowledge that every line was scanned for hidden meanings by the secret police. His letters showed the family man, full of solicitude for those he loved, occupied with Dorothea and with Edmond's military career. Anna replied in kind.

At the elaborate ceremonial inducting the new young ladies-in-waiting, the grand master of ceremonies introduced Dorothea—and the others, one by one—and each took her oath of office. Then Talleyrand, in his ceremonial role as vice-grand-elector, presented the group to Their Imperial Majesties. "You would have been proud of Dorothea. She was dazzling," he informed the grand duchess. "Her pregnancy was disguised by a special Leroy creation" —clouds of silver tulle, embroidered with cornflowers and made adjustable by a row of cleverly arranged diamond safety pins.

Dorothea's duties as lady-in-waiting were quite specific. When the empress left the Château for her daily drive, Dorothea and the others rode in a separate carriage behind. When the empress was on public display, Dorothea stood directly behind Her Imperial Majesty, whether at receptions, troop reviews, state dinners, the opera, whatever.

Dorothea was on her initial, three-month tour of duty when the court made its annual move to Fontainebleau. Talleyrand was included in the imperial party and quartered in the same palace wing, so he and his niece had a chance to get acquainted at last. As with Prince Czartoryski earlier, age inspired trust, and Dorothea was attracted to the older man. She was awed by *l'oncle*'s vast experience and knowledge of the world, his brilliant conversation and intelligence. Talleyrand, for his part, was enchanted. Like her mother, Dorothea talked and listened well—and laughed at the right moments—and he soon decided that there was not another soul in the château with whom he could enjoy so much good conversation.

One morning, *l'oncle* showed Dorothea Herr Tiedge's latest poem, which Anna had enclosed in a recent letter. Dorothea glanced at it and was unimpressed. Herr Tiedge managed to shake poetry out of his sleeve whenever it was needed, but he was hardly in a class with Goethe, no matter what Aunt Elisa—who should know better—might think.

"I think we should reply by sending her a copy of the verse making the rounds here, eh?" *l'oncle* suggested.

> The sex of the infant, the hope of the fatherland,
> Even for the Emperor is still a secret.
> For the first time in his life,
> He doesn't know what he did.

"You know," Dorothea retorted, "the Emperor is positive the baby will be a boy." Talleyrand chuckled, and she joined in.

On her return to Paris, Dorothea decided to visit the famed seer, Mme. Lenormand, who was the present rage. Like her friends, she took elaborate precautions not to be recognized and sent her chambermaid ahead to make the appointment under a false name. To complete her incognito, she arrived unescorted—ladies of quality never went out alone—and in a hired hack, which she picked up some distance from the rue Grange-Batelière, rather than in her own liveried equipage.

The walls of the soothsayer's apartment on the rue Tournon were covered with huge bats; stuffed owls peered down from bookcases, cabalistic symbols were everywhere, and a skeleton perched on a stool in a corner. A door creaked open and the celebrated sibyl appeared. Bedecked with an outlandish fur cap, she resembled a monstrous toad, bloated and venomous, and had one walleye. Dorothea followed her into the study, where the usual rigmarole ensued. After Dorothea volunteered her birthdate and favorite colors, the old crone consulted charts of the stars and the moon, then an untidy mass of papers full of intersecting lines. She murmured some mumbo jumbo and gazed into a crystal ball. Her enigmatic prophecy so puzzled Dorothea that she remembered it as long as she lived. The prediction that she and Edmond would separate did not startle her. But what did the seer mean when she said that Dorothea would become allied with a person who, by his influential position, would enable her to play an important political role?

Anna returned from Löbikau well before the end of the year, and was on hand to welcome her grandchild, Napoleon-Louis, when he was born on March 13, 1811. For Dorothea's sake, the grand duchess hoped that the baby's arrival might bridge the growing gap between the young parents, although the disparity of their interests and tastes was painfully evident. The excitement of life in Paris and in the imperial court continued to provide sufficient distraction to make Dorothea's marriage tolerable, but any long-term accommodation was increasingly jeopardized by Edmond's irresponsible behavior—his heavy gambling, extravagance, and avid pursuit of the opera *rats,* those winsome members of the Academy of Music's corps de ballet.

The imperial couple agreed to act as godparents, but they

were unable to appear at the christening because of their own imminent blessed event. Seven days later, while he was dining with the grand duchess, Talleyrand received the message France was expecting: "Marie-Louise is in labor." He rushed home, donned full court regalia, and proceeded to the Tuileries to await the imperial offspring with other dignitaries whom protocol convoked.

Anna, whose invitation to a small entertainment for the empress's visiting uncle was automatically canceled, slept fitfully that night, one ear expectantly cocked for the cannonade announcing the long-awaited infant's arrival. The next morning, the air in her boudoir was redolent of hot curling tongs and the scent of those various oils for rejuvenating the skin that Paris excelled at concocting, and Anna was examining the mouth-watering assortment of the latest fashions and fripperies spread out to tempt her by the first tradespeople to appear, when the official salvoes commenced. "One, two, three . . . nineteen, twenty . . ." Everyone in the grand duchess's room was counting. There was a dramatic pause after the twenty-first boom, and they held their breath.

"It's only a girl!" Anna's maid cried out in disappointment. Was Josephine's sacrifice in vain? But the gunner at the Invalides had a sense of humor—or of history. For the cannon soon resumed and continued the 101 rounds specified for a boy.

Two months later, François Charles Joseph Bonaparte— l'Aiglon (the Eaglet)—was baptized at Notre Dame in a ceremony that the emperor decreed should be the greatest of his reign —he intended it to solidify the empire and to do so borrowed and adapted prodigally from previous similar Bourbon functions. This time Dorothea and Charles-Maurice participated officially.

From where Anna and her friend the Princess Tyskiewicz sat in the great Gothic cathedral, she could barely make out Talleyrand limping along with the other grand officers of the empire on the heels of the heralds-at-arms, pages, and chamberlains. The solemn procession moved up the cavernous nave, redolent of the transplanted forest of evergreens, the masses of hothouse flowers, and the wax of thousands of candles, to music from the enlarged orchestra and choir behind the altar. Then came the Eaglet's regalia: the taper with its velvet sheath decorated with bees and roses, a magnificently embroidered baptismal veil, and the salt-cellar—each piece carefully carried by a woman of the imperial household. Three others brought the godparents' distinctive symbols—the silver-gilt bowl, the towel, and the ewer. Finally, under a canopy surmounted by ostrich plumes and aigrettes—"That must have cost a pretty sou!" the Princess Tyskiewicz nudged Anna—came the star of the show, his long lace robe wrapped in a cloth of gold ermine-lined cloak, and draped across his chest the wide red ribbon of the Grand Cross of the Legion d'Honneur. The emperor and empress followed, happy to play a secondary role under the circumstances. Marie-Louise was literally covered with diamonds; even the sleeves and border of her robe were made of diamond vermicelli. "That superb eight-strand pearl necklace she's wearing was a gift from the emperor on the evening of the imperial baby's birth," Anna remarked, putting down her lorgnette. She had succeeded in locating Dorothea, bringing up the rear with the empress's other ladies-in-waiting.

Recalled from his post in Saint Petersburg for the solemn occasion, the French ambassador came out frequently to the Château Neuf, formerly the pavilion of Henri IV at Saint Germain-en-Laye, which Anna had purchased and restored for summer use, for long talks with his old friend Talleyrand. Although he was intensely loyal to Napoleon, the ambassador felt as keenly as Charles-Maurice the need for an end to the perpetual warfare that was impoverishing France and bleeding it to death. Both men were disturbed at France's perceptible drift toward a rupture with Russia and hoped that the Eaglet's advent might cure Napoleon's lust for conquest and induce him to settle down and consolidate his gains for his son's sake. But certain straws in the wind indicated persistent imperial preoccupation with Eastern Europe.

On August 15, when Talleyrand returned to the Château from the Tuileries after paying his respects at the annual dual celebration, the Fête of the Assumption and Napoleon's birthday, it was late. He handed his valet his dress sword and plumed hat but did not take time to change into something more comfortable. Instead, he hurried directly into the library to tell Anna some important news. Napoleon had dressed down the Russian ambassador before the entire diplomatic corps. The emperor caught him completely unaware and left him beet red.

The next day, the emperor's absorption with Russia—and his pent-up annoyance at Talleyrand for openly voicing disapproval of his Continental policies—probably triggered a second, recorded, public scene. At the sight of Dorothea, the tsar's subject, innocently attending the empress, the emperor peevishly berated the young woman for Edmond's latest folly. "Madame, how could your husband spend 10,000 francs for cameos?"

"S-sire, Your Majesty has been ill informed. M-my husband has not been that foolish." Dorothea's stammer betrayed her agitation.

Ignoring her, Napoleon turned to his chief of staff, who was standing alongside. "You ought not to tolerate these things by one of your aides-de-camp. Even so, this nonsense is more excusable than many another he has committed." The marshal bowed his head without saying a word. Napoleon went on. "At any rate, as you well know, I haven't paid any attention to these poor Périgords for some time."

Dorothea's indignation broke down her usual reserve and she spoke up without being addressed—a cardinal sin of protocol. "S-sire, my husband and my uncle have at all times served Your Imperial Majesty with zeal. It rests with you to make further use of them. S-surely their earlier services deserve that Your Imperial Majesty s-should not ridicule them." She was blushing at her own temerity and on the verge of tears, and ignored etiquette to rush from the room.

At dinner, every courtier assiduously ignored Dorothea. But the one thing Napoleon admired, especially in women, was independence, and her courageous stand forced home the absurdity of his attack on the young imperial lady-in-waiting. The next noon, the emperor invited Dorothea to sit at his table for lunch, and later, when the hunt stopped for tea in the middle of the forest, he passed a bowl of fresh fruit to her himself. This renewal of imperial esteem, which brought the fickle courtiers fawning to Dorothea's side, was not, however, extended to Talleyrand, who soon had more direct evidence of continued imperial displeasure.

Anna-Dorothea was sitting in the library at the Château Neuf some weeks later finishing a needlepoint billfold for Charles-Maurice, and he was helping his adopted daughter, thirteen-year-old Charlotte, with her history lesson. (It is not known positively whether Charlotte was actually the daughter of friends, as Talleyrand claimed, or the daughter of Talleyrand and Catherine—born out of wedlock. One thing is certain; he and Catherine both adored her and spoiled her outrageously. Some of Talleyrand's most charming letters are those he wrote to her.)

The early fall sun, red as a cider apple, had sunk in the west, and darkness pressed down like a thick wet sack when a footman appeared. Anna was annoyed. She did not care to be disturbed when she was with the family, but when she learned an officer from the minister of police was at the door asking for M. de Talleyrand, the grand duchess had him shown in at once.

The captain, hat tucked respectfully under one arm, bowed ceremoniously and handed Talleyrand a dispatch. Leisurely, Charles-Maurice slit open the envelope dripping with seals and read the contents, his pale face as sphinxlike as ever. It concerned Catherine. His wife had seen the duke of San Carlos again, despite the emperor's express command to the contrary. Although there was also an imperial injunction forbidding their correspondence, Catherine had managed to remain in touch with her paramour. When she was passing through Ain, which was near Bourg-en-Bresse, where the Spanish duke was residing, still in banishment because of their liaison, the forty-nine-year-old woman disguised herself in the clothes of one of her male attendants and visited her lover. As a result, Catherine had been exiled to Talleyrand's property in the Ardennes. The minister warned that Napoleon threatened to send Charles-Maurice there also, if he could not control his wife.

Anna was speechless with indignation. How dare Catherine bring scandal on the house of Talleyrand by making a public spectacle of herself! And how ridiculous of Napoleon to blame Charles-Maurice. The grand duchess was shocked at the pettiness of Napoleon's growing tyranny. But the minister of police's admonition revealed the extent of the emperor's irritation, and Talleyrand dared not ignore the message. He told the captain to wait outside for a reply and dragged himself over to the cylindrical marquetry desk. Rolling back the top, he sat down and started to write. Several hours and innumerable drafts later—after reading aloud and reworking each line with Anna—Charles-Maurice had one that satisfied him. Only after he had sent it off with the officer personally would he consider food.

Since Talleyrand ate only one meal a day, Anna had had a footman keep two tureens—one full of bouillon, the other with a succulent, aromatic matelote (a sort of bouillabaisse)—simmering on gleaming silver *réchauds*; several covered trays rested along-side. Charles-Maurice lifted the napkin from a platter of sandwiches, opened each until he found one with ham, and popped it into his mouth. Meanwhile, Anna mixed him a glass of red wine and water, which he sipped slowly. He wanted nothing more. After a catnap, he let his faithful valet shave and dress him, and at 5:00 A.M. Talleyrand was in his carriage headed for Paris and the minister of police's levee. The affair was quickly settled to his satisfaction. In keeping with the dignity of the family name, Catherine was permitted to return to Paris to the hôtel Matignon with the understanding that she live there in semiretirement, and nothing more was said about any punishment for Talleyrand.

The grand duchess was the real winner. For Charles-Maurice profited from Catherine's escapade to live increasingly apart with Anna. On the surface, the pattern of their life at Saint Germain-en-Laye was a quiet one. As at Löbikau, Anna spent a lot of time outdoors. So did Talleyrand. Astride a small chestnut mare, Charles-Maurice rode daily with his daughter under the tall oaks of the nearby forest, swinging his crop, now fast, now slow, as he concentrated on European problems. Talleyrand's musician-in-residence was on hand for Charlotte's piano lessons and entertained Anna and the others in the evening by playing personal compositions or improvising. Around midnight, tea was enjoyed with a few neighborhood friends; Anna prepared coffee for Charles-Maurice. He drank very few spirits and preferred his superb mocha, so the grand duchess had his majordomo show her how to prepare the special blend, which was sent out fresh daily from the hôtel Matignon. It was a hotter autumn than usual, and after their guests left, the two would move out onto the terrace where the scent of stock and rare, night-blooming nicotiana perfumed the still air. The widened Seine flowed silently below the gentle slope at their feet, with distant Paris asleep in the moonlight. This was one of the quiet corners of the day that Anna enjoyed the most, discussing current events alone with Charles-Maurice. International politics was a vast, exciting game in which she had enjoyed participating ever since Grand Duke Peter sent her off as his special ambassadress to Warsaw. And here she had a front-row seat at the drama being played out at the heart of the French empire.

The Château Neuf was now a nest of anti-Napoleonic intrigue. Secret opposition to the emperor's foreign program—and to the probable opening of an eastern front—was growing, especially among the higher echelons of the army. Anna's own disappointment with Napoleon had been increasing by leaps and bounds. The spell of imperial achievements had worn thin. She disliked the emperor's dictatorial methods and no longer trusted his proclaimed aims. The grand duchess had seen firsthand the harsh treatment accorded the occupied countries she traveled through the previous year en route to and from Löbikau. Hardship stories that family and friends were forever repeating during her stay in Central Europe further altered her original vision of Napoleon as the savior of the world. She also sensed a change in the tsar's attitude toward Napoleon.

Napoleon did nothing to check her current reactions. Once he detected a whiff of opposition, his gracious welcome to the grand duchess chilled, and the imperial disapproval was shown by his indifference to her. Such treatment made her resentful—Anna was nothing if not spoiled—and this, coupled with her disillusionment, developed in time into implacable hostility. Subjected to Charles-Maurice's clear, concise reasoning, Anna was gradually viewing the emperor through his eyes.

A patriot first and foremost, Talleyrand was playing a dangerous game, working behind the scenes to foster a spirit of resistance among Napoleon's frightened allies and satellites in order to achieve the peace he felt France—and Europe—needed. Metternich, as Austrian ambassador to Paris, had been the first foreign official to learn that Europe had an unexpected friend in Talleyrand, long before Charles-Maurice's conspiratorial meetings with Alexander I at Erfurt in 1808. And Talleyrand had remained secretly in contact with the Ballhausplatz ever since. It is impossible to ascertain whether Anna ever discovered that the diplomatic pouches of an attaché in Paris's Austrian embassy regularly contained information from "Monsieur X"—Talleyrand's nom de plume—for which Vienna was paying handsomely.

Exactly when she learned of Charles-Maurice's parallel Saint Petersburg–oriented activities is also a mystery. Ever since the spring of 1810 the tsar had had two representatives in the French capital: the ambassador, who was officially accredited to the emperor, and a counsellor, Count Charles Nesselrode, who was secretly accredited to the hôtel Matignon with an autographed letter from Alexander. The counsellor's secret communiqués to Saint Petersburg henceforth carried the information "Cousin Henri"

—Talleyrand's Russian code name—intended for the tsar. By the fall following the Eaglet's birth, the grand duchess was unquestionably au courant of the steady flow of information to the tsar, for the counsellor was frequently at the Château Neuf. And when Napoleon's secret police suspected the counsellor of espionage, and he was recalled and replaced by an intelligence officer from the Russian imperial guard, this new young colonel, who was likewise put secretly in touch with Talleyrand by a holograph from Alexander, was as welcome at Saint Germain-en-Laye as his predecessor had been.

The grand duchess did not blink an eye at Charles-Maurice's disclosures—just as she apparently chose never to think about the many accusations, often repeated within her hearing, that Talleyrand was venal. She did not consider him a traitor because dictatorship made any legal opposition to the emperor impossible. For Talleyrand's efforts to be most effective, he needed continuous, updated information not only from the Tuileries but from the farthest reaches of empire, and here Anna could help. She would be his eyes, ears, and voice in the east. Her personal correspondence with Tsar Alexander, the grand duchess of Weimar, the Prussian royal family, and others who mattered in Central European courts was at his disposal, not only to cull facts but to transmit messages and propagate his views with the people who counted there. Wilhelmina, Paulina, and Joanna, staunch anti-Bonapartists, were also well situated to be of assistance.

The winter proved a disquieting one for Anna. Her correspondence with the tsar was larger than normal, for more and more letters sent over her signature were composed in their entirety by Charles-Maurice. Talleyrand wanted to be sure that the tsar did not forget the need for a close understanding with Austria. And he wanted the tsar to realize that for Russia to get the requisite European backing, Napoleon should bear the odium of beginning the war that Talleyrand hoped was to put an end to the French emperor's passion for conquest.

But a large portion of Anna's letters to Russia were personal, and written in a futile attempt to discover why most of her Russian income should have been suddenly and inexplicably blocked by complicated litigation. Anything as prosaic as a shortage of funds was beyond the grand duchess's comprehension. She entertained as frequently and luxuriously as ever and was amassing gargantuan debts. Nor was she the only one. France as a nation was also in economic straits. After a poor harvest, the price of bread soared, and severe famine was causing considerable unrest. Talleyrand too was pinched, like many Parisians, and forced to ship the fine library which was his prize possession off to London for auction.

To discount rumors about the country's financial plight and to hide his war preparations—though almost every day when Anna went for her afternoon drive, she passed troops on the boulevard setting off for the east—Napoleon insisted that the court's social activity be as brilliant as ever. Imperial fêtes of varied description succeeded one another uninterruptedly. There was not one night when a concert, a play, a masquerade, or an entertainment of some description did not follow billiards, écarté, and whist at the Château, until Anna's head ached and she no longer tried to attend every Tuileries function.

With the year running downhill, imperial misgivings about Talleyrand's activities revived, and for the first time extended to the grand duchess. One forenoon, Anna and a group of her friends were in her luxurious apartment on the rue Saint Dominique enjoying a fascinating lecture by Dr. Gall. To illustrate a point he wanted to make, the inventor of phrenology was removing some specimens from one of his five trunks when the door burst open with a loud clatter, and the minister of police strode in unannounced. The learned German was so startled that he upset the containers, and skulls toppled out in every direction. The women jumped to their feet as if they had spied a mouse, shrieking and pulling their short trains up tight to escape the rolling heads.

The minister had been riding by, and when he noticed a large number of parked carriages and coachmen in the street in front of Anna's hotel, he decided to investigate, on the off chance he might be able to confirm Napoleon's suspicions about the grand duchess's goings-on. When the ancient footman repeated, with quavering insistence, that Madame la Duchesse was not at home to any visitors, the minister was convinced that he had caught Anna red-handed. He brushed the bent old servitor abruptly aside and rushed headlong into the salon. Staggered at the spectacle that confronted him—and for which he was responsible—the poor man stammered that he was a great admirer of the celebrated doctor and wanted to hear him talk. Mopping his brow in embarrassment, he slunk to the nearest chair to listen to the termination of the discussion. But this invasion of the grand duchess's privacy served notice that she, as well as Charles-Maurice, would have to be extremely careful in the future.

The secret police was stepping up its arrests, and not solely because the emperor had become overly sensitive to criticism. There were other reasons for its accelerated activity, as Anna soon determined. The same week as the minister of police's visit to Anna, a young colonel from the Russian embassy, who was due to leave Paris on a periodic trip to Saint Petersburg, stopped at the grand duchess's to say farewell and collect a letter of hers for the tsar. A few hours afterwards, one of his colleagues was at the door demanding to see Madame la Duchesse at once. The footman reported that the man was terribly agitated and claimed it was an emergency.

It was. The secret police had just arrested the colonel's secretary, but the frightened attaché had managed to slip out the back door while the agents were still in the colonel's bedroom. No, the man replied to Talleyrand's questioning, nervously twisting his hat by its brim, he did not think he had been followed to the rue Saint Dominique. And yes, the attaché assured them, the colonel had gotten off safely about an hour before. Anna was relieved. The colonel's work for military intelligence was no concern to Charles-Maurice and herself, but what if the true nature of their correspondence with the tsar came to light? Talleyrand sent the shaken attaché back to the embassy with instructions to keep them apprised of developments. There was no point in losing sleep over idle speculation; first it must be determined what had been discovered.

Sufficient evidence of the colonel's spying was unearthed to justify official disregard for diplomatic immunity, and some of the Russian embassy servants were jailed. The trail did not stop there. The clerk in the war ministry who had been feeding the colonel army secrets was tracked down, summarily sentenced, and so speedily executed that Anna was apprehensive for days. Whenever she heard an unfamiliar carriage roll into the courtyard, she rushed to the window to see whether the minister of police would emerge to arrest her. She did not relax until Talleyrand appeared, several weeks later, with an agreeable surprise.

Half sitting on the desk in the library as he often did—his

bad right leg draped over the edge, the other braced on the parquet to support himself—Charles-Maurice permitted himself the briefest of half smiles. No wonder. The state had agreed to purchase the hôtel Matignon, and La Muette as well. Anna was delighted. The sale of these two properties, the large town house and the château on the outskirts of Paris, would rescue Charles-Maurice from his continuing financial embarrassment. But more important, Napoleon's required approval of the sale meant that the emperor had no further suspicions of Talleyrand, in spite of the recent espionage scandal.

This was even more evident when Napoleon called Talleyrand to the Château and asked him to undertake a crucial confidential mission to Warsaw. The emperor needed maximum Polish support in the forthcoming conflict with Russia, and only Talleyrand possessed the requisite experience—as well as the highly placed Polish friends—to assure this. Charles-Maurice agreed to go. But word of his upcoming assignment trickled out. Napoleon jumped to the conclusion that Talleyrand was responsible and was so furious that he immediately dispatched another in his place. Matters were not helped when twenty-four hours later the postal director in charge of censoring the mail discovered that Charles-Maurice had recently drawn a large draft on a bank in Vienna. The emperor ordered him to the Tuileries and thundered, "Is Austria trying to bribe you?" Talleyrand truthfully replied that he had been preparing for the proposed Polish post by getting the foreign currency he would need there.

The emperor ordered the leak traced. When the trail led to the salon of the vicomtesse de Laval, a member of Charles-Maurice's seraglio, the emperor was positive his original supposition was correct. Talleyrand must be the culprit. As a warning to him and to teach society busybodies and newsmongers in general a lesson, Napoleon ordered the hostess in question into temporary exile.

Anna was thunderstruck. She was sure Mme. de Laval had never opened her mouth. Since the grand duchess was leaving before too long for Löbikau, and since there was no possible way to get the imperial injunction revoked, surely the emperor would permit the vicomtesse to postpone her departure date so the two women might travel together. Indeed not. Under no circumstances. "I dislike women who meddle in government affairs," His Imperial Majesty replied. "I won't have the Vicomtesse off with the Grand

Duchess. The latter is fond enough of intrigue as it is, and would do endless mischief if she were worked on by the Vicomtesse."

When the secret police finally exposed the wife of the foreign minister as the responsible party, Napoleon rescinded the innocent vicomtesse's sentence and ordered the culprit to apologize to Talleyrand. The guilty woman had been afraid that Charles-Maurice—the former foreign minister—would acquit himself so well in Warsaw that he would be returned to the foreign office and her own husband ousted. The extraordinary, Machiavellian lengths to which she was willing to resort to keep her husband in office constitute an object lesson for anyone interested in the frenetic behind-the-scenes politicking that transpired at the highest levels of empire.

The emperor's discontent with troublemaking females had not run its course. With war against the tsar imminent, he toyed with the idea of exiling the grand duchess, a Russian subject. Instead he sent the minister of police to Talleyrand to express indignation at certain of Anna's remarks and determine what was holding up Her Excellency's planned departure. The imperial inference was clear, but Anna had no intention of being hurried. Besides, she faced an unusual problem—for her. The grand duchess's long-standing financial difficulties with Saint Petersburg had resulted in a mountain of bills, and at the first hint that she might set forth for home, her creditors went to court to prevent her departure. They were convinced that if she left France, they would never see a sou of their money again. But the emperor preferred the grand duchess to be on her way and ordered that a satisfactory financial accommodation be reached.

With the advent of warm weather, Charles-Maurice's seraglio was scattering to the countryside for the summer. Talleyrand so orchestrated their departures that every afternoon for almost a week, he arrived at a different hôtel, stowed a hamper stuffed with the famed pâté of red pheasant and truffles from his Périgord estates into the waiting carriage, and escorted another of his *chéres amies* part way on her trip. Anna left after the others, and Talleyrand and Dorothea accompanied her as far as the first relay post, where she must change horses. She was heartbroken that Charles-Maurice should take her departure so philosophically, and she wept a good deal that first day in the great berlin heading eastward.

With Maman, with whom Dorothea remained on bittersweet terms, in Löbikau that summer of 1812, and with Edmond, now a colonel, headed east to join the Grande Armée—it reached the Vistula on May 1, and Russian forces were engaged before the end of July—Dorothea left her children, fifteen-month-old Napoleon-Louis and two-month-old Dorothea-Charlotte-Emilie, at Rosny, the family estate and moved into *l'oncle*'s new Right Bank residence at 2, rue Saint Florentine. Henceforth she divided her time between the hôtel Saint Florentin, which was as princely as the hôtel Matignon but lacked a park, and Talleyrand's château at Saint Brice, which was in the forest of Montmorency, near enough to Saint Cloud to enable her to commute when the court moved there to avoid Paris in the summer heat. For like other members of both imperial households, Dorothea was required to work alternating three-month periods.

At nineteen, the last traces of the immature, underdeveloped child bride had vanished, but Dorothea's appearance—with her haughty features and enormous eyes—was still too unusual to be called pretty. Although she adopted the court vogue of heavy makeup, the rouged circles painted on her pale cheeks, like on a doll's, did not detract from the velvety softness of her face. Dorothea's well-trained, eager mind, far more questioning and independent than her mother's, delighted Talleyrand as much as her improved looks. She had a surprising maturity of judgment, coupled with a refreshing absence of preconceptions and prejudices—although she never forgot her due as a princess. The deference she accorded *l'oncle* and her genuine interest in his ideas and convictions beguiled the cynical, hardened statesman, and he was challenged by the opportunity to shape his young niece's thinking. She had come to regard him as the most fascinating man she had ever known and was filled with admiration for the agile pragmatism that had assured his survival in a position of authority through so many upheavals, from the Revolution, by way of the Directorate and Consulate, to the Empire.

Dorothea considered her marriage a parody and did not find any compensation for its shortcomings in motherhood. Like the grand duchess and her eldest sister, Wilhelmina, she was drawn to politics. Her former interest in Prince Czartoryski sprang more from the mind than from the heart, and was in large measure motivated by a desire for involvement in important current events.

These months spent in close contact with Talleyrand, even though they were the stagnant days of his semidisgrace, offered tantalizing visions of a new and different life, unlike any she had imagined, and killed the slightest possibility of her ever establishing a modus vivendi with Edmond, her philandering, unreliable husband.

At the birth of her second child, the emperor, as a mark of favor and esteem—in marked contrast to his present attitude toward her mother—had promoted Dorothea to a higher category of lady-in-waiting, with double the emolument and additional duties. She was starting her second stint in her new position when the court returned to Paris in the fall.

Gloom spread like pea soup fog over the capital. Every home there had some beloved one with the Grande Armée and had a map stuck on the wall to locate, with pins, his approximate whereabouts in the unknown vastness of Russia. Official communiqués were intermittent, and Napoleon was deep in enemy territory when the tsar's dread ally, winter, struck.

The end of November 1812, Bulletin XXIX exploded like a bomb across the pages of the official newspaper, the *Moniteur,* spreading the news of the emperor's defeat and the French rout at Berezina:

> The cold began. . . . More than 30,000 horses died in a few days. We had to destroy a goodly part of our guns, our munitions and our food supplies. [We were] almost without cavalry, artillery, or transportation. . . . The enemy sought to take advantage . . . it occupied all the crossings of the Berezina. . . . The combat became brisk . . . .
> The army without cavalry, weak in munitions, [was] horribly fatigued by fifty days of marching. . . . The army needs to . . . remount its cavalry, artillery and supply wagons. . . . Rest is its first need.

Dorothea found disaster on this gigantic a scale hard to believe. Only yesterday—or so it seemed—she and the rest of the empress's household participated in a victorious Te Deum in Notre Dame to celebrate the taking of Moscow, and the great government buildings had been illuminated by tens of thousands of little oil-filled pots for the citywide celebration that followed.

Marie-Louise appeared no more personally affected by the

frightful calamity than Dorothea, and the imperial schedule for the afternoon remained unaltered. When Dorothea accompanied the empress to an art exhibition, their carriage passed crowds gathered wherever Bulletin XXIX was posted. Most of the people were listening carefully, anxious to catch some particle of hope they might have missed, while the few who could read the dramatic communiqué did so, over and over, for the benefit of latecomers. One question was on everyone's lips: Where was the emperor? Dorothea was one of the first to find out.

The following night there was a loud pounding—instead of the customary scratching—on the door of the empress's suite at the unheard-of hour of midnight. Seconds later, two unshaven men bundled in furs thrust open the paneled doors and hurtled in. Dorothea, who was about to leave, shrieked for help and dropped her reticule and wrap to try to bar their way. To silence further outcry, the shorter of the two invaders flung open his greatcoat. It was the emperor—and, with him, the Grand Master of the Horse, *l'oncle*'s good friend, the former ambassador to Russia.

As the bottle green court carriage with its coachman and footman in imperial livery took her home, Dorothea mulled over the emperor's dramatic arrival. She was unaware of what Talleyrand was up to, for he and Anna—when Maman was in Paris—never discussed the emperor or imperial policy in front of her, in order not to place the girl in an awkward position as a member of the empress's household. But Dorothea was no dummy, and she must have suspected that *l'oncle* was far more active than he pretended to be. She wondered what he would make of Napoleon's unexpected reappearance, but she was unable to find out, for when she was deposited at the door of the hôtel Saint Florentin, the lackey there informed her that "Monsieur" was still out. So Dorothea hastily scribbled a few lines relating what had occurred and rang for *l'oncle*'s trusted valet to give them to him before he retired.

Next morning, while the Invalides cannon were still barking to announce the emperor's return, a Tuileries page appeared with word from His Imperial Majesty that Edmond was in good health and had escaped from the converging Russian armies. That same day, Talleyrand had a long chat with the Grand Master of the Horse, who confided that the emperor had talked about Talleyrand more than once when the two—accompanied only by an interpreter and the faithful imperial Mameluke, Rustam—raced west across Europe. Napoleon admitted that the grand duchess of Courland's "society machinations" had infuriated him, and he held Charles-Maurice responsible.

His Imperial Majesty might continue to question Talleyrand's loyalty. But there was still insufficient evidence to formulate charges of treason against the one man Napoleon now needed because of the universal respect he commanded abroad. So twice within the next seventy-two hours the emperor called Charles-Maurice in and offered him the foreign affairs portfolio. Both times Talleyrand refused, and angry words followed. The emperor's external policy was contrary to Talleyrand's personal conception of the glory and happiness of France. Before the end of the month, Talleyrand and Napoleon had still another quarrel, and this time, the emperor mentioned the grand duchess and specifically "her schemes" with the tsar. Fortunately, His Imperial Majesty was convinced these were Anna's, not Talleyrand's, doings. With the emperor once more in residence in the capital, criticism sank to a whisper, and conspiracy crept underground.

CHAPTER EIGHT

Wilhelmina & Metternich
1813 - Early 1814

WILHELMINA WAS FLOUTING CONVENTION, not with her disorderly private life—Vienna was even more permissive in this regard than Paris—but with her attempts, like those of her mother and her aunt Elisa before her, to break out of the mold that society created for its own. To administer personally the huge domains she had inherited—Nachod and Sagan—as Wilhelmina was doing, was unusual for a woman of the day, but conceivable. However, in marked contrast to her mother, who was attracted to interesting people, regardless of their fields of endeavor, the consuming passions of Wilhelmina's life were current events and Continental affairs. And unfortunately the extent of her activity in these fields could only be indirect.

Wilhelmina possessed a thorough understanding of the complex history and the ruling courts of Central Europe from firsthand acquaintance with many of the leading actors, and was kept better informed than most contemporary statesmen through her far-flung network of family and friends. Reinforced by her prominent social position and unlimited wealth, the duchess of Sagan was a behind-the-scenes factor to be reckoned with in Vienna by the time Napoleon was marching eastward to avenge his Russian fiasco in early 1813. For more top-level government matters were resolved in the drawing rooms of the crème—as the highest aristocracy in that most hierarchic of cities was called—than within the austere walls of the foreign office.

News was hard to come by, and since much could be gleaned at drawing-room gatherings from the guests' private letters, ministers and their aides regularly went the circuit to supplement their mail pouches. Frustrated diplomats—and especially the French ambassador in Vienna—were forever fulminating about the petticoat politics of the Austrian salons and the resultant speed with which rumors circulated in Europe.

Forty-year-old Chancellor Metternich was in his element in society and knew how to make society—that is to say, women—an element in his success. Outrageously good-looking, with a detached, arrogant air, he had a tall, splendid physique, a patrician head topped by lightly powdered blond hair, a fair complexion, blue eyes, and a long, thin, eagle's nose. He had known Anna-Dorothea in Berlin, and he knew the duchess of Sagan, who was seven years younger than he, from her Dresden days when he was ambassador there. He had learned to admire her sharp mind as well as her beauty. The chancellor needed a forum for his unpopular foreign policy. So increasingly Metternich left the white stone foreign office across from the imperial palace when his day's work was done, traversed the square, directed his steps across the Minoritenplatz, where the trees' branches were slowly showing feathery spots of green, and continued the short distance to Wilhelmina's luxurious apartments in the Palm palace.

Tempers were growing sharp there over the issue of war. Metternich was adamantly opposed. Peace was his primary aim and then to reestablish Austrian prominence and the European balance of power—which were synonymous in his eyes. "The first step," Metternich repeatedly stressed to Wilhelmina, "is for Austria to switch from an unwilling French ally to an armed neutral without outraging the moral sense of Emperor Franz. There is no need to destroy his son-in-law, Napoleon, to achieve this. But patience is required to bide time for the auspicious moment to change camp." As he explained this, the handsome chancellor fingered the Golden Fleece, the highest order of the Austrian empire (which he had received for arranging the glittering marriage of the Austrian archduchess, Marie-Louise), which gleamed conspicuously from the ribbon round the neck of his somber, otherwise unadorned coat.

Wilhelmina disagreed. She was convinced that war was inevitable. Never. Metternich was adamant. Not if he could help it.

During this tense period of his watchful waiting for the European scene to unfold so Austria might make a move, Metternich needed a confidante to share the terrible anxieties of his high office. Early in his marriage the chancellor, a ladies' man, had established a modus vivendi that suited him, if not his wife, Laure—though she was so madly in love with Metternich that she readily understood how no woman could resist him. Laure and their numerous children would always have a prominent role in his life, but Clemens found it impossible to live without *une amie* who would devote herself to him, body and soul, night and day, to the exclusion of everyone and everything else. And Metternich was turning more and more to Wilhelmina, whose long liaison with Prince Alfred Windischgratz seemed to be ending—as near as he could tell.

When an aroused Prussia signed a treaty of allegiance with the tsar and then declared war against France in 1813, Wilhelmina was convinced that Austria's hour had struck. She was determined to do everything possible to push Metternich into this new anti-Napoleonic coalition. (Tantalizingly, from the point of view of a biographer of Wilhelmina, a large number of letters between the duchess of Sagan and the chancellor dating from this decisive spring are missing—destroyed by Wilhelmina at Metternich's specific request, probably when he was editing his *Memoirs*. Since the diary of Gentz (who was the chancellor's spare brain) had the pages dealing with the same critical period also ripped out, we have only the unwavering view of himself as the farsighted nemesis of Napoleon that the chancellor chose to will to posterity. We lose the political woman in the background who was trying to change the dove of this spring and summer into a hawk.)

After an inconclusive battle at Bautzen in Saxony May 20–21, the Prussians and Russians retreated toward Silesia, and the French emperor unexpectedly asked for an armistice. Napoleon's subsequent acceptance of Austria as mediator was a triumph for the chancellor's strategy.

The time for decision was at hand. Metternich must move nearer the war zone immediately to facilitate communications, and he selected Gitschin in Bohemia as the best location for Emperor Franz and himself. It lay between Dresden, where Napoleon's headquarters were located, and Reichenbach, where the Russian and Prussian general staffs and thousands of their troops were, and was temptingly near Nachod, where Wilhelmina always spent the summer months. She was headed there on the morrow, and Clemens stopped by around midnight to bid her a hasty good-bye and tell her of his plans.

As fingers of light in the west indicated approaching dawn, Metternich, Emperor Franz, and a single aide set off—in such a hurry that the chancellor forgot the black china-wood box holding his money and travel necessities. The skies clouded over, the weather turned foul, and their speedy light carriage, harnessed though it was to the swiftest horses in the Hofburg stables, bogged down axle deep in mud. Impatient over the delay, the chancellor was so anxious to arrive that they did not stop to sleep the second night but pressed on.

Wilhelmina traveled north more leisurely. When she reached Ratiborzitz, her small, pale yellow manor house, which she preferred to the mammoth, gloomy castle where she and her sisters had once lived, she found a note awaiting her from the chancellor with word that the armistice was official. It had been signed at Pleiswetz on June 4. Metternich was relieved, but Wilhelmina was annoyed. She wanted Austria to plunge into the fight on the side of the Allies at once, and she knew the chancellor would use the two-week respite of the armistice to renew his efforts for peace.

The lull in the fighting afforded the tsar's sisters, who were visiting relatives not far off, a chance to see Alexander. So a nearby castle, Opocno, was hastily dusted out and placed at their disposal. Since Wilhelmina's manor house was on the tsar's way there, he sent a courier ahead to announce that he would be pleased to dine the next day with the duchess of Sagan, the only one of Anna-Dorothea's daughters whom he had never met.

The impending arrival of the archangel Gabriel could not have appalled Wilhelmina more. She always lived simply when she was in the country, and as luck would have it, the one butler she had brought with her was prostrate with a high fever. In despair she sent a messenger to the chancellor, six hours distant at Gitschin, with a scribbled S.O.S. and hastily dispatched her intendant on a fast horse to some of the hundred-odd hamlets on the estate to commandeer as many hands as possible to help in the emergency. Other servants were detailed to go the rounds collecting food. Then Wilhelmina donned an apron, tucked her long blonde locks under a bright kerchief, and hastened into the salon to supervise moving furniture around.

She was still busy late that night, helping out wherever needed, when she heard the welcome clatter of horses' hooves. Relieved, Wilhelmina darted into the kitchen where a swarm of peasant women bustled about, their sleeves rolled up, joking, laughing, chopping, slicing, cooking amid an aromatic medley of paprika, anise, and other exotic spices. One of the chancellor's aides-de-camp and a footman in the Metternich livery hastened in, dragging several bulging hampers. But Wilhelmina looked in vain for the pastry chef she had requested.

The emperor's could not be spared and the chancellor did not have one with him, Metternich's aide apologized. But the bald officer hastened to reassure her, removing his hat with a sweeping flourish, that he himself was a jack-of-all-trades. So there was no cause for worry. He started gingerly unpacking case after case of bonbons, sugared almonds, cakes, macaroons, and tiny sweet souf-flés, only to find that everything had been shaken to bits by the speedy trip over rough country roads. Undaunted, he sat back on his haunches, licked his gooey fingers, and explained Metternich's fall-back plan—to mask the sorry-looking mess with a rich sabayon sauce and ceremoniously unveil the result as a new dessert created expressly in His Imperial Highness's honor. Tired though she was, Wilhelmina burst out laughing. How like Clemens to think of that.

Metternich did not consider it proper to dine with the tsar before their formal meeting at Opocno forty-eight hours later, but similar niceties did not disturb the Chevalier Friedrich von Gentz. Serving presently as the chancellor's private secretary, the pub-licist could not bear to miss an informal rendezvous with the Tsar of All the Russias and arrived early the next morning from Gitschin, nattily attired in tight leather breeches and high patent boots, which would have done justice to the chancellor's tall, supple figure but looked ridiculous on so tiny a man. An old Berlin acquaintance of the grand duchess's, Gentz had a finger on the pulse of the vari-ous anti-Napoleonic forces congregated in Prague, Toëplitz, Karls-bad, and as far afield as Silesia and even England. Wilhelmina had never seen the chevalier—a title she knew the redheaded Jew had preempted, like the *von* in his name—without dark glasses and a high, black stock wrapped tightly under the chin of his crumpled, ageless face. Gentz, who preferred young men—and loved money most of all—was heavily perfumed and always shivering, either from having caught cold or from fear of catching one.

Somehow, Wilhelmina managed to get Ratiborzitz ready, and at 5:00 P.M., the appointed hour, she and a reception committee of flag-waving Nachod citizens were waiting to greet Alexander at the entrance of the long drive that led through the centuries-old beech forest to the schloss. The tsar appeared astride a black charger, resplendent in a white uniform that showed off his wasp waist to perfection, his chestful of medals trapping the sun's late rays. He was preceded by a regiment of six-foot imperial guards and accompanied by Austria's former foreign minister, Count Stadion. Upon reaching Ratiborzitz, Alexander strolled around to the back to admire the tranquil Aupa, which flowed from the snowy heights of the Mountains of the Giants in the misty distance across the meadow below, where an occasional stork rose, legs tucked underneath, to skim away over the treetops.

As etiquette required, the table in the pink-and-gray dining room was laid for the tsar in solitary splendor. But Alexander insisted they must eat together. The table was quickly reset, and the imperial blue eyes exuded affability as he gallantly toasted "the Grand Duchess of Courland and her four daughters, the Courland Graces."

Alexander wasted no time in setting the record straight. He assured his hostess that contrary to rumor and certain people's wishes, he had not had a hand in Princess Dorothea's engagement. Wilhelmina smiled pleasantly. One did not contradict the tsar, but she knew he was lying.

It was quickly evident that today's meeting had been carefully engineered by Count Stadion. Violently opposed to Metternich's peace policy, he was familiar with the many rumors linking the chancellor and the duchess of Sagan, and knew that Wilhelmina was a rabid Francophobe. Since Metternich and Emperor Franz were the only two doves of importance who were still undecided about Austria's joining the Allied war effort, the count explained to Wilhelmina, "It is imperative, Your Excellency, that you do what you can to bring the chancellor into line." Alexander concurred. She must help. "I am sure the Duchess understands"—the tsar's tone was suddenly icy—"even though she now considers Vienna her home." Alexander dropped the curtain of social amenities and, as he had with her mother at the time of Dorothea's engagement, obliquely threatened confiscation. For Wilhelmina was still technically a Russian subject, although she was far less vulnerable than Anna because the bulk of her inheritance was not included in the family's Russian holdings.

There was nothing about the meal to reveal Ratiborzitz's inadequate staff. The fish, caught fresh in the Little Elbe, was delicious; the hams for which Prague was famous lived up to their reputation. And at the end, when Metternich's aide-de-camp, disguised as the maître d'hôtel, personally supervised the serving of the "macédoine à l'Alexandre," Wilhelmina smiled up at him gratefully.

She poured coffee in the library, and Alexander, after examining at length the superb Nymphenburg porcelain decorated in trompe l'oeil on display in a rococo Bavarian corner cabinet, sat down beside her to chat. Chevalier von Gentz took a pinch of snuff, then glanced at the latest journals neatly stacked on a table, while Count Stadion preferred to smoke a small pipe, so he adjourned to the next room. After leafing with interest through some of her father Grand Duke Peter's collection of fine etchings, the tsar took his leave, although Wilhelmina had adroitly, and courageously, avoided any commitment regarding Metternich.

Exhausted though she was, she did not forget her nightly note to Alfred Windischgratz. She reminded him that no matter how crowded the manor house might get, his suite—bedroom, study, and sitting room, adjoining her boudoir—was his alone, always. Despite Clemens's wishful thinking, Wilhelmina had not split with the young prince, but had patched things up—as so often in the past. Some of the nagging imponderables of their four-year-old affair crept into her letter. Was she too independent to suit Alfred? Or too old? Was she on a dead-end road? As the head of one of Austria's most distinguished Catholic families, Windischgratz must marry someday to perpetuate the line. Yet she was twice divorced and could no longer bear children.

Metternich arrived late at night, after Wilhelmina had already retired. The following morning, the two took their café au lait together at a table set in a sunny corner of her bedroom. Wilhelmina's slender waist and small, high breasts were set off to perfection by the bright Bohemian dirndl she adopted in the country, peasant attire Clemens had never seen her wear before. The duchess of Sagan always gave the impression of height because of the imperious way she carried herself. But she was tiny, like her mother and sisters, and would joke, with her brown eyes flashing, "I am every bit as tall as my *bête noir* [Napoleon]."

"Aren't you afraid you'll put on weight?" Clemens teased, watching her spread lavish amounts of rich, freshly churned butter on her third slice of bread.

"No. Should I be?" Wilhelmina, who loved to eat and never gained, made the wry little face that so amused Metternich. He termed it *"si gentille"* (so pleasant). She repeated the tsar's conversation at dinner, and listened attentively while Clemens detailed his idea for a peace congress in Prague.

Then he set off for Opocno, two hours distant, and Alexander. The tsar agreed to participate—for a price. Should the Prague meetings abort, Austria must automatically join the war against the French. If the proposed congress was to carry any weight, Prussia too must participate. So in order to save time, since the armistice was due to expire, Metternich immediately dispatched an aide to invite the Prussian chancellor to Ratiborzitz, and rushed back to meet him there.

The schloss was soon echoing with their heated discussions. Should some point require special stressing, the Prussian ambassador to Vienna, who had accompanied his superior, poked his sharply creased face toward the latter and repeated it, enunciating as clearly as his lisp would permit, so that his deaf colleague might read his lips.

For Wilhelmina, as for her mother, Anna, this was life at its best—at the epicenter of decision making. She sat beside a small fruitwood sewing table, in whose tiny multiple drawers she kept her colored silk threads, listening and embroidering. More than once, Wilhelmina thought her head—and the men's, too—would burst at the din, until finally she arose and, pushing open the long doors leading toward the gardens, suggested a short walk before the sun set. A little fresh air should clear everyone's thinking.

Their parleys resumed. There were several moments later in the evening when—as he gratefully acknowledged in a subsequent letter—the chancellor expected the talks to erupt, like Vesuvius, in an explosion of anger and bad feelings. Instead, Wilhelmina again offered a welcome interruption—this time, tea—and proposed afterwards that her guests retire and start afresh the next morning. They did, and as Wilhelmina anticipated, a good night's sleep on Ratiborzitz's goose-down mattresses and the rustic quiet, punctuated only by the usual farm sounds, produced the desired calming effect. An agreement was reached, and Prussia in turn consented to send a delegate to Prague—for the same stiff price as the tsar's. Austria must declare war if the congress failed.

To reciprocate her recent hospitality, the tsar invited Wilhelmina to Opocno. But Alfred's last letter indicated he was jealous of her success with the handsome, philandering Alexander, so she feigned one of her sixty-hour migraines and stayed home. Gentz went in her stead and returned at dawn the next day, with word that the tsar was looking forward to another meal at Ratiborzitz that very afternoon. The little chevalier was in his element with so many important people coming and going. "What a signal honor, Your Grace! Two imperial visits within the same week! Paris, Vienna, Berlin and Saint Petersburg sink away in importance compared with Gitschin, Reichenbach, Ratiborzitz, and Opocno. Here we are," he gloated, rubbing his hands together as if he were washing them, "in an area forty kilometers in length and not as a wide—and right at its heart, where the fate of the entire Continent is being decided."

Wilhelmina was not equally thrilled at the prospect of a repeat imperial visit. But with the tsar to wish was to command. Fortunately, Metternich's father's chef was passing through the district en route to London, and the chancellor, who had been alerted to the tsar's plans, requisitioned him.

Sidetracked to Ratiborzitz to help out, the old retainer arrived armed with a brief explanatory note. "Don't thank me," Clemens wrote. "I am sending the family chef selfishly, employing every measure at my command to prevent you from forgetting me."

By the time the imperial party appeared, a cold rain was whipping across the terrace, and the gilt-and-white porcelain stoves were lit in every room to drive out the dampness and chill. Wilhelmina and her guests were barely seated at the table when her intendant rushed in excitedly.

"Your Grace! The Cossacks are cutting down the oaks along the river bank! They're burning them for firewood!"

Their commander, the tsar's brother, Grand Duke Constantine, a homely man with Tartar features and a flattened hairless skull, jumped to his feet. Pulling out a sword, he glared around with a nearsighted squint, searching for his coadjutant, and yelled, "Get out there! Hang every one of the devils who has laid a finger on the Duchess's trees. Hang them from the oaks!"

"I'd rather they cut down every one of my trees than that a single man be hanged!" Wilhelmina burst out.

Alexander intervened. Both Cossacks and trees were spared, and the rest of the visit passed without further incident.

Clemens's letter the following morning contained startling news. Napoleon had summoned him to Dresden. And he was going because if the Prague congress was to succeed, France must also send a delegate.

Two days later, Wilhelmina profited from a brief lull in the rainy weather to enjoy the terrace with her house guests, Gentz, the Prussian chancellor, and the Prussian ambassador. The quartet was discussing the meeting taking place at that moment in the Marcolini palace in Dresden and speculating on what Metternich and the French emperor were saying to each other, when Wilhelmina heard the clank of spurs and looked up to see Prince Alfred Windischgratz smiling at her. She was overjoyed that Alfred had taken advantage of the brief armistice to visit her. But after another seventy-two hours passed without any sign from Metternich, Wilhelmina found herself listening to the young prince's chatter distractedly; like Gentz and her two other guests, she had one ear cocked for the hoofbeats of a courier's horse. What was happening at Dresden? Why did not Clemens write? He had never expected to be gone this long.

The rain resumed and never stopped. Rivers and streams flooded. Wilhelmina would have preferred to remain comfortably indoors, listening to the drops pelt the windowpanes and the wind rattle the doors. But Alfred, who was leaving on the morrow, was restless. So she accompanied him on a long horseback ride in the downpour.

Thursday and Friday came and went before Wilhelmina heard from Metternich. He requested that a relay of four horses await him halfway along the road to Gitschin the next morning and added, "I am bringing a windfall of good news for the curious denizens of Ratiborzitz."

The Russian foreign minister, Count Nesselrode, was alerted and appeared shortly before Metternich's coach swept into view. Wilhelmina sat silently listening while Metternich briefed the anxious officials about his two marathon encounters with the French emperor. The trip had been well worth the anguish and the effort— and the new, deep purple shadows under the chancellor's eyes. With the fate of Europe at stake, he had successfully negotiated French participation in the forthcoming Prague congress.

Concluding his report, Metternich announced, as casually as if he were predicting the daily sunrise and sunset, that at Napoleon's request he had arbitrarily extended the armistice deadline twenty days longer than the Allies had agreed upon. There was a moment of stunned silence while his audience digested this startling disclosure. Then pandemonium reigned. The Prussian ambassador paced angrily up and down, his heels clicking staccato each time he reached the end of the Aubusson rug and hit the parquet; the Russian foreign minister planted himself before the Prussian chancellor and complained in a loud voice. That statesman, with the helpless expression of the deaf, cupped his hand to his ear and kept demanding, "Why delay? Our armies are set." Gentz, who was standing alongside, stirred yet another of his innumerable powders into a glass of water—this one was to quiet his nerves. What the others did not know, and what Metternich had no intention of revealing, was that Vienna's troops were not yet at combat readiness and needed this extra time as much as Napoleon did.

More than once, two of the men, gesticulating madly, broke off the tumultuous discussion and rushed into the adjacent library for a whispered consultation. At length, Wilhelmina put down her needlework and interrupted diplomatically. "Gentlemen, may I propose an armistice of my own making?" She reached for the bell and ordered refreshments.

Sunday saw another stormy session over the truce extension. Whenever the conversation got overly turbulent, the duchess of Sagan's warm humor or quick remark successfully turned the talk to safer channels. Each diplomat knew that the opposing military forces were so delicately balanced that without the Austrian "Whitecoats," Napoleon could not be beaten in the field, and by nightfall Metternich won grudging approval for his unilateral action. The Austrian chancellor did not consider the peace conference a feint to gain time, as certain latter-day historians interpreted it. Should it fail, however, as Wilhelmina and the others anticipated, the Austrians were irrevocably committed to march.

The past months had constituted a turning point in Metternich's career—and in his private life. A few short years before, when Metternich had stepped into the chancellery, once-proud Austria was one of Napoleon's humble satellites; today he had successfully upgraded her position to that of European mediator and balance wheel. He also found himself in love with the duchess of Sagan. They had long since bedded down together. One evening, Clemens desired her. Wilhelmina felt a similar urge—and that was that. Wilhelmina attached little more importance to the physical act of making love than to eating a good dinner. Both were to be enjoyed.

But now Clemens, though an experienced Lothario with a connoisseur's appreciation of the opposite sex, found himself experiencing emotions he never knew existed before. He wanted Wilhelmina exclusively, not for a few weeks but forever, and wished he knew the exact status of her liaison with Alfred.

Because Metternich expected to depart with the others, he stayed up late, after every other candle was out and the schloss was dark and peaceful, writing Wilhelmina to express his feelings. Then he tore the letter up. He preferred to talk to her. With the exception of Gentz, her other guests had departed at daybreak, and Metternich should have too. He had urgent work to attend to with Emperor Franz, but with the Prague conference on the agenda, Clemens was not sure when he might see Wilhelmina again. So he remained.

It was clear, for a change, and Clemens led Wilhelmina onto the rain-washed terrace. "Wilhelmina, I've always respected your intelligence and tact, but never so much as in these past forty-eight hours. I felt so alone when I returned from Dresden. I took a tremendous responsibility when I extended, unauthorized, the armistice period. You sensed this and gave me encouragement and understanding, even though you didn't agree with my stand. Otherwise, I could never have withstood the barrage of arguments—and invectives—hurled at me. You and you alone supported me. Oh, my dear!" He took her in his arms. "I don't know if you love me, but I love you from the bottom of my heart—and much more than I should for my own good."

Gently Wilhelmina released herself. "Clemens, you are my dear and trusted friend." She smiled affectionately at him. "What more can I say?" she asked softly in her warm alto voice. What more could she say—and be honest with herself?

"We've known each other for many years. Why didn't we find each other long ago? I want you to be mine alone—not for weeks but forever!" Metternich continued.

Wilhelmina put her finger to his lips to stop further talk, though she was deeply moved. Gentz was approaching to remind the chancellor that it was late. They must be off.

No one knew better than Metternich the distinction between the bonds of marriage and those of love. How many times would this complex man explain to Wilhelmina that he had married to have children, not to satisfy the desires of his heart. To emphasize —and illustrate—the way he kept his life and feelings compartmentalized, with his wife and family in a place apart but never forgotten, Clemens had showed Wilhelmina the extravagant snuff box set with sixteen huge diamonds that Napoleon had presented to him on his departure from Dresden—a *tabatière* far more magnificent than the customary tribute the occasion called for. The chancellor was sending it to his wife. He wanted her to have the stones pried off and used to enlarge her necklace from three to four strands.

Given their social and moral code, Wilhelmina understood Clemens's need to reveal this gift. But she still found the transformation of her old friend's affections hard to believe, even when he repeated, from Gitschin, "I cannot imagine life without you."

This letter was among the first of an extensive exchange over the next fifteen months that would illuminate the true relationship beween the pair, the significance of which liaison was not even guessed at until the letters' accidental discovery in 1949. They were in a black box bound like a book with gilded edges, and inscribed on the spine in Metternich's handwriting was "Letters of the Duchess of Sagan." For security at the outbreak of World War II, the box had been secreted with the Metternich archives in a walled-up cellar underneath the brewery of the Cistercian Abbey on the Metternich estate at Plass in Bohemia. These letters stand out as the frankest, most probing and most emotional—even with allowances for the romantic sensibilities of the period—of all the chancellor ever wrote to anyone. And he had a voluminous correspondence.

Wilhelmina's reply was hardly the one Metternich was seeking, but her solicitude for his feelings showed behind each carefully phrased sentence.

> If you know a word, dear Clemens, that says more than
> emotion, sensibility, gratitude, friendship and tenderness,
> I beg you, use it. That will give you some idea of the way
> I felt when I got your letter. . . . If our relationship is
> not what you desire, still it has its good side . . . and allow
> me the satisfaction of believing that I may sometimes lighten
> your position, make you forget, for a moment, the burden
> you bear, that burden that is very nearly the whole world.

By the time the chancellor reached Prague, most of the other delegates' wives had joined their husbands. His wanted to also, but Metternich did not suggest she come. It was Wilhelmina he desired, Wilhelmina whom he importuned to meet him there.

The Duchess of Sagan continuously postponed her departure. First it was because of a visit from her sister Paulina. Then a Biron cousin arrived. But more important, she kept expecting Alfred to return. When he did not, and it was evident that he would not, she set forth, anticipating that the young prince might show up in Prague.

Wilhelmina's coach rattled into that city, one of the continent's oldest, at dusk, and she was surprised to find it packed like on a carnival day. Joyous crowds slowed the carriage to a crawl, and she signaled her coachman on the box to inquire the reason for so much rejoicing.

"Wellington's great victory at Vittorio, that be what we be celebrating," replied a stout burgher trudging alongside with a small red-cheeked child clinging to each hand. "And shouldn't that put a nail in old Boney's coffin!" he prophesied gleefully.

Wilhelmina was held up at one narrow crossing in the labyrinth of crooked medieval streets by a troop of comedians dragging a small portable stage around the corner. The milling around of laughing, applauding spectators detained her long enough to witness most of the anti-Bonaparte pantomime. Then her horses were straining up the hill and she looked back, her ears deafened by the sound of firing rockets, to admire the spires of Prague's convents and baroque palaces etched against the sky by the leaping bonfires.

The Biron family's Karmelitergasse residence had been sold two years before, so Wilhelmina had begged an apartment in the beautiful Wallenstein palace from the proprietor, a friend. It was located near the Schönborn palace, in the Mala Strana, where Clemens was lodged. The minute he learned of her arrival, the chancellor swept his deskful of work into a drawer, shooed the last official visitor out the door as gracefully as possible, and hurried on foot to welcome her.

The seasons were topsy-turvy. There had been no spring and now, after so much rain, it had turned unbearably hot. Whenever he had a free hour, Metternich took Wilhelmina for a drive in the countryside to cool off. She also went shopping with him to select a bonnet and gown for his wife, taffeta for dresses for his daughters, and special chocolates for his favorite, the oldest girl, and his only son.

The days melted away, like the delicately flavored ices served following the main courses at dinner. But the French delegate failed to take his seat at the green baize-covered table with his Prussian, Russian, and Austrian counterparts, and the chancellor was unequivocally committed to war if nothing was resolved by August 10. As he waited that inflexible deadline, Wilhelmina was the one person Metternich could talk to who understood him—even if they did not agree. She appreciated the chancellor's dilemma. His heart told him to keep trying for peace; his mind, that this was foolishness.

Finally the long overdue French representative did arrive—minus the necessary credentials—and that evening Metternich admitted to Wilhelmina that Napoleon must have sent him improperly documented to stall for time. Upon leaving the Wallenstein palace later, Metternich persuaded Gentz to get a breath of fresh air with him. The city gates were long since shut and the streets deserted, citizens and visitors alike either in bed or silently going about their nocturnal affairs. The pair descended the hill, skirted the Gothic Cathedral of Saint Thomas, and traversed the ancient Maltese Square under the shadow of Saint Nicolas Church. They passed little shuttered shops and sgraffito-decorated houses, pillared balconies, inner courtyards, and great baroque palaces with intricate armorial bearings blazed on their entries, and lingered as they crossed the medieval Charles Bridge, its balustrades lined with age-stained statues, its twenty-four colossal arches spanning the murky Moldau.

This was not the first time Metternich had walked the streets after midnight to confide in the little bespectacled chevalier, but Gentz had never seen the chancellor so disturbed. From this distance it is hard to say whether Metternich was more upset by the French emperor's intransigence or by Alfred's arrival, hard on the heels of Napoleon's emissary, and Wilhelmina's subsequent confession that the main reason she had come to Prague was in the hopes of seeing Windischgratz before he set forth on active duty. Startled by her frank disclosure, Clemens labeled her feelings for the young prince maternal, and Wilhelmina conceded that she could not be sure if they were or not. Wilhelmina was the first woman ever to have evaded the chancellor, and Clemens, who prided himself on complete self-mastery, was as tormented and jealous as an adolescent in the throes of first love.

Gentz was worried about Wilhelmina's distracting effect on the chancellor. The congress was stalled. The point of no return was drawing near, and Metternich must be clearheaded for the decisions ahead. Yet Gentz knew that Metternich was passing sleepless nights. The redheaded chevalier had repeatedly tried to warn him about this femme fatale. Wilhelmina had already had many affairs, and Gentz was sure she would have many others, but he was too tactful to say so. Instead, Gentz retreated to safer ground and pointed out that the chancellor's feelings for the duchess of Sagan were no secret. Was Metternich aware of the bad impression this created? The image he projected? The powerful chancellor of the Austrian empire was a man at the summit of power. He must never admit himself prey to any of the frailties of ordinary man—like unrequited love.

The chevalier's advice went begging. Metternich's feelings got the upper hand. Tension on a professional level was part of his job. To endure it simultaneously on a personal one was to make a bad situation worse. The day before the congress's deadline, the chancellor for once took advantage of his position and sent Alfred out of town with a dispatch to Emperor Franz in Brandeis, a mission sufficiently prestigious to lull any suspicions Wilhelmina might have about the timing of the prince's departure—or Clemens's hand in it. Metternich got Wilhelmina to himself by this ploy, but she was poor company. Sick with concern about Alfred's imminent battlefront exposure, her thoughts were elsewhere, and she was not to be cheered.

On Tuesday, August 10, a distinguished array of guests assembled in Metternich's Schönborn palace salons, impatiently awaiting midnight. At last the door of the famous Gothic clock on Prague's Town Hall sprang open and out stepped the wooden figures of the twelve apostles to bow and retreat, one by one, with each stroke of the clapper. "The Congress is at an end!" Gentz proclaimed, and the Russian and Prussian negotiators leaped to their feet, jubilant. Slowly, reluctantly, Metternich walked to the great flat-topped desk where the Austrian declaration of war lay waiting. Wilhelmina held out the pen. The chancellor took it and solemnly signed the document, turned, and extended his hand to the commander in chief of the Austrian forces to wish him success in the campaign ahead. Then he dispatched a waiting aide with an order that the great signal fires be lit on the crest of the hill above, in front of the Hradschin palace, to relay through the velvety black starlit sky across Bohemia their message of impending bloodshed and carnage.

Wilhelmina, her eyes luminous with tears, lifted her flute of champagne to exchange a silent toast with Clemens before joining the rest to drink to Allied victory. Only she knew the extent of her own role in bolstering the chancellor's courage when he was wavering in his commitments.

With the Allies on the move, the tsar was coming to the ancient Bohemian capital and wished to dine at Ratiborzitz en route. Wilhelmina hurried home for her third command performance and was pleasantly surprised to be greeted by two of the chancellor's liveried footmen and his principal aide-de-camp, who handed her a sealed envelope. "I wish I were this letter," Clemens wrote. "Don't please the tsar too much—just sufficiently to follow him back to Prague." Bearing in mind Wilhelmina's dilemma on Alexander's two previous visits, Metternich had anticipated she would again require domestic assistance.

After her imperial visitor left, Wilhelmina rode over to dreary Nachod where she was lodging her Aunt Elisa and the poet Tiedge, and the three climbed to the top of the castle's lookout tower to watch the high-stepping war-bound Prussian troops cross the Bohemian border with Friedrich-Wilhelm III trotting at their head. Then country life resumed its somnolent pace.

The doctors could find little wrong when the chancellor fell ill a short time later, and he sent word to his wife that he had only a cold. But he told Wilhelmina a different story. He romantically claimed that his malaise was due to longing for her and so alarmed the duchess of Sagan that she replied at once.

Wilhelmina's feelings toward the chancellor had been slowly evolving, isolated as she presently was at quiet Ratiborzitz, with ample time to reflect on their past weeks together—and on his repeated declarations of love. It was comforting to have the number-one man in the Austrian empire—after Emperor Franz, of course —madly in love with her. His repeated confidence in her judgment was flattering . . . his Olympian good looks . . . his thoughtfulness . . . all added up in Clemens's favor. Glancing down once more at the sheet lying open on the desk before her, Wilhelmina's eye caught the motto she had embossed on her stationery years before:

Such was love in the golden circle,
One can never find it again
But one continues the search.

This eternal quest for happiness, was it not the leitmotif of her life?

The memory of previous happy days Wilhelmina had spent with Alfred here at Ratiborzitz flooded back. "I think it would not be possible to love you more than I do today," she had written Windischgratz then, recalling long walks they had taken in the woods together. "Now, following these same paths evokes [those] precious hours. . . . There, you stopped to look at me—here I took your arm—there we chatted." Once again, Wilhelmina thought of her frequent recent quarrels with Alfred and of her increasing desire to fix her affections permanently on a man on whom she could rely. Could she be falling in love with Clemens?

The skies opened up once more, confining Wilhelmina indoors. Torrents of rain blotted out the meadow at the foot of the hill, and she insulated herself with layers of shawls and woolens against the damp and chill. Rumor proved even more of a depressant, and she ordered her father's fine library, porcelains, and other collections packed and shipped off, for fear Ratiborzitz and Nachod might be sacked as Sagan had been earlier. Her overriding concern about Windischgratz's safety added to her woes. She could not sleep and fell prey to one of her sixty-hour migraines.

Clemens wrote Wilhelmina regularly. Because of communication problems, and the necessity of meshing diplomatic as well as military operations in order to prevent the tsar from assuming supreme command, the chancellor decided that the three Allied sovereigns and their principal ministers must follow the armies. To set Wilhelmina's mind at ease, Metternich instructed Gentz, whom he was leaving behind to direct public opinion as editor of the *Prager Zeitung,* that he must keep the duchess of Sagan posted with advance copies of all releases.

To get the news as fast as it reached the bespectacled chevalier, Wilhelmina determined to return to Prague. Impulsively writing Metternich that she would join him anywhere he wished, she set forth in her cumbersome travel berlin. Tagging along behind was a fast little calèche and extra horses, should the need arise to evacuate the city hastily. The trip, which normally took about thirty hours at this season, stretched into a long nightmare for the duchess, who was accompanied by only a personal servant and Hännchen, her faithful lady's maid, who had been with her forever —and who was seven and a half months pregnant.

The continuous rain turned the roads into a quagmire. More than once the carriage slithered to a halt, stopped by officers who forced the coachman to back into some scarcely visible spur and wait interminable hours in the dreary downpour while wagonloads of troop reserves lumbered noisily along. Because there was no moon, travel at night, which was difficult at best, became extremely precarious, and caissons mired right and left in the oozing mud made the narrow road almost impassable in spots. When her own berlin got stuck, Wilhelmina was sure they would be there until doomsday. Fortunately, a captain in charge of a regiment of soldiers marching behind came to the rescue and ordered his men to unhitch her frightened, exhausted horses and dislodge the duchess's vehicle. Worn out by the untoward mishaps, her nerves on edge, Wilhelmina's ears rang with hair-raising tales of pillaging deserters and brigands. Their second night on the road, when they were once again held up by military convoys and she saw several shadowy figures approach, Wilhelmina was positive the three women were about to be raped and their throats slit. But nothing happened, the men continued past, and she arrived in Prague shortly before the gates closed the next day.

Gentz's jewel of a chef had an excellent hot supper ready in Gentz's suite adjoining hers in the Wallenstein palace, and amid a pile of mail awaiting her perusal, Wilhelmina recognized two addressed in Clemens's fine, clear hand and sealed in bright blue with the personal intaglio he used on her correspondence in lieu of his readily identifiable family crest. Rapidly scanning the small sheets, folded like a book, she was pleased that Clemens, who had not yet had time to receive her letter, likewise proposed a rendezvous and suggested Laun, which was located halfway between Prague and Toëplitz, where the chancellor and the Allied sovereigns were quartered.

Wilhelmina took off early the following morning. Relays were sent ahead, and at Metternich's suggestion, Gentz accompanied her as a safeguard. Whenever they passed a wagon piled high with wounded and dead soldiers, the victims of the recent heavy fighting at Külm, Wilhelmina's thoughts reverted to Alfred. But this was not the moment to think of Windischgratz. Besides, Clemens had taken time to track down the prince, and in his last letter he had assured Wilhelmina that his rival was safe and well.

Metternich had sent staff ahead to prepare four rooms at the Inn of the Brown Deer to receive her, and after advising Emperor Franz, King Friedrich-Wilhelm III, and the tsar that the most urgent personal affairs demanded his attention, he managed to arrive in Laun shortly after Wilhelmina did.

They enjoyed the pleasures of sex unabashed and Clemens relaxed during his first break in many anxiety-fraught days. The chancellor's chef prepared elsewhere a mouth-watering veal roast which an aide-de-camp then served in their tiny salon, and the two lingered over coffee. Clemens took his cognac neat while Wilhelmina, as usual, preferred to place a sugar lump on a spoon, dip it briefly in the liquid in his small glass, and then suck the slowly dissolving crystals. Languidly savoring the warmth-giving brandy as it touched the tip of her tongue, Wilhelmina managed to impart, even to that insignificant act, a sensual quality.

Wilhelmina laughed until the tears rolled down her cheeks when Metternich regaled her with the latest anecdote concerning his waggish valet. The man was straight out of Molière, and that morning he had made such an infernal racket pulling shut the windows, folding back the louvers, arranging everything for his master's toilet that the chancellor could not have slept had he wanted to. Actually, Clemens confided, he was lying there, wide awake, thinking about seeing Wilhelmina later. "Well! How funny!" Metternich mimicked his manservant's comments when he at last opened the bed-curtains. "Does Monsieur always sleep with his eyes open?"

There were serious moments, too. Wilhelmina's eyes clouded over as she listened to Metternich recount the horrors of the lost battle of Dresden and the Prussian victory on the Latzbach. What if Alfred had been there?

Without thinking, Wilhelmina invariably shut the door between their rooms if she left him, and to Clemens's bafflement, she would knock before returning. When Clemens asked why she bothered to close it in the first place, Wilhelmina shrugged. She really could not say, any more than she knew why she continued to address him with the formal *vous* (you) face to face, or in her letters. She still had some inner sanctum Clemens had not yet breeched, but he was confident she loved him and would come to fill the place he held ready for her in his heart.

Back once more in Prague, Wilhelmina was appalled at the never-ending stream of wounded that poured through the city and overflowed at every street corner, leaving stranded the mutilated and those too sick to continue homeward—poor souls who could only hope that warm-hearted burghers would take pity on them. Pleased to find one small way to help in the war—there was so little a capable woman was permitted to do—the duchess of Sagan single-handedly established and equipped, with her own funds, a hundred-bed hospital. She supervised its day-to-day operations, pressed some of her coterie into service, and inspired others to start similar units. The chancellor helped where he could, from Allied headquarters. He also interceded with the tsar, at Wilhelmina's request, for more merciful treatment of those unfortunates the Russians took prisoners and whom they forced to walk, days on end, with inadequate nourishment.

By one of Fate's quirks, the Russian prince who had been Wilhelmina's second husband was on Alexander's staff at Toëplitz. Metternich, who was in daily contact with him, confessed:

> I . . . see in him a crazy fool who bought a lottery ticket and carried off the grand prize. Scarcely does he have in his possession what would have made the happiness of any reasonable . . . man than he squanders his fortune. . . . I would like to shout at him, "What a great imbecile you are."

Occasionally, Wilhelmina attended to small errands for Clemens. And because the stench of death from Toëplitz's cramped medical facilities was overpowering, she sent him a little silver pocket flask to hold vinegar to protect him from the omnipresent fumes.

Wilhelmina's rooms in the Wallenstein palace bulged at the seams. Her generous Cour hospitality never faltered, although good food was scarce, and she was eating her share of dried fish. A bonus attraction was the latest Allied bulletins, for the arrival of the chancellor's courier at Gentz's apartment next door was Prague's biggest daily event, and Wilhelmina was the first to be informed of the dispatches he brought. She also had a group of friends and hangers-on who did nothing from dawn to dusk but visit the other salons and coffeehouses and return each night to transform her drawing room into an arsenal of gossip while Wilhelmina and the few women present scraped lint for her wards.

The Allied armies must soon move westward, and with them, their general headquarters. But the chancellor, who learned through Gentz that Alfred had been in Prague for another long weekend, could not leave without seeing Wilhelmina. Emperor Franz did not say a word when the chancellor told him he must return there briefly. The tsar was the inquisitive one. Alexander asked Metternich more than once where he was off to and remarked, pointedly, that he hoped the chancellor had a good excuse for leaving on the eve of the camp's breakup. Apparently Metternich lied unconvincingly, for instead of replying, Alexander winked and wagged an imperial finger in mock warning.

To preserve the chancellor's incognito, Gentz alerted the watchman at the city gates to let him pass and borrowed rooms for him in an inconspicuous rear courtyard of the nearby Fürstenberg palace. Clemens arrived laden like Father Christmas. "Direct from the Tsar's commissary!" he exclaimed, handing Wilhelmina a large carton of caviar. "And here are your favorite imperial chocolates." He took another box from the aide standing respectfully alongside with a big armful of packages. "I know you can be won by attentions, and I don't want to be remiss." And to amuse her, Clemens produced at the dinner table a copy of an indiscreet letter written by one of Napoleon's marshals, which had been found in a bag of captured mail. It had already gone the raucous rounds of Allied headquarters and explained, in detail, how the famous French officer hoped to make his unattractive wife produce handsome children by concentrating his thoughts on his beautiful mistress while performing his connubial duties.

Wilhelmina was once more amazed—and touched—that the chancellor could find time for her, overwhelmed as he was with his immense responsibilities. They had a marvelous two days together, and after a gay late supper, Metternich was off on the tedious twelve-hour drive back to Toëplitz.

It was not long before Wilhelmina was downcast again. "Don't worry about Alfred," Metternich wrote, accurately diagnosing her depression from afar. "This war could lead us as far as the Rhine without his risking anything more than fatigue." The chancellor generously forwarded her letters to Windischgratz by special courier and did the same with the young prince's rare replies to Wilhelmina.

Metternich managed to steal one more long weekend in Prague, and Wilhelmina listened eagerly their first evening together while Clemens discussed the altered European scene. For England had decided to join the coalition and wage all-out war against Napoleon, and Bavaria, the most important state of the Rhineland Confederation, was soon to follow suit—as Wilhelmina had predicted. These talks about war, day-to-day events, the form of the future, all the things that vitally interested her, were what Wilhelmina enjoyed most about being with the chancellor. As for Metternich, he had written her earlier:

> With my guidance you know—and understand—our
> problems far better than any of [my] Ministers. . . . I like to
> to see the reflection of my words in your eyes when I discuss
> politics. For it tells me that you comprehend me and follow
> me, even if you don't agree.

Their days together sped past. One morning Metternich accompanied Wilhelmina on her hospital rounds, and hearing her address a few words to each patient in his native tongue—Metternich himself spoke five languages, but women in their circle rarely knew more than one, and French—he was struck anew by her linguistic ability. Wilhelmina had already surprised him earlier that summer when they were on horseback in the Nachod woods, and she stopped to chat with the peasants in the local dialect, which she had learned when she summered there as a teenager. It was unheard of for princesses to converse with peasants, but Wilhelmina always took a personal interest in hers. One of their rendezvous was broken off, abruptly, when Hännchen sent word to the Schönborn palace that she was having labor pains. Throwing a coat over her shoulders, Wilhelmina rushed home and served as midwife for the illegitimate infant.

Then Clemens had to leave, and it would be months before they would see each other again because the Allies were starting an offensive. His road north was so encumbered with transports and war material that even the chancellor's new carriage was stalled, and Metternich was forced to stop at dusk. While waiting for the moon to rise before proceeding further, he wrote Wilhelmina. "My head and my heart are overflowing—with *mon amie* and Europe; with Europe and *mon amie*. Guess which one predominates?"

During the succeeding days and weeks, Wilhelmina was adrift

in a sea of anxiety, torn by her feelings—one minute for Clemens, the next for Alfred—unable to sort out her emotions. Only with Chevalier von Gentz could she talk freely—at least about the chancellor. But the heavily perfumed redhead was too inquisitive a neighbor. In search of privacy, Wilhelmina moved into the rooms the chancellor had vacated in the rear of the Fürstenberg palace. Gentz was glad she did. The ceaseless chatter of her guests coming and going in the hall outside his apartments in the Wallenstein made him nervous. On the other hand, he was proud to be the chancellor's sole confidant where Wilhelmina was concerned and felt duty bound to keep his patron informed about the duchess of Sagan's various activities. Therefore, he continued to call on her daily.

The chevalier did not approve of her string of admirers and catalogued "the Duchess's Illegalities"—suitors would seem to be a more accurate term—for Metternich. There were so many: a young British diplomat; a handsome Russian officer of the imperial guards, lately released from the duchess's hospital and still convalescent; a much-decorated British diplomat who was recuperating from serious wounds received at Külm; the duchess's first husband, who was hanging around threatening suicide if Wilhelmina did not get him a suitable commission.

One night shortly after midnight, Metternich's exhausted, mud-spattered courier stumbled into Gentz's apartment with word of a great Allied success. Withholding several tidbits to dine out on—because of his access to confidential information Gentz was the season's most sought-after guest—the chevalier hurriedly dashed off a note and sent a lackey scurrying around to Wilhelmina with the good news before he started work on a special edition of the *Prager Zeitung*.

Within twenty-four hours, Wilhelmina received her own eye-witness report from Clemens himself; it had been written on the night of the Leipzig victory and was accompanied by a strategic map to make it easier for her to follow the action. His description was so graphic that she felt as if she were standing beside Metternich on a nearby ridge with the king, the tsar, and the emperor, watching the tide of half a million men surge back and forth. Clemens concluded:

> Alfred is well, *ma chère*, and we have won the battle of the world. . . . What a singular thing the heart is, and what a frightful situation I find myself in! With so many things on

my mind, I still make myself attend to yours. Do you know what concerned me the most? The fear that something might happen to Alfred. I followed him with my eyes as much as possible.

Wilhelmina replied at once, congratulating Clemens as if Leipzig were his personal victory. And when a grateful emperor elevated the chancellor to hereditary prince, Metternich's droll valet appeared at his bedside the next morning and demanded gravely, "Will Your Serene Highness put on the same suit Your Excellency wore yesterday?"

Metternich felt he was ordained by Fate to defeat Napoleon. As the Allied armies and headquarters followed hard on the French emperor's fleeing heels, he exulted, "My hour has struck at last. I am triumphing and Providence has destined *mon amie* as my recompense."

The last thing Wilhelmina wanted to be was Clemens's manifest destiny. How could she tell him that she loved him if she herself was not yet sure she did? If Alfred, facing death daily on the battlefield, still tugged at her heart? On the other hand, she did not want to relinquish the security of Clemens's love. If only the chancellor could love her a little less.

Tormented by her conflicting emotions for the two men, Wilhelmina took to bed with a migraine. The first day she was able to lift her head from the pillow, she propped herself up and sent for her portable writing table. She must answer Clemens. But the effort was too painful. She could only scribble, "Tell yourself, *mon ami,* that my heart is sincerely devoted to you." She could not write another word. Exhausted by her efforts, Wilhelmina dropped the quill, rang for Hännchen, handed her the almost blank sheet to send off, and slid miserably back under the covers.

These few lines in which Wilhelmina once more spoke in terms of friendship reached Metternich at Weimar, as he was setting forth on a day's tour of inspection. Greatly upset, he tucked the note in the pocket of his caped overcoat and pulled it out to reread several times while he hastened to and fro. Circulation was difficult because the roads were cluttered with the paraphernalia of war. He was toppled from his carriage and finished his work on horseback. Bruised and bone weary, and deeply concerned about Wilhelmina, the chancellor returned to his lodgings to find both an English and a Bavarian courier impatiently waiting for him to sign important dispatches so they could depart. The Prussian ambassador was also there to consult with him. But the chancellor kept all three on tenterhooks at his elbow while he wrote Wilhelmina. Clemens terminated ". . . as soon as I can sweep my tiny room clear of the twenty-five other people crowding in . . . I am going to bed . . . to dream of you, I hope."

That same fall of 1813, Dorothea was feeling poorly. Edmond had been in and out of Paris on leave intermittently the preceding spring and summer, and she was well along in pregnancy. Her last confinement had been a hard one, and this time she was extremely ill and spent a good part of each day on her chaise longue.

But she bundled up well in the greatcoat she had lined with the remnants of the bundles of sables the tsar had given her as a wedding present and watched with Talleyrand from a balcony of *l'oncle*'s hôtel overlooking the great, festively decorated Place de la Concorde the day the Emperor's chief of staff presented Marie-Louise with twenty captured enemy flags Napoleon sent her from the battlefields. Through his private underground, *l'oncle* knew that the victory being celebrated was a minor one and that it had been deliberately blown up out of proportion to soften the blow of another defeat, which would be announced shortly. The crowds were exultant at the stirring military pageant, a type of ceremony at which the First Empire excelled, but who knew what those cheering masses would do when they learned that France was on the verge of invasion? How would they react when they discovered that Napoleon was already mustering new troops, composed more of boys than of men, for the defense of the fatherland? Even Talleyrand himself found that hard to believe.

Napoleon no sooner returned from the front than he sent for Charles-Maurice and offered him the ministry of foreign affairs again. This time certain conditions were attached. Charles-Maurice must officially separate from his wife, Catherine. "I can no longer compel foreign ambassadors to call on her," the emperor declared. Talleyrand must also shut his door to certain of his troublemaking friends: Napoleon singled out the grand duchess of Courland by name, and one or two others whom he considered "intriguers." Whatever His Imperial Majesty's intentions were when he included these stipulations, he should have foreseen that any man as proud as Talleyrand would reject interference in his personal life. Talleyrand, for his part, was relieved to be handed so easy an out and once more declined. He felt the emperor was too vulnerable to be allied with any longer.

Because she was worried about the outcome of the imperial interview, Dorothea was waiting up for Talleyrand even though it was late when he got home from Saint Cloud. So *l'oncle* suggested that she join him in his study on the entresol for a chat before retiring, something they frequently did.

Talleyrand settled himself in a comfortable armchair before the fireplace and propped his bad right leg on a stool while Dorothea fixed his mocha the way he preferred it. Like Maman, she had learned the trick from the majordomo. Strangely enough for a man who considered good conversation an essential part of living, *l'oncle* enjoyed silence too. At length, he related what had occurred. Then he fell quiet once more, twirling his gold-and-ivory lorgnon as was his wont when preoccupied. Dorothea was so impatient for further information that she committed the unpardonable sin of pestering him with questions. She ought to have known better.

Without saying a word, Talleyrand picked up a candlestick and dragged himself over to examine a self-portrait that Anna-Dorothea, who had just returned from Löbikau for Dorothea's upcoming accouchement, had had painted in Saxony. Leisurely he finished his inspection, decided to move the painting, tried it in several locations, then propped the grand duchess up on the mantel to smile down at him. Talleyrand then eased himself back down into his favorite spot and bent over to pet his new King Charles spaniel, which he had named "Carlos" with characteristic humor— after his wife's paramour. Finally, he glanced mischievously at the young woman standing fidgeting before him. He would teach her to rush him.

"You were saying, eh?" he drawled. Before Dorothea could reply, he went on, "Oh, don't bother me about your emperor. He's finished." He drew out of his pocket a journal printed in England. "Here. You can read English." He handed her the paper, which he had received through an informant at the censor's bureau. Talleyrand had the best unofficial news-gathering service in the entire capital. "Read this paragraph."

It was an account of a recent London dinner party given by the prince regent in honor of the duchesse d'Angoulême, the daughter-in-law of Louis XVIII, and described the dining-room draped in the Bourbon colors, sky blue and white—with a centerpiece of white lilies, the Bourbon flower. After studying it, Dorothea looked at *l'oncle* in amazement. He took the article and folded it carefully, adding with the exquisite, sly smile that only he possessed, "Oh! How stupid you are!"

Talleyrand pushed aside the Louis XV gilded bronze screen, twisted and lit the newspaper, threw it into the fireplace, and crossed the shovel and tongs on top to prevent any ash from flying up the chimney. As a statesman, he knew how to destroy a secret secretly. It was very late when he rang for a footman to light Dorothea to her apartment on the ground floor.

Swollen by the surplus baggage wagons necessary to accommodate the needs of a king, an emperor, and a tsar in the field, Allied general headquarters flared out like a vast peacock's tail behind its swift-moving westbound armies. In order that Wilhelmina hear from him regularly now that he was on the move, Metternich suggested that she return to Vienna, where couriers would be riding daily. But a half-promised—and never realized—visit from Alfred before he rejoined his new company detained her in Prague several extra weeks. When Wilhelmina did set forth, worry over Windischgratz's whereabouts coupled with five grueling days of winter traveling conditions wreaked havoc on her nerves.

Wilhelmina arrived before her staff expected her. Setting foot inside the vast Palm palace, she was assailed by the musty, damp odor of unopened, unheated rooms—made even chillier by the loftiness of their gilded ceilings. Instead of the customary gay bouquets clustered in profusion throughout, there was only furniture draped ghostlike in white sheets, pictures covered in dark cloth to protect them from the sun's rays, crystal chandeliers encased in navy blue dust bags.

This lugubrious welcome and the normal disorder attendant upon arrival—the unpacking of the luggage wagons and the rumbling noise as servants dragged upstairs trunk after trunk crammed with clothes and barrels full of fine porcelain, bibelots, and family portraits that accompanied Wilhelmina everywhere—increased her depression. And she came down with one of her famous migraines.

Her head throbbing, she was lying wretched and miserable in

her bedchamber, which Hännchen had hermetically sealed against sound and light, when the chancellor's Christmas package arrived. Clemens had sent a handsome brown leather portfolio with golden locks and hinges prematurely, so it would not be late, and tied to the accompanying tiny key was a note of instructions written on gay holiday stationery, painted over with jolly little angels:

> Each compartment will contain a year of my correspondence. One day I want your heirs to know that you have been loved as you merited. Your image has sustained, in the moments which decided the safety of the world, a man who was called directly to influence Destiny.

No tribute could have pleased Wilhelmina more.

Christmas was family time and an especially gay season in Vienna. The windows were rattling an accompaniment to the city's innumerable church bells, heralding noon, when Wilhelmina's three foster girls, home on holiday from Mme. de Brévillier's "Institute for Aristocratic Ladies," trooped in to greet their "*Chère Maman.*" For their sake, Wilhelmina pulled herself together. As one of the three was to relate fondly, years later, anyone who saw the pretty duchess of Sagan bounce out of bed the next morning in her nightdress, ribbons and blonde locks flying, to do a funny barefoot dance on the carpet, then jump back under the covers and pull them over her head, would have had a hard time recognizing one of the style setters of Viennese society.

The three girls were normally kept in the background and brought up apart, as the Courland princesses had been—but with more affection and a more rounded education. Wilhelmina made an exception during the holidays, and she and her sisters, Paulina and Joanna, sandwiched the customary holiday treats into their own busy schedules. Shrieks of laughter and joyous voices echoed through the spacious quarters, and Wilhelmina abandoned herself to the Christmas spirit for the children's sake. But more than once the two twelve-year-old girls, coming unexpectedly into her boudoir, found the duchess of Sagan sobbing. Another time, Marischel, the eight-year-old, searching for "*Chère Maman*" for a game of blindman's buff, found her staring transfixed at a new portrait hanging on the bedroom wall. "Who is she? Do I know her?" she asked, looking first at the likeness of a girl about her foster sisters' age, then, wonderingly, at Maman, whose eyes glistened with tears. Wilhelmina shook her head and convulsively hugged Marischel.

The pervasive holiday atmosphere and the children's gaiety made the thought of distant, unattainable Vava—Wilhelmina's illegitimate daughter by Baron d'Armfelt—more than Wilhelmina could endure. Gustava was still in distant Finland with the same d'Armfelt cousins who had raised her since birth on Wilhelmina's money. So carefully was Vava's existence hidden that there was never a whisper about her by even the duchess of Sagan's most carping critics. But Wilhelmina wanted her daughter back.

Might Metternich use his intimacy with the tsar to restore Vava to Wilhelmina's aching arms? After all, Finland, where the child was, belonged to Russia. Wilhelmina, who never hesitated to ask favors of the chancellor—for herself and others—had trouble broaching the subject. Wilhelmina sat down at her desk and began, "When you told me, once, that all the events of my life were known to you, I believed I might be able to spare myself the embarrassment of talking about this . . ." And could go no further. She tried another time. "I am well convinced of the zeal with which you will render me a great service . . ." And again stopped. Then one day, crying so hard that tears blotted each word, Wilhelmina confided to Clemens "the secret that means more to me than anything in the world," and beseeched his help.

This was not the most propitious moment for Metternich to request anything of the tsar. The more the Allies' campaign against Napoleon neared a finale, the closer to the surface surged the power struggle between the chancellor and Alexander for control of the war's last stages and results, and the more frequently the two quarreled. One day the pair almost came to blows over the route their armies should take. But, the next morning—the day Clemens received Wilhelmina's letter about Vava—a temperamental Alexander received Metternich, the chancellor reported, "like a mistress after a bad case of the sulks," and embraced him affectionately. "I feel positive this would have given you far more pleasure than it did me," Clemens continued, "but I seized the opportunity to intimate I had a favor to request. I will do everything possible to restore our child to you."

Metternich from that letter on referred to Vava as "our child." He considered both the girl herself and the secret of her existence as two more links tying Wilhelmina to him.

CHAPTER NINE

The Grand Duchess & Talleyrand
1814

JANUARY 16, 1814—THE MORNING AFTER Metternich talked to the tsar about Vava—started in the best possible way for the grand duchess because there on her breakfast tray was a billet from Charles-Maurice. She was in her town house, 24, rue du Faubourg-Poissonnière, on the Right Bank, where she had moved to be nearer Talleyrand's hôtel Saint Florentin. Talleyrand enclosed the written authorization she had requested to visit certain galleries of the Louvre which were closed to the general public and gently chided her, *"Mon Ange,* I don't like to have you thank me for something. In my mind, my heart, and my imagination, we have such a community of interests that you are using of yourself when you use me."

They had expected to spend the day together. Instead, Talleyrand was unexpectedly summoned to the Château. Napoleon created a terrible scene, belaboring Charles-Maurice before the entire cabinet. But His Imperial Majesty had nothing specific for which to reproach Talleyrand, other than the same persistent rumors that he had been plotting against the regime, and after the rest of the ministers left, Napoleon recalled Talleyrand and proposed that he treat with the Allies on the emperor's behalf. Talleyrand, who was convinced Napoleon was doomed, refused.

"He who denies me his services today is necessarily my enemy!" the emperor shouted.

Charles-Maurice thought his hour had struck and that he would surely be sent to the prison at Vincennes, as Napoleon had often threatened. So he took the precaution of going home and burning any incriminating documents and letters before hurrying to Anna's to urge her to do likewise. The storm had momentarily passed, but the pair dared not relax their vigilance, and most of Talleyrand's billets to the grand duchess henceforth ended with the postscript "This is to be burned." Fortunately for history, in most cases they were not.

Three days later, word reached Paris that the enemy had passed the Meuse. And at the end of the month, Napoleon summoned his cabinet, Talleyrand, and the other imperial officers to Fontainebleau, where he invested Marie-Louise with the regency before rejoining the army. It was a mournful ceremony, Talleyrand reported to Anna. The empress was to stay in Paris, and as long as she did, Paris would remain the safest place in France. There was no reason to be nervous yet, but they must be prepared for any contingency. Should Marie-Louise leave, Talleyrand would take the necessary precautions in order that his family, too, could depart at a moment's notice, for he wanted them sheltered from any troop movements that might make the capital difficult to live in. "In times like these," Charles-Maurice concluded, "one loves better than ever his loved ones. I find I can endure anything when I'm with you."

Metternich, who hated war, was surrounded by it on every side, and while the Allied armies were fighting their way to Paris, he and the other diplomats continued peace parlays. "I have not had five minutes which I could dispose of for anything that did not influence the fate of several million men," he reported to Wilhelmina. "I have spent a whole day cutting Europe into bits like a piece of cheese. . . . I've had so many things on my conscience that I'm exhausted." But long after midnight, the chancellor found it relaxing to forget public affairs and think about his return to private life.

> Then I hope to find you truly mine, without remorse, pain or a backward glance. I love you in France as I did when I was in Germany and as I did when I was in Switzerland. *Toi et toujours toi et rien que toi* [thou, always thou, and only thou]—that is my motto.

Because he continued to forward the prince's mail with the Ballhausplatz's special courier, Metternich was aware how seldom

Alfred wrote and considered the clocklike regularity of his own correspondence a potent weapon in his long-distance courtship.

His letters were an even greater source of comfort to Wilhelmina in Vienna than in Prague, for she disliked the situation she now found herself in with the princess von Metternich. She did not wish Clemens's wife to think she was brazenly trying to hide their affair by a pretended intimacy with her, and it was only to please Clemens that she often accompanied her sisters, the princess's long-standing friends, on their visits to the chancellery apartments.

Wilhelmina did not understand how Clemens could simultaneously adore her and care for his wife. However, at Laun, he had explained, "It is the ménage that kills love in a marriage. Another sentiment replaces it, a feeling that becomes especially powerful once there are children, but it is no longer love."

At Clemens's request, she borrowed Gentz's *English Peerage* and chose a new motto for the Metternich coat of arms, which had not yet been revised since he had been created a hereditary prince. Metternich wanted future generations to know that it was selected by the duchess of Sagan, "whom I loved one hundred times more than life itself, in the most glorious moments of my life."

Wilhelmina found the Austrian capital's anti-Metternich bias disturbing. Because its influential inner core disagreed with Clemens's desire to negotiate for peace, Metternich sent Gentz back to arrest this trend, and under the chevalier's editorship, the Vienna *Beobachter* faithfully featured Clemens's repeated diplomatic successes at Allied headquarters. Wilhelmina was proud of his glory. "I don't know if I can explain what I feel," she wrote him.

> It is not easy—but, for example, I can't help a feeling of
> pride when I am out walking at Ratiborzitz and the sun
> unexpectedly spotlights a lovely scene. What is certain is that
> I love your glory because it is yours. . . . My heart would
> not know henceforth how to forget to share your pains,
> pleasures, your success—and all that touches you closely
> or distantly.

Metternich's stock soared and his picture was seen in the best salons. At last Wilhelmina too could display his portrait without undue gossip, and she hastened to Antaria's in the Köhlmarkt to purchase a copy of his latest official likeness. When she hung it over the mantel, her sister Joanna decided there was a leer in the right eye. That was easy to rectify, Clemens riposted, when Wilhelmina relayed Joanna's criticism. "Remind me, the next time I sit, to be painted without any eyes at all."

Clemens was forever searching wherever they stopped for gifts to send her, and Wilhelmina's desk bore mute testimony to the Allied march west. Everything on its burnished mahogany surface —the timepiece encased with a thermometer in a glass block, the delicate bone-and-silver inkwell, the paper cutter and accompanying folded ruler of intricately carved Indian wood—came from Metternich. He wanted Wilhelmina to feel comforted and warmed by his innumerable attentions, as though he were physically present.

But all was not smooth sailing in Wilhelmina's long-distance romance. One evening, the staff officers assigned to the present Allied headquarters at Langres amused themselves with tales of amatory conquests. A Russian officer, his tongue loosened by the excellent native champagne, topped the group with a titillating replay of how the beautiful duchess of Sagan had not only personally nursed him back to health in her Prague hospital, but had slipped into bed with him as part of the cure. To verify his story, the captain passed about a needlepoint wallet that he claimed Wilhelmina had made for him, together with a billet-doux, supposedly hers, which had already made the rounds of the entire Semenovsky Guards.

Clemens had been trying to ignore the scandalous accounts reaching him from his wife and friends, intimating that Wilhelmina was finding solace with various admirers, but this was too much. Devoured with jealousy and wounded pride, the tormented chancellor blasted off a letter—which he sent by special courier—berating Wilhelmina for carelessly leaving herself open to gossip and for the pain she was causing him.

Indignant that Clemens should believe this slander, let alone waste time repeating it, Wilhelmina sent off a sizzling response with neither salutation nor ending. She termed the accusation "disgusting" and demanded to see the original letter. Since it had already been seen by a whole Russian regiment and a portion of the Allied armies as well, it should not be too precious an object to be available as proof. Her blistering reply reached Metternich at the climax of a crisis-ridden week when he needed to husband his strength and energy. Instead, he was so disturbed that after tossing and turning half the night he rose and wrote, demanding pardon. "My life is tied to the history of the world, and to my relationship with you, and our relations, *mon amie*, are more difficult to arrange than those of Europe."

With the emperor away and news scarce in Paris, the Tuileries was the best source of information, so Talleyrand dined nightly with Anna-Dorothea at 5:00 P.M. on the dot before hastening to the Château in his emergency capacity as a member of the regency council. There was the customary facade of official entertainments. The grand duchess appeared at a lavish fête given by the visiting queen of Naples, Napoleon's sister, in white tulle with a thick girdle sprinkled with violets; garlands of the same flower were clipped in her hair by diamond laurel leaves, and around her neck dangled amethysts and precious stones. Dorothea also attended, making her first public appearance since the birth of her second son. None of the several thousand guests present that evening in the Château's theater, which had been turned into a ballroom for the event, seemed aware that three enemy armies—Russian, Prussian, and Austrian—were marching on the city, alternating fighting with attempted peace negotiations.

Like most of Paris, Anna and Talleyrand led as normal lives as possible. Charles-Maurice was inordinately fond of children, and Anna often met him at the rue Grange-Batelière, where he stopped regularly to check on the newest Talleyrand addition, Alexander-Edmond, named after his godfather, the tsar. Dorothea's older boy, Napoleon-Louis, almost three, was the French emperor's godchild. There was no longer fresh milk for little Dorothea, not quite two, and her brothers, and no more cream for the adults because the army had impounded *l'oncle*'s cows at Saint Brice. When Anna and Dorothea complained, Talleyrand warned that conditions would get worse before they got better. The military had also requisitioned the grand duchess's horses, leaving her with only one. Fortunately Talleyrand, as vice-grand-elector, was permitted to keep a pair, for it was impossible for him to walk any distance.

When rumors reached the capital that the emperor had suffered a severe setback at Troyes, the arch-chancellor canceled his Tuesday reception for the first time since coming to power fifteen years before. But Talleyrand still felt there was no hurry about leaving

Paris. An expert navigator, the crafty statesman was not yet sure what the wave of the future might wash ashore, and he was cautiously keeping his options open, awaiting the course of events. As one member of his seraglio commented cryptically, "Whatever course Charles-Maurice chooses to follow, nothing he does would surprise me—except an error of taste."

Finally, Talleyrand needed room to maneuver without worrying about his family's safety. Four days after his intimate friend Caulaincourt, the Grand Master of the Horse, undertook negotiations with the Allies at Châtillon—the role Talleyrand had refused—Charles-Maurice sent Anna a charming miniature of the Virgin with instructions "to place it above your bed to protect you from danger wherever you are. I love you with all my soul—in harsh times as well as in gentler ones." The following morning he handed her into her carriage, and she was off for Rosny, Edmond's rosy brick château overlooking the Seine northwest of Paris, to join Dorothea, who had already left with her youngsters and a battery of nurses and maids. Charles-Maurice's wife, Catherine de Talleyrand, and several elderly family friends soon followed, carrying a trunk full of Talleyrand's clothes. Should Charles-Maurice be caught short and have to leave the capital in a hurry, he could travel light.

Anna and Dorothea did not find living together again under the same roof as difficult as in the past. A fragile equilibrium, fabricated from their reciprocal feelings and admiration for Talleyrand, bridged the gulf existing since childhood between mother and daughter. Anna had been pleased at the friendship flowering between *l'oncle* and his niece during her recent long absence at Löbikau. Had not dear Charles-Maurice written her, "When one does not have what one loves, one knows how to love what one has." There was no reason for jealousy. Dorothea was, in the grand duchess's eyes, still an immature adolescent—her baby.

Blücher, the Prussian general, was within twenty-four hours of Paris when the emperor, outnumbered almost five to one, wheeled unexpectedly and defeated several Allied detachments. Napoleon was drunk with hope, and when one of his aides tried to moderate his elation, the emperor replied in his barracks-room argot, "The lion isn't dead yet. It's too early to piss on him." A shrewd gambler, His Imperial Majesty promptly raised the ante for Caulaincourt's peace mission at Châtillon. But this was only a momentary ray of sunshine in an imperial picture painted in the most somber of tones. And the wildest rumors were the order of the day.

Talleyrand urged Anna to believe only what he himself wrote and promised to let her know in ample time should danger threaten. She lived for his daily letters, which remained calm, with a rare, anguished cry over the humiliation of seeing France at the mercy of invaders: "One would have to be without an ounce of French blood not to suffer horribly from all the evils and all the humiliation our unhappy country is experiencing." Some came by the regular twice-weekly post. Others, which Charles-Maurice deemed more important, were entrusted to a confidential secretary who commuted on horseback between the two residences.

Rather than risk committing to paper the story of the police minister's latest unannounced visit, Talleyrand instructed his courier to relate in person what had happened. The grand duchess gasped when she learned how that official had appeared at the hôtel Saint Florentin long after midnight, eluded footmen and servants, and crept upstairs unannounced in an unsuccessful effort to catch Talleyrand conspiring. That was all the grand duchess needed to hear. What was she doing secluded in the dreary countryside with a houseful of women and children when dear Charles-Maurice was in danger in Paris? When the center of action was in the capital? Invasion or not, she was returning at once.

Talleyrand was overjoyed to see Anna and touched that she wanted to share these perilous times at his side. "Ah, *ma Chère*," his billets would henceforth echo, "I can bear everything when I am near you. . . . In times of anxiety, one needs to be near those one loves and you . . . are the first and tenderest interest of my love."

The lack of accurate news was so baffling that Talleyrand, who remained the best-informed man in Paris, had arranged a private code with the Grand Master of the Horse in order to keep abreast of the negotiations the latter was conducting at Châtillon. The emperor had no more devoted friend than this official, his former ambassador to Russia, who was willing to keep Charles-Maurice secretly posted because the diplomat hoped that Talleyrand could help force Napoleon to accept peace.

It was equally crucial to know the disposition of the Allied leaders if they won. Would they leave the country free to choose its own form of government? With whom would they treat? Talleyrand had lately received a smuggled excerpt from the *London*

Times that reported that the comte d'Artois—Louis VIII's brother—had left London and was somewhere on the Continent. Was there any chance of a Bourbon restoration? Or did Metternich prefer a regency for Napoleon's son, l'Aiglon? After all, since Franz I was l'Aiglon's grandfather, that would place the Austrian emperor's chancellor in a dominant position. Talleyrand was personally opposed to this solution because he knew Napoleon would always be behind the door, listening and awaiting another chance.

What did the tsar want? Before Christmas, Alexander favored putting Prince Bernadotte of Sweden, one of Napoleon's former marshals, on the French throne. But now? Even Anna did not know. And the last letters that had succeeded in reaching her from the east mentioned that Alexander had taken to reading the Bible daily and was increasingly leaving cabinet meetings to consult it for guidance.

Talleyrand felt it was extremely dangerous to be at the mercy of conflicting rumors. A whist crony, the minister of Baden, had found a way to get the answers Charles-Maurice was seeking, and the two men met at the hôtel Saint Florentin the evening following Anna's return to discuss particulars. Anna watched the nervous tics crisscrossing the birdlike face of the wiry diplomat—a grand seigneur whose family tree was traced to a cousin of the Holy Virgin—as he outlined his plan. Heads would roll should his scheme miscarry. It was one thing to talk treason, another to enter into active communication with the emperor's enemies. Nonetheless, a mutual acquaintance, Baron Vitrolles, a confirmed Royalist whom Anna also knew, was willing to undertake the perilous mission of penetrating the enemy lines to arrive at Allied headquarters. The Baden minister intended to supply Baron Vitrolles with the names of two Viennese sisters whose favors—the minister coughed and glanced discreetly in the grand duchess's direction—he had once shared with Metternich's predecessor at the Ballhausplatz. The women's names were to be written on a piece of paper small enough to insert in the Royalist's watchcase, in invisible ink that would appear only when the scrap was held over a candle. The minister would also furnish the emissary with the carnelian seal engraved with his family coat of arms that was presently dangling from his watch chain. These two items would clearly identify the Royalist to the former Austrian foreign minister as having come from the Baden diplomat.

While Charles-Maurice silently weighed this information, slowly tapping the brace on his bad right leg with his cane, Anna replenished the visitor's *kümmel*. The conversation resumed.

How did the Baden minister plan to accredit the baron with the Russians, Charles-Maurice wanted to know. The diplomat shrugged. He had not thought that far yet, but this should not pose a problem since the Russian foreign minister was his cousin— as well as a friend of Talleyrand. Was the foreign minister familiar with his cousin's handwriting, Charles-Maurice demanded. The diplomat nodded. So Talleyrand suggested the latter send him a note.

Anna rang for paper. A footman materialized, drew up a small rosewood table, removed several jeweled gold snuff boxes and a miniature Dürer drawing on an easel, replaced them with writing necessities, and discreetly withdrew. Half leaning against the mantelpiece, as he often did to keep the weight off his bad right foot, Charles-Maurice dictated while the diplomat wrote, on a small square of notched stationery bordered in gray, the famous equivocal message that the Russian foreign minister would declare, years later, decided the Allied march on Paris: ". . . You are walking on crutches when you could make use of your legs to greater advantage." He was signaling to the Allies that the road to Paris was free; the capital was defenseless; they would be welcome.

Dear Charles-Maurice. As Anna sat there listening, was she reminded of the monkey in the fable who would not risk singeing his paw to get the chestnut, but let the cat do it for him? On the face of it, only the Baden minister accredited Baron Vitrolles to the Austrian and Russian officials. There was nothing to implicate Talleyrand, who was too cautious even to see the baron.

A single problem remained. What if the Baden minister should encounter difficulty at the outset and be unable to convince the intended emissary of Talleyrand's support?

"Let me know." Anna spoke for the first time. "I will talk to the Baron"—and protect Charles-Maurice from incrimination. "I have known him ever since he lived in an émigré colony near Löbikau during the Revolution."

The Baden minister bowed and took his leave. Somewhere a distant clock struck three.

Napoleon's world was crashing. Daily, Talleyrand visited the minister of police, the prefect of police of Paris, the postmaster general in the main post office, and often the foreign ministry, taking advantage of his privileges as vice-grand-elector to see the government reports—and also gather unofficial nuggets of information. In mid-March, the English entered Bordeaux and that city declared for Louis XVIII. Two days later, Charles-Maurice informed Anna that the peace negotiations at Châtillon had finally fallen through. Events were outracing one another.

Dorothea's next tour of duty as imperial lady-in-waiting was due to start shortly. But Talleyrand was so concerned about her safety that he forbade her to leave Rosny and started spreading rumors of her illness in order to manufacture an acceptable alibi for her impending absence from court.

A week later, on Saturday, March 26, the menace of invasion hung in the Paris air. Friends who came to the small salon attached to Talleyrand's loge at the Comédie Française to enjoy an ice during the entr'acte of Beaumarchais's *Barber of Seville* had been delayed by the throngs of peasants driving their livestock before them into the comparative safety of the city's suburbs.

Talleyrand deemed it essential that the empress leave the capital before the Allies entered. If she did not, he was convinced that the tsar, who fancied himself a knight-errant, would rush to lay his sword at Marie-Louise's feet and gallantly pronounce her regent. So en route back from the theater, he stopped at the home of a member of his seraglio to deliver a letter he had purportedly received from her brother, who was in the Royalist unit fighting alongside the Allies. It was very bitter—"We're coming, determined to purge France of the assassins of the Royal Family. . . .", that sort of thing. And Talleyrand told his friend that she could render an invaluable service to the Royalist cause if she would read it to the minister of police. Talleyrand knew his world. He counted on the content's vindictive tone to frighten the police official, who would frighten the empress, who would in turn frighten Joseph Bonaparte, Napoleon's brother, now king of Spain and the emperor's spokesman in the regency cabinet.

Then Anna and Charles-Maurice continued on their way. Snow was gently falling but it was mild out, and the runner preceding them through the narrow rue du Faubourg-Poissonnière exuberantly tapped a tattoo on the corners of the houses as he passed, with the tip of his torch. The carriage rolled to a halt in front of the grand duchess's hôtel. Talleyrand stepped out slowly and turned to hand her out. Anna looked down at Charles-Maurice's face, illuminated by the flickering flambeaux held by the footmen. Like a city under siege, all life was hidden behind those hooded, impenetrable eyes, and Anna's question, "Who wrote that letter?" was stillborn. She recalled their conversation the previous evening. "What opinion do you think posterity will have of me, eh?" Charles-Maurice had queried, reflectively twirling his gold-and-ivory lorgnon. Before Anna could reply, he went on, "People always talk too ill or too well of me. I enjoy the honors of exaggeration. So be it. I want people, for centuries to come, to discuss what I have been, what I have thought, and what I wanted."

Sunday, marshals Mortier and Marmont were fighting desperately against the Allies, close at hand, but that evening the theaters were packed. Talleyrand found the court in excellent spirits. Marie-Louise gave the order to cut the envelope holding the playing cards, and he played whist with Her Imepiral Majesty.

The next day, Monday, the twenty-eighth, an emergency meeting was called at the Château to decide whether the empress should leave the threatened capital. It was past midnight before the session broke up, and Talleyrand stopped by to brief Anna. King Joseph had opened the session with a letter from Napoleon. Declaring that there was no more miserable fate in history than that of Astyanax, taken prisoner by the Greeks, the emperor preferred his son at the bottom of the Seine rather than in the hands of France's enemies. When the opinion of each member present was polled on what course of action to follow, Talleyrand stated unequivocally that the empress should remain. Anna was confused. She thought Charles-Maurice wanted Marie-Louise to go. So he did. But the wily statesman, who was forever proclaiming, "Speech is given man to disguise his thoughts," knew that Joseph mistrusted him. Had Talleyrand advised the empress's departure, she undoubtedly would have remained. Instead, she was leaving.

Early on Tuesday, Anna received word that Talleyrand must be present at the imperial departure. The snow had turned into a dreary downpour by the time he sent a second message. Marie-Louise and l'Aiglon had left. A third advised that it was wisest for

Dorothea to remain at Rosny, and reminded the Grand Duchess she was expected for dinner.

The boulevards were so crowded with fugitives thronging into Paris that Anna had a hard time getting to the hôtel Saint Florentin on time. There was the usual large number of guests at the table. Even before dinner was over, the great salon upstairs was filled with anxious visitors. They had learned of the empress's departure and wanted to chart a personal course of action. When was Talleyrand leaving to follow her to Blois? Should they depart too? Would the Russians sack Paris the way the French had Moscow?

On Wednesday morning, the news ran the streets that marshals Mortier and Marmont were staving off a Prussian-Russian attack with their backs to the walls of the city. The growling of the distant cannon was clearly audible as Anna drank her café au lait, yet she could not find a word about the fighting in the *Moniteur*. The most prominent story on its front page was the queen of England's cold. She thumbed through the official journal again, then tossed it aside in disgust.

Callers, who arrived while she was still dressing, told of spectators filling the chairs that lined the main boulevards to watch the columns of men march forth to join the embattled army. Some of the grand duchess's circle who did not plan to flee had already hired masons and carpenters to build special hiding places for their valuables; others were having diamonds sewed into clothes linings.

Late in the afternoon, Talleyrand appeared. A truce had been declared within the hour. The city was surrounded and the Allies had moved in from the suburbs and were already at the gates of Clichy and the Trône. If the capital was to be saved the horrors of an assault, the moment had come to negotiate, so he was remaining in Paris. Charles-Maurice's mind was made up. He was casting his weight on the side of Louis XVIII, although he did not know whether the Bourbons considered him friend or foe.

Anna was appalled. It was treason for any Grand Dignitary of the Empire not to follow Marie-Louise, and Napoleon was like a rubber ball. The Emperor had bounced back more than once in the present campaign, and he might do so again. But Talleyrand had devised an ingenious—and he hoped foolproof—scheme to stay behind and yet be absolved of blame for so doing.

As Anna anticipated, a woman was cast in the farce's leading role. Promptly at 6:00 P.M., Charles-Maurice and his accomplice set off to call on the latter's cousin, the prefect of police. When the pair arrived at the prefecture on the Quai des Orfèvres, Talleyrand's pretty companion did all the talking. "Monsieur de Talleyrand is divided between two duties. On the one hand, he is obligated to rejoin the empress and the rest of the Regency Council. On the other, if he leaves Paris, who will remain behind to deal with the invaders and act as a go-between?" The young Royalist fluttered her hands, the picture of hopeless despair. "All the important officials must not leave. Who else in Paris knows the foreign rulers, their generals and ambassadors? Who else can carry any weight with them?"

"True, true," the gruff prefect conceded. "But I fail to see how I can help." He looked questioningly at Talleyrand. That gentleman, for the one and only recorded time in his long life, stammered, stuttered, and appeared to be so upset that he was at a loss for words. The police prefect's fingers drummed impatiently on his desk. There were more important matters awaiting his attention.

His cousin replied, "Monsieur de Talleyrand has come to ask for advice. I suggested that he pretend to leave and that you might issue orders to turn him back at the city's gates."

The prefect demurred. He wanted no part of this dangerous game, but to be polite, he pointed out that his concurrence was not necessary. "The various gates of Paris are being patrolled by the national guard. Your husband is in charge of one of their divisions. You need only determine where he is stationed and alert him."

She did as suggested. And Talleyrand, preceded by his secretary, departed with much fanfare—only to return home with a great show of indignation a few hours later. Imagine! he hastened to write the empress. He had been refused permission to leave!

So far, so good, a brief billet advised Talleyrand's *Cher Ange*. Now, how was he going to let the tsar know he was still in Paris— without being caught in the act of communicating with the enemy?

Around midnight, Talleyrand went to the hôtel Pérégeux, Marshal Marmont's home on the rue Paradis, ostensibly to inquire whether his chances of rejoining the empress at Blois had improved. As Charles-Maurice had anticipated, the tsar's two commissioners were there to sign the French capitulation. They were astonished to find Talleyrand still in the capital. Charles-Maurice feigned similar surprise and begged them to lay his profound respects at the feet of the Tsar of All the Russias.

When Alexander received Talleyrand's message, he understood it because Baron Vitrolles had successfully gotten through earlier. The next morning, Thursday, the thirty-first, he sent his foreign minister, Count Nesselrode, to Talleyrand's levée, which was held at the unheard-of hour of 6:30 A.M., with word that the tsar would see the French statesman after the Allied parade.

The grand duchess was on a balcony at the hôtel Saint Florentin early that afternoon to watch the foreign troops in red, white, blue, and green uniforms, with plumes and tassels waving and military bands blaring, clatter over the cobblestones of the still unfinished rue de Rivoli to the Place de la Concorde. The weather cleared, and the rain-and-snow-washed square sparkled in the rays of the spring sun. Parisians were out in their finest to see the first conquerors to invade Paris in centuries, and greeted the handsome, beaming Tsar Alexander and King Friedrich-Wilhelm III as they rode into view, flanked by towering Cossacks—Emperor Franz I and Metternich were still boxed in by troop movements somewhere near Dijon—with enthusiastic huzzahs. Alexander's green hat sported a magnificent cascade of cock feathers, his white uniform was trimmed in massive gold braid, and his feet rested in stirrups of wrought gold. The grand duchess recognized his gray mare as the one Napoleon had given him in happier days at the Erfurt Conference.

When the review was over, the tsar strode across the great square toward the hôtel Saint Florentin in the corner. Several hours earlier, his foreign minister had reported an anonymous warning that the Elysée palace, where His Imperial Majesty intended to lodge, was mined. So Alexander had accepted Talleyrand's timely offer to stay in the hôtel Saint Florentin instead. Not all historians agree that Talleyrand was responsible for this nefarious rumor, but the tsar had the dominant Allied voice, and with Alexander under his own roof, Charles-Maurice was in a position to screen visitors and prevent any undesirable, inopportune ones. The new kingmaker believed in leaving nothing to chance. He was also counting on the grand duchess to convince Alexander that any decisions Charles-Maurice made were the correct ones.

The tsar greeted his host cordially. "You have my confidence and that of my Allies. We do not want to settle anything until we have heard from you. You know France, its needs, and its desires."

Anna took special pains with her toilette that evening. Her maids had removed the cane cover from the Louis XV canapé-shaped tub and filled it with warm water. The grand duchess was soaking in it, her face covered with a mask of Josephine's special almond-pâté-and-cucumber salve (which the former empress recommended for tired skin and had given her the last time Anna visited Malmaison), when a loud commotion in the inner court broke her revery. A maid whom she sent down to inquire the cause came back with stars in her eyes. A whole troop of Cossacks were there—in their wide pantaloons and tall bonnets, with long whips hung round their necks and horses as small as ponies. They had been sent as an honor guard by the tsar to assure that the grand duchess was not molested, their captain announced importantly, and they were to stay as long as Alexander was in Paris.

Anna smiled. How thoughtful of Alexander. Of course, she was a Russian subject. All boded well for her immediate usefulness to dear Charles-Maurice.

Word had leaked out that the Allied sovereigns planned to attend that night's performance at the Academy of Music, and Paris's Opéra on the rue Louvois was a sea of Bourbon blue and white. Every Royalist who could beg, borrow, or steal a ticket appeared. The hall was fragrant with lilies, the Bourbon flower—in the women's hair, in their bonnets, in garlands around their necks—while the men sported white cockades, resurrected from some hidden cache, in their hats. Anna arrived early for once and was seated with her friend, Marie-Thérèse, the princess Tyskiewicz, in Talleyrand's permanent loge, which faced the imperial one, before the tsar and King Friedrich-Wilhelm III appeared after the second curtain. Charles-Maurice sat directly behind the two sovereigns but could have seen little of the performance. Every time Anna looked that way, the tsar was whispering in his ear; then Talleyrand would dispatch another of the numerous aides who were standing rigidly at attention in the back of the box and were continuously being replaced as fast as they disappeared, like figures in a shooting gallery at a country fair.

The program was not the announced one. Talleyrand had ordered a substitute, for it would never do to present Persuis and

Lesueur's *The Triumph of Trajan,* which contained the famous march composed in honor of Napoleon's resounding Prussian victories. As the audience was filing out at the end, several enthusiastic young Royalists shinnied up the columns on one side of the stage and sent the massive Napoleonic insignias on top of the velvet curtains crashing down with a reverberating thud.

By the time Anna and the Princess Tyskiewicz reached the rue Saint Florentin, Talleyrand's mansion was ablaze from cellar to garret with twinkling candles; its ground-floor antechambers held a multilingual swarm. The magnificent ceremonial staircase with its delicately spiraled wrought-iron balustrade and landings filled with sculpture and paintings was so crowded that Anna was almost pushed into one of the giant Russian imperial guards who were posted, two to a riser, now that the tsar was in residence. Talleyrand was already closeted with the Prussian king and Alexander, and every nook and cranny, every window bay of the pale-gray-and-crystal Salon de l'Aigle—with its life-size gold-leaf eagles supporting golden medallions in each corner of the ceiling—was filled with gesticulating, arguing dignitaries, both Allied and French.

The next morning, Friday, April 1, Anna was having her face cleansed—a maid was patting it with a little bag fragrant with chamomile, elderberry, and linden blooms, which she dipped from time to time in a bowl of hot milk—when an unexpected early caller arrived, the tsar's homely, bald brother, the Grand Duke Constantine. Anna had not received her usual billet from Charles-Maurice, and she was interested to learn about the proclamation, prepared largely by Talleyrand in advance, that the official poster hangers had plastered on Paris walls as the first light streaked the sky. The Allies refused to treat with Napoleon or any member of his family, but they were determined not to take advantage of their victory, her visitor explained, so they were leaving the French free to select a temporary body to administer the country and prepare a new constitution. Talleyrand, who as vice-grand-elector had the requisite authority to convoke the Senate, had already called an afternoon meeting for this specific purpose.

And only summoned those senators he was sure of, Anna was willing to wager. Continuing the conversation, she disappeared behind a shoulder-high screen where she was helped into one of the elaborately simple costumes that were in vogue for morning calls. She soon reemerged, buttoning the sleeves of a becoming gray wool outfit trimmed in black passementerie while a patient maid tagged behind, trying not to step on the small train while fastening the last hooks and eyes. One girl sprayed her with essence of lily of the valley while another woman arranged the veil of a close-fitting toque around her coiffure. Anna's guest departed, and she went to the hôtel Saint Florentin to pay her respects to his brother, Alexander.

That afternoon, a rump session of the Senate—63 of the 141 members—met in the Luxembourg palace with Talleyrand presiding. The only dignitary of the empire present, Talleyrand maneuvered to be chosen as head of a provisional government of five. He then dictated the choice of the other four, including his friend the Baden minister, and immediately installed them in three of the six rooms on the hôtel Saint Florentin mezzanine that he had reserved for himself when he gave Alexander the top floor. Within twenty-four hours Charles-Maurice had transformed himself into the most powerful man in France and made his home the nerve center of Europe.

Patriotic qualms prevented some lawmakers from appearing when the tsar received the Senate in the hôtel Saint Florentin's Salon de l'Aigle before the dinner Talleyrand tendered in their honor. If Charles-Maurice retaliated by substituting actors, as gossip had it, they looked sufficiently like the genuine articles, attired in the official senatorial costume of yellow-silk-lined, gold-embroidered jacket and coat and white trousers, to fool His Imperial Majesty.

Anna had an extended chat with Alexander that evening, and Princess Marie-Thérèse Tyskiewicz, who witnessed their prolonged tête-à-tête in an alcove of the overflowing salon, whispered, "All Paris is convinced that you prearranged your Tsar's stay here at the hôtel Saint Florentin." Anna did not gainsay her.

On Saturday morning King Friedrich-Wilhelm III came to pay his respects to the grand duchess, and at noon Anna received her first note from Charles-Maurice since the Allies reached Paris. He wanted Dorothea to return from Rosny. She must come by way of Aubergenville, and a detachment of Cossacks would await her at the relay post of Saint Germain that midnight to escort her through the various roadblocks and into the city. Dorothea would be an additional adornment to the hôtel Saint Florentin, and Talleyrand did not want to overlook any detail that might keep the tsar happy. The continued goodwill of temperamental, volatile Alexander was not easy to guarantee, but crucial at this critical juncture.

Talleyrand had declared, "The return of the Bourbons is a principle; anything else is an intrigue." He felt that Louis XVIII, the legitimate ruler, possessed the moral authority necessary to impose a peace treaty on the defeated country and give it the stability and position that was its due.

But Talleyrand had not yet convinced the tsar that Louis XVIII should succeed to the throne—and Napoleon was not yet reconciled to abdication. The Senate might have docilely deposed the Bonapartes, but Napoleon had not abandoned hope of fighting on and remained at Fontainebleau with 60,000 loyal troops who must somehow be separated from him.

On Sunday, the third, Charles-Maurice was back on schedule with a billet on Anna's breakfast tray. Would his *Chère Amie* please advise him as soon as Dorothea arrived safely? He expected them both for dinner.

On Monday, Talleyrand's tiny, crabbed handwriting raced triumphantly off the amber-scented blue sheet. "Marshal Marmont has just capitulated. It is the result of our proclamations and papers. He no longer wishes to serve Bonaparte against the fatherland." This meant that the army had deserted the emperor. And after an all-night argument, Charles-Maurice had persuaded the tsar that a regency in favor of l'Aiglon was not viable.

Anna must have drawn a sigh of relief. Charles-Maurice had won, and the time was at hand to send for Louis XVIII's deputy, his brother, the comte d'Artois.

A disgruntled imperialist inveigled indignantly against Marmont that evening in the Salon de l'Aigle. "The Marshal is a disgrace to the flag. The effects of what one has the impertinence to call the initiative of defeat—"

"*Mon Dieu!*" Talleyrand suavely interrupted. "That only proves one thing—Marmont's watch was fast. It was set ahead of everyone else's."

Overhearing him, Anna was greatly relieved. The strain was easing. Dear Charles-Maurice was his witty self once more. And she, too, had good news for him when they managed a brief aside. For the tsar looked with favor upon a marriage uniting the houses of Romanoff and Bourbon, to cement a solid future between the two countries—a matter she had discussed with Alexander at Talleyrand's request.

Within forty-eight hours, Napoleon signed an unconditional surrender. The Senate quickly passed a new constitution calling Louis XVIII to the throne, and on Friday, the eighth, Talleyrand wrote Anna, "I'm looking forward to the moment when, if you will permit me, I can once more pass my time with you whom I love with all my heart."

This year the Greek Orthodox and the Roman Catholic Easter coincided, and the grand duchess and Dorothea had a ringside view from the hôtel Saint Florentin of the service that was performed in the Place de la Concorde at an altar that had been especially constructed there at the tsar's request. The day was cool, with the brilliance of a polished diamond, and a few cotton-ball clouds hovered lazily overhead. Anna was not religious herself, but as she looked at the great square packed with people of every faith kneeling there celebrating the end of bloodshed, she could not have helped feeling an immense surge of pride in Charles-Maurice's role in terminating the carnage—and she knew she had been helpful to him with the tsar. Anna believed in and trusted Talleyrand blindly. Whether he was motivated by a desire to serve France and the cause of Continental peace or—as many historians still think— by personal reasons, including revenge for Napoleon's abuse, she never bothered to analyze.

The transportation bottleneck around Dijon had been broken at last, and upon their arrival in Paris this same morning, Metternich, the Prussian chancellor, and the British foreign secretary hastened to the hôtel Saint Florentin to work out the final details of the abdication treaty. Metternich found that his absence had handed Alexander what Metternich had until then successfully denied him: effective control of the Allied leadership.

With Alexander's Lenten fast at an end, the three sovereigns and assorted dignitaries were guests at what Talleyrand euphemistically called "a family dinner." Since Catherine de Talleyrand was not among them, Charles-Maurice had requested his brother, Archambaud, to be present so that the latter's daughter-in-law, Dorothea, might do the honors, and she did, sitting slender and poised facing *l'oncle* across the fabulous vermeil service.

Anna was next to her old Berlin friend Metternich at the table and agreed to select hats for him to send his wife and oldest daughter. She was well aware of his affair with Wilhelmina and happy to receive firsthand news of her oldest daughter, as well as word of Joanna and Paulina. The pair discussed at length Napoleon's proposed place of exile.

"M. de Talleyrand agrees with me that Elba is too near the Continent he has troubled so grievously. Someone suggested America, I understand, but . . ." The chancellor raised his hand with an expression of resignation and glanced significantly at Alexander, who was adamantly opposed to this.

"America?" Someone overheard the grand duchess reply. "Wouldn't James and Dolley Madison have a fit!" Anna gave the tinkling laugh Metternich remembered so well. Then she fell silent. Listening to the wind instruments tucked in a corner playing a melody from Gluck's *Iphigenia*, she recalled Talleyrand's instructions to his resident music director. "Nothing serious should be heard tonight, mind you. I suggest something soothing that will not require concentration or take my guests' minds from the conversation."

It would never do for Louis XVIII's brother to return after almost twenty-five years in exile and find France's provisional government housed on the floor underneath a foreign ruler, let alone in the home of a married priest, the former bishop of Autun, who had been so long associated with the Revolution. Therefore, the tsar moved over to the Elysée palace, accompanied by Talleyrand's celebrated new chef: On the theory that the way to Alexander's heart lay, in part, through his stomach, Charles-Maurice was loaning him Maître Câreme.

As president of the provisional government, Talleyrand welcomed the comte d'Artois at the capital's gates at Bondy, and Anna and Dorothea attended the subsequent Te Deum at Notre Dame that same Tuesday night. While "Monsieur"—as the king's brother was known—slumbered peacefully in Marie-Louise's former Tuileries suite, Napoleon attempted suicide at Fontainebleau. But the prussic acid salts he swallowed had lost their strength after having hung in a little bag around his neck for the past six years, and he was soon en route to Elba. Napoleon traveled alone, without Marie-Louise or l'Aiglon, for the Austrian emperor forbade his daughter to follow her husband.

Talleyrand sent Anna the news. *"Mon Ange,"* he continued:

You scolded me a little yesterday. I didn't merit it, but your scolding gave me pleasure. I like to see the person I love have spirit. . . . You must let me berate you occasionally, to work off the small irritations I endure during the day.

This note disturbed Anna. The returning Royalists lived on their resentments. They had learned nothing and forgotten nothing and were endlessly complicating Talleyrand's herculean task. Anna worried about dear Charles-Maurice. She had noticed of late how drawn his pale face was from lack of sleep. He must take better care of himself—or else let her take care of him. The tenderness and affection with which he surrounded her was in stark contrast to the tempestuous, emotional nature of her earlier affairs with Batowski and d'Armfelt. It was also eminently more suited to— and more satisfying in—these autumnal years of her life. The grand duchess was fifty-three.

Anna did not see how Charles-Maurice managed to do everything his official job entailed and still not neglect her or his responsibilities as the head of the house of Talleyrand. He found time to sign the agreement for the marriage of his adopted daughter, Charlotte, who was now sixteen, to his nephew the baron de Talleyrand—thereby legally assuring her of the name that was probably her birthright and keeping her substantial dowry in the family— and gave a family dinner in her honor. The minute Louis XVIII crossed the Channel and landed in France, before the king had time to name the royal households, Charles-Maurice requested that Edmond be selected as one of His Majesty's aides-de-camp and Dorothea as a lady-in-waiting to Madame, the First Lady of the Bourbon Court. (Since the king was a childless widower, his official hostess was the wife of his nephew, the duc d'Angoulême.) By return courier, Edmond was elevated instead to brigadier general, but no mention was made then—or ever—of Dorothea, "ma petite Italienne," as the monarch used to call her when he dandled her on his knee at Mitau years before. Probably the post was refused because Louis XVIII did not want a former imperial lady-in-waiting serving at the Bourbon court.

Talleyrand was not sure what reception to expect when he went to Compiègne to greet the returning sovereign, whose recurrent bouts of gout were slowing his journey. So before going, he secretly removed—and burned—any compromising correspondence between himself and Napoleon that could be found in the archives of the former imperial cabinet in the Louvre.

Louis XVIII was friendly. Adroitly, His Majesty shuffled out of sight the Revolution and everything that had happened since and flattered Talleyrand at his most susceptible point—the ancient nobility of the Périgords. However, Anna felt it was a better indication of the monarch's true feelings—and a bad omen for any future working relationship between the two men—that Louis XVIII did not receive Talleyrand at once, but made him wait a full three hours before granting him an audience.

On May 3, the day of the king's formal entry into Paris, Anna was awakened early by the sound of drums summoning the national guard to arms. Security was so heavy that flowerpots on windowsills and carriages other than those in the official cortege were forbidden along the royal route, which was beautifully decorated with white standards ornamented with blue tassels covered with fleurs-de-lis. The minute the king set foot inside his capital, the intrepid Mme. Blanchard, a famed aeronaut, ascended in her balloon—which got caught for one breathtaking moment on a statue of Henri IV, then freed itself—and released a flock of doves to wing their way across the skies as symbols of the longed-for peace.

The following afternoon, Anna and the Princess Tyskiewicz witnessed the parade of the Allied forces along the quais led by the tsar's brother. Out of deference to their ailing guest of honor, the sovereigns themselves did not march with their troops but appeared at an open window of the Louvre. The unwieldy Bourbon bulk was stuffed into a sturdy armchair in front of the Austrian emperor and the sad-faced Prussian king while the tsar, standing conspicuously in the foreground, did the honors. But Wellington stole the show. After winding up a most successful Peninsular campaign, he surprised the high command by arriving in time to ride with the British contingent, and the sovereigns craned their necks every bit as much as Anna did for a first glimpse of this fresh Allied hero.

In the evening, society shuttled between Charles-Maurice's, Anna's, and the British embassy. At the hôtel Saint Florentin, Catherine de Talleyrand, more voluminous and less voluble than ever, now lorded it over the Salon de l'Aigle, seated with her feet resting on a gigantic cushion on which she had embroidered the arms of the comtes de Périgord to remind those present that she was Charles-Maurice's wife, regardless of what position the grand duchess of Courland—or her daughter—might assume. There was a cosmopolitan scene at Anna's, while Wellington stole the show at the small ball hosted by the English ambassador for *tout Paris,* dance division. The grand duchess felt duty bound to meet the new star at once and managed an appearance in the wee hours; even then, guests were still queued up to shake Milord's hand and congratulate him on his elevation several hours earlier to dukedom.

In the midst of this frenzied activity, little Dorothea-Charlotte came down with a severe case of measles. Busy as *l'oncle* was, he made it a point—with Edmond on duty out of town more often than in—to stop by the rue Grange-Batelière daily to see how his goddaughter was progressing. Anna thought Charles-Maurice was taxing himself needlessly, adding one more item to his already surcharged schedule, for the two-year-old had passed the crisis and was receiving the best possible care.

But within the week, the small patient had an unexpected relapse and took a turn for the worse. *L'oncle* was shocked and sent his personal physician to keep a round-the-clock vigil and report to him. That good man so alarmed Charles-Maurice that he awakened Anna the following morning with an earlier billet than usual, in which *l'oncle* seemed as worried about his niece as he was about his godchild. Anna must keep Dorothea at the rue du Faubourg-Poissonnière and not let her go home. The doctor warned that Dorothea, who had still not regained her strength after a difficult pregnancy and accouchement, was not strong enough to withstand the shock of seeing her daughter so ill. "If Dorothea could accomplish anything by being at her bedside," Talleyrand concluded, "I wouldn't say a word."

That same evening the sick child died. And Dorothea retreated into a shell, inconsolable.

CHAPTER TEN

Wilhelmina & Metternich
Spring-Summer 1814

WILHELMINA WAS HAVING A HARD TIME living with herself because she did not wish to mislead Clemens. He could not bear the thought of sharing her with anyone and wanted her exclusively, and Wilhelmina was still not completely convinced she wanted to terminate her relationship with Prince Windischgratz. As for her "four English Nelsons," as she jokingly referred to the young bloods from the British embassy whom Vienna enjoyed gossiping about, Wilhelmina was not serious about any of them. But she did wish the chancellor would love her as a flesh-and-blood woman with assorted weaknesses instead of putting her on a pedestal like some goddess in a shrine.

Their long-distance quarrel was not helped by the twenty days required for an exchange of letters, but in due course they made their peace. She found herself at last addressing him as "Tu" (thou) in their correspondence, and the lock of her hair she presently sent him would be kept, together with her letters, in the same black box that lay on a shelf in Metternich's study in the Ballhausplatz for many long decades.

Clemens sent her firsthand news from Paris about her family. He reported that the grand duchess was "astonishing for her age, and nobody would be surprised to find himself in love with her!" He did not find Dorothea, whom he had last seen as a child in her mother's Berlin salon, pretty. Dorothea was too "bosomy" for his taste. He preferred the duchess of Sagan's figure—"She has too much of that of which you have not too little"—and he informed Wilhelmina, "Both your noses are *respectables, mais je respecte* yours more. *Mon Dieu!* What don't I like about you?"

Clemens urged Wilhelmina to join him in Paris, but she could not make up her mind to accept his invitation, even if she found the money for the trip. Her hospital in Sagan, which she had established several years before to care for wounded German resistance fighters, was still in operation and proving a serious drain on even her vast resources. However, she would need clothes for the forthcoming congress in Vienna, so would Metternich ask Maman to order several court gowns, ball robes, and blouses for her and please advance the money if the grand duchess—who still had not straightened out her snarled finances—was unable to pay for these purchases?

When Wilhelmina at last agreed to come, she did so in good part because she knew Alfred was in Paris, although she had not heard from him recently. Since the chancellor warned that the roads were not yet safe for unescorted ladies and Gentz was unavailable, Wilhelmina pressed into service one of the junior British attachés who were always under foot. Frederick Lamb accompanied Wilhelmina and Paulina—Joanna was to follow—as far as Munich, and they arrived at Anna's hotel, where they were to stay, nine days later, on May 15, 1814, the afternoon of Metternich's forty-first birthday, as Wilhelmina had promised.

Unfortunately, Wilhelmina's reunion with Clemens was hardly the happy occasion she had anticipated. For in the interim, busy-body Gentz had felt duty bound to send the chancellor a copy of an Austrian secret police bulletin detailing Wilhelmina's presumed liaison with the young Englishman who traveled partway west with her and Paulina. When the chancellor angrily greeted her with this accusation, Wilhelmina riposted that a gay flirtation was the right—"nay, the duty"—of any woman. And what, pray tell, about *tout Paris*'s claim that Metternich had renewed an old love affair of his own? With the wife of one of Napoleon's generals?

But it was seven months since they had last seen each other in Prague, and propinquity after so long an absence can work miracles. And did. Metternich wrote his wife that M. de Talleyrand was monopolizing the Courland princesses, and they were seeing everything under his aegis—although their family reunion had been dampened by the tragic death of Dorothea's small daughter and the young mother's inconsolable grief. But it was simply not true, as Clemens maintained, that he had seen them only three times. Paulina and Joanna, perhaps yes. Wilhelmina, however, he saw almost daily, whenever he could break away from his endless meetings.

Paris that mid-May was like a blushing bride, and Wilhelmina saw its beauty through the eyes of Clemens, who loved the French capital. Sipping white wine outdoors at fashionable Tortoni's on the corner of the rue Taitbout, they watched smart Parisiennes in the latest mode—audacious frocks with enormous patterns and equally big bows and clumps of flowers on their small, narrow pokes—mingling with the crowds of foreigners. Boulevardiers sauntered past in well-cut coats of gray twill and matching black-braided trousers, a fashion that was fast replacing form-fitting culottes.

Wilhelmina and Clemens strolled through the Louvre amid the incredible art treasures that Napoleon had looted from French-occupied Europe; they walked along the quais under a green bower of chestnut trees and visited antique shops, seeking rare pieces for the chancellery apartments and the Metternich villa at Rennwegg, which were both being redecorated for the congress. As the collection of astronomical clocks and scientific instruments he kept in his office bore witness, Metternich's personal selections were more often the result of curiosity than of true artistic dis-crimination. He appreciated Wilhelmina's exquisite taste and con-sulted her on several wagonloads of purchases—furniture in the latest Empire style from the celebrated cabinetmaker Jacob, gold and silver objets d'art from Biennais, fine porcelains and Thomire bronzes, Caffieri andirons, upholstery and silk from Lyons.

Wilhelmina accompanied him to Leroy, who kept a dummy made to the princess von Metternich's measurements from her years in Paris when Clemens was ambassador, and helped select three trunkfuls of clothing for her, including a handsome redingote exactly like the one Marie-Louise had worn the day Metternich visited her at Rambouillet. To salve his conscience for not per-mitting his wife to join the unending stream of diplomats' wives converging there—she would be more useful in Vienna preparing for the expected raft of fall visitors, the chancellor claimed—he and Wilhelmina also picked out one or two frocks from Victorine, the new star on the couturiere horizon. Material was also in-cluded so that Clemens's favorite, his oldest girl, might have one of her mother's new Paris outfits copied.

Before Wilhelmina's arrival, Clemens had already collected a number of bêtises (silly extravagances) for her—diamanté shoe buckles from Grancher's Le Petit Dunkerque, an ivory fan inlaid with little chips of diamonds from Friese and Devilliers, and from another boutique specializing in luxurious novelties, a jeweled mechanical monkey that played a violin and matched the one the tsar had presented to the former Empress Josephine at Malmaison the previous week. And when they were out shopping together and Metternich bought gifts for his wife and oldest daughter, he often bought the same for Wilhelmina.

Nearly always they ended their evenings at the hôtel Saint Florentin, where the soirées now concluded with dancing because that was the tsar's favorite pastime. That, at least, was one thing His Imperial Majesty did well, Metternich grumbled. He was very concerned about his deteriorating relations with Alexander and the trouble the temperamental Russian ruler was causing in the parleys winding up the permanent peace treaty with France. If Wilhelmina had missed their politics-oriented tête-à-têtes during the long months they were apart, Metternich missed mulling over his problems with her. As they sat discussing each day's occurrences, he once more appreciated her intelligence and realized what an excellent sounding board she made. Wilhelmina listened well and expressed her views with a clarity that was a delight.

This was not the fashionable season by Faubourg Saint-Germain standards. The aristocracy was preparing to retire to its chilly, damp châteaux, made habitable by the summer warmth, and entertained little, but the cosmopolitan diplomatic circles were as lively as ever. Because of the grand duchess's close ties with Talleyrand and the tsar, the three Courland princesses should have been assured of a warm welcome everywhere.

But twice-divorced Wilhelmina would not soon forget her sorry experience at the English embassy. The wife of the British foreign secretary nearly fainted when she inquired the name of the stunning blonde sitting farther down the table, the one who had come with the Austrian chancellor, and her dinner partner, Prince Louis de Rohan, casually replied, "She's my former wife." In Vienna, the crème's laissez-faire attitude toward its own had spared Wilhelmina many problems she might otherwise have faced. In Paris, Wilhelmina discovered there were ancient-regime homes where she was persona non grata, and for the first time, she realized the social awkwardness of her situation.

There was another cloud on Wilhelmina's horizon as well: Alfred. Where was he? Windischgratz was not in the French capital as she had been led to believe he would be—and for a good reason. Wilhelmina's last letters to Clemens before coming west showed that she had yet to make a clean break with Alfred, in spite of her promises to the contrary. And Clemens was afraid to have Wilhelmina see the handsome prince covered with new, well-deserved decorations—he had developed into one of the Allies' most admired cavalry officers—before Clemens was reassured of Wilhelmina's love. So the chancellor had Windischgratz sent to Turin as Emperor Franz's personal emissary to the king of Sardinia. Whether Wilhelmina realized Clemens had a hand in Alfred's departure or even asked about it is not known.

Wilhelmina agreed to follow the chancellor to England, where the Allies' consultations about the forthcoming Congress of Vienna were to be held as soon as the Treaty of Paris was signed. And so Clemens felt confident things were going his way, both in diplomacy and in love. If Wilhelmina was not entirely his yet, she almost was, and before leaving Paris he went to Chaumet's in the Palais Royal arcades to select a gift to commemorate the fact. After being shown a number of beautiful pieces, the chancellor settled on a delicately wrought gold bracelet and ordered engraved, inside, the date Wilhelmina first surrendered to him.

When the jeweler's apprentice delivered the present, Wilhelmina had a considerable struggle to decipher the short accompanying note. For Clemens had playfully resorted to mirror writing and compiled a questionnaire:

Requests   *Replies*

(1) Give me a *pledge of will* in London
(2) Always wear my bracelet
(3) Take Alfred's off forever
(4) Take it off, to put it on again
(5) Tell me when our relations will be entirely re-established [Clemens and Wilhelmina had had another tiff]
(6) Wear the little medallion I gave you

> What have you answered?
> Many good things!
> Do tell me yes _____
>   no _____
>
> —Wednesday, June 1, 1814

Before Wilhelmina could reply to Clemens, she must hear from Alfred. She wrote offering Windischgratz his freedom. He must decide what was best for him and make up her mind for her. Wilhelmina lacked the strength to part with Windischgratz forever when Clemens was promising no more than a long liaison.

The Channel packet was held up by adverse winds and took longer than customary for the crossing. As soon as they landed, Wilhelmina and her sisters, Paulina and Joanna, continued straight through to London. But the evening was well advanced before Metternich was able to break away from a state reception to welcome the duchess of Sagan. When he did appear, in his superbly cut, waist-hugging dress uniform, heavily embroidered in gold and bespangled with glittering decorations, his splendid figure and well-turned calves showing off to singular advantage in his tight white breeches, silk stockings, and black satin *escarpins,* Wilhelmina once again thought he was surely the handsomest man in Christendom.

The chancellor, like the British, was agog at the carryings-on of the recently widowed Grand Duchess Catherine of Oldenburg. "Cathou," as Alexander called his favorite, twenty-six-year-old sister, closely resembled her imperial brother in looks, but was not pretty. She had preceded him to London by a good three weeks, supposedly to prepare the way for the tsar's arrival, but more probably on an inspection tour of matrimonial candidates. Since Cathou was not a run-of-the-mill visitor, everything she did was subjected to the glare of publicity—and was vitally important to Metternich as an index of on-going British-Russian relations. So he regaled Wilhelmina with a blow-by-blow account of how Cathou had given full rein to her Slavic love for mischief and managed to offend nearly everyone she met, from the prince regent on down.

Upon her arrival, His Royal Highness had come to pay his

respects, and Cathou had kept him waiting a scandalously long time. Later, at dinner at his home, Cathou had insisted that an Italian trio, which had barely set bows to strings, stop, "Immediately! Music makes me vomit!" The prince regent was understandably annoyed, and his initial impressions of the Russian grand duchess had never changed.

Official London's reactions to the Romanoff family were not improved, Clemens continued, when Alexander sneaked into the city incognito, although he was fully aware that thousands of tickets had been sold for grandstand seats to watch his official entry. Grand Duchess Catherine was at the Pulteney Hotel in Piccadilly, and she persuaded her brother to lodge there too, rather than at Saint James Palace, where a suite had been especially redecorated for His Imperial Majesty. Matters were further aggravated when Alexander remained to dine with his sister instead of going to Carlton House where he was expected. When Alexander finally did put in an appearance, the prince regent introduced him to his mistress. The tsar bowed coldly, but said nothing. Knowing Alexander was deaf in one ear, His Highness repeated her name loudly. The tsar bowed again and silently resumed examining with his lorgnon a fetching young thing he had spotted at the opposite end of the salon. As the indignant regent withdrew, with his plump marquise on his arm, Alexander turned his glass on her portly, disappearing rump and remarked to the Russian ambassadress in a distinctly audible voice, "She looks mighty old." Since then, the tsar and the prince regent had not been able to stand the sight of each other and made little effort to conceal the fact.

Alexander, instead of translating the average Britisher's warmth for him as Jack the Giant Killer—old "Boney" had been their public enemy number one—into a diplomatic success, ignored his capable foreign minister's lead and chose as mentor Cathou, who continued to startle and astound. The brother and sister's outrageous behavior had already stiffened backs in the circles that counted, and the imperial reservoir of goodwill was fast emptying. These incredible imperial capers held the potential for significant Allied policy shifts for the chancellor, who was not anxious to exchange Napoleon's stranglehold on Europe for a Russian bear hug. As Wilhelmina was quick to grasp, the chancellor, by skillfully exploiting the situation and subtly stimulating the traditional British mistrust of Russia, now had a God-given opportunity to tighten the bond between England and Austria. For London, like Vienna, considered a balance of European power the best guarantee for Continental peace.

Before Metternich left Wilhelmina on her first evening in the British capital, he reminded her that the old queen stayed at Windsor with mad George III, so there was no British court, properly speaking. In order to appear on the invitation lists for the official celebrations in honor of the visiting galaxy, Wilhelmina and her sisters would have to be presented at one of Her Majesty's Drawing Rooms, which occurred on the queen's rare visits to the capital. Therefore, the Courland trio must call on Countess Merveldt, the Austrian ambassadress, at once so she could arrange this. It would not be easy to do and might require time, the chancellor warned, since social ostracism for divorce was at its peak in the best British society because of the shocking open separation between the prince regent and his wife, Princess Caroline.

Because of her irregular marital status—and because of the devious diplomatic hand the chancellor was playing—Wilhelmina's London visit was a fiasco from start almost to finish. Instead of long, leisurely hours together, during which Wilhelmina had hoped to resolve their personal affairs, she had only bits and pieces of Clemens's time, sandwiched in between this conference and that meeting, this ball and that fête. And their rendezvous, when they did manage to meet, were generally late at night, far away from the public eye—a novel experience for them both. Unfortunately, Clemens had spoiled Wilhelmina so thoroughly that if he did not appear daily, she felt abused and, worse than that, neglected. He had to attend never less than three or four functions each afternoon and evening, to which Wilhelmina believed she should be invited. But how could she be, when the Austrian ambassadress, who held the key to Wilhelmina's Drawing Room presentation, was apparently afraid of compromising her husband's position at court, and so was conveniently out each time the sisters came to call?

Wilhelmina had to take a back seat while Metternich, like the other Allied dignitaries, came in for his share of popular acclaim. Several hundred women, "dressed to scare you," Clemens wrote his wife, were always pressing around at the various parties. Even the Londoners in the street recognized his carriage when it came to a halt in front of Carlton House and would surround him, hands outstretched for him to shake. Metternich had done his homework well and not only presented the regent with the Golden Fleece, Emperor Franz's highest award, in diamonds, but also made him honorary commander of the specific Hussar regiment that boasted the most gorgeous of the Austrian army's various uniforms. For a prince who enjoyed dressing up like Prinny did, nothing could have been better calculated to please. The bestowment of a military command, while commonplace on the Continent, had never been done before in England and the red tape involved was endless. But it was well worth the effort. The delighted prince regent set the royal tailors to work round the clock, and His Highness's expansive corseted backside in his new field marshal outfit was a sight to behold.

If only Metternich could be as sure of Wilhelmina as he was of his personal success and his diplomatic strategy. She had not yet signed the pledge of will he had sent her before coming to England, and the petulant tone of her notes mounted: "We expect you for dinner, dear Clemens, although I don't believe it, for you will surely find some other engagement during the course of the day."

Unfeelingly, he admonished, "Share my happiness, *mon amie,* but do not irritate it."

Sad and depressed, with her thoughts more and more in the past, Wilhelmina wrote Alfred a letter full of tender memories. She was obviously still deeply torn between the two men, but she repeated what she had already written from Paris. The decision to make a clear break rested with Windischgratz.

Fortunately for Wilhelmina, when her young British admirer Frederick Lamb, who had accompanied her as far as Munich, learned that the duchess of Sagan was continuing on to London, he importuned his father to entertain her. After several of his son's insistent letters, Lord Melbourne did so. No doctor could have prescribed better medicine. Wilhelmina, who had taken to her bed with a migraine, accepted though her head still throbbed, and Hännchen artfully rouged her pallid cheeks. After dinner at Melbourne House, the other great Whig homes of the regent's opposition opened their doors, and life looked brighter.

The visiting rulers and their ministers went to a performance of Edmund Kean in *Otello* at the Drury Lane Theater; so did the Courland sisters—but in separate boxes. The sovereigns were at

Ascot. The Courland trio was too, but not with them. When the crowned heads, accompanied by two uniformed bands, were rowed down the Thames on an elaborately festooned barge to the Royal Military Academy at Woolwich for an artillery demonstration, the three sisters were in the gay flotilla—in a boat with the duchess of Somerset, an old friend of Wilhelmina's who had just returned from abroad. Still, this was not the same as being in the official party with Clemens where Wilhelmina felt she belonged. When the Austrian ambassadress, after Wilhelmina's third unsuccessful attempt to call, sent a footman around with a few cold lines advising that there was no possibility of a presentation until after the monarchs' departure, Wilhelmina was outraged. She was unaccustomed to such insulting treatment and forwarded the communication to Metternich with a sharp note demanding he intercede immediately.

Why Clemens had not done this earlier is not clear, but he did so now, and within twenty-four hours an invitation appeared for the three to curtsey before the old queen at the last Drawing Room of the season. Wilhelmina was an instant success, and the enchanted regent saw to it that the duchess of Sagan, Paulina, and Joanna were included at the remaining official entertainments. At the last ball, Wellington danced the polonaise, Prussia's leading field marshal performed a country dance, and Wilhelmina laughed until the tears streamed down her cheeks when his elderly Russian counterpart, not to be outdone, leaped to his feet and contributed a Cossack dance, nodding, whinnying, and stomping like a horse.

Driving back to her hotel with Clemens after the final military review, Wilhelmina found Metternich relaxed for the first time since her arrival in England. Clemens might not have settled the various Congress of Vienna issues as he had hoped, but by now even the Tory cabinet was offended by Alexander, and the chancellor had gone a long ways toward wresting the coalition control back from Russia.

But a bombshell was awaiting Wilhelmina on her desk: a furious letter from Alfred. It had not been written in reply to either of her two letters—the one from Paris or the more recent one from London, both asking the young prince whether he wanted his freedom. He had not had time to receive either. Nonetheless, she had her answer. He did.

Windischgratz had returned to Vienna, expecting to find the

duchess of Sagan. Instead, he was greeted by a swarm of vicious rumors coupling her with the young British attaché. When he learned, in addition, of her compromising trip to Paris and then on across the Channel to be with the chancellor, Alfred decided he never wanted to see Wilhelmina again. Wilhelmina answered at once, defending herself against any reproaches for her conduct in Vienna and pointing out that she had come to Paris in large measure because she expected to find Windischgratz there—not off in Turin. Face to face with the stark reality of losing Alfred, Wilhelmina nostalgically recalled their happy past together. She must see him once more, and would be back in the Austrian capital shortly.

With no official meetings scheduled in Paris, Clemens and Wilhelmina made the most of their few days there together en route to the Austrian capital. Metternich enjoyed eating out, something he never did in Vienna—at Véry's, in the Palais Royal arcades, or at the chic Café des Aveugles, where an orchestra of blind musicians played—then strolling leisurely home along the moonlit Seine with ample time, for once, to talk things over. If Wilhelmina had come to consider a third marriage a social necessity—as one London letter to Windischgratz would indicate—such a decision would automatically rule out Alfred, who must marry to perpetuate his line. And there is no clue as to whether she discussed or even hinted at marriage to the chancellor.

But for a man whose avowed ambition was to be the heir of Kaunitz, Empress Maria-Teresa's great chancellor, a divorce from the woman who was Kaunitz's only grandchild was a clear impossibility. Emperor Franz, a family man himself, and the crème, who were very straitlaced in these matters and whose support Metternich needed, would forsake him. Metternich simply wanted Wilhelmina, too. He did not want to give Wilhelmina up. He did not want to share her with Alfred—or anybody. And he reminded her that he was still awaiting her answers to his questionnaire.

Then Clemens was off to Vienna, taking along his chef, who had followed him in the field from the start and whom Metternich had placed in Talleyrand's kitchen to brush up his repertoire for the forthcoming congress. Wilhelmina planned to follow with her sisters and Maman, who was en route for her annual Karlsbad cure. But at the last moment, Wilhelmina was delayed by an unexpected final sitting for her newest portrait by the celebrated artist Gérard.

When Wilhelmina crossed the customs barrier at Lambach, she was handed a letter Clemens had written, en route, thanking her for their Paris interlude, which had given him renewed strength. A few such hours could make one forget whole epochs of privation and suffering, and Clemens was still too mesmerized by Wilhelmina, who had been his guiding star through the terrible crises of the past year, to get along easily without her. *"Mon amie, I am yours,"* he concluded. "My fate is no longer in my hands. I do not regret having placed it in yours." But she must also be faithful to him. When Wilhelmina reached Vienna, Clemens would not regret having placed it in yours." But she must also be faithful to him. When Wilhelmina reached Vienna, Clemens would not come to greet her. He would not write her. He would not make any effort to see her. She must decide once and for all between him and Alfred. If she came to Clemens, her appearance would signal surrender to his terms.

Wilhelmina knew what this meant. The key to the Europe of the future was in the chancellor's hands, and he alone intended to turn it. So he would never divorce his wife. He loved Wilhelmina more than he had ever loved any other woman and wanted her completely—body, soul, and mind. In return, she should have his devotion. Their lives were at a fork, and the path they took was up to Wilhelmina.

Metternich was as good as his word. Upon arrival at the Palm palace, Wilhelmina found no letters with the chancellor's special seal. She looked in vain for his flowers. Every time she heard a carriage enter the mammoth courtyard, she stopped what she was doing, expecting a footman in Metternich livery to enter with a bêtise from Clemens. None appeared. Perhaps Clemens did not expect her back so soon. But the following day and the next, there was still no sign from him. The chancellor meant what he said. When she sent over to the Ballhausplatz apartments the princess de Metternich's new Paris frocks—they had not been ready when Clemens departed and so Wilhelmina had brought them with her—she enclosed a few formal lines reminding Metternich how equivocal her situation was.

Vienna was empty at this season. Alfred was at Tächau, his Bohemian estate; her sisters Paulina and Joanna were still at Karlsbad with Maman; and the crème were scattered—at their schlosses or taking the cure at one of the Bohemian spas or at nearby Baden. Most of Wilhelmina's friends preferred this gay little watering place, and the Metternich family always passed the summer months there because it was a scant two hours distant.

Lonely and blue, Wilhelmina decided to rent an apartment in Baden too for the remainder of the summer and took the pleasant drive out through one of Austria's best wine-growing districts to see what was available. The next morning Gentz, who had learned of her arrival—he made it a point to be the first to know everything—appeared at her inn and angrily berated Wilhelmina for her irresponsible behavior toward Metternich. How could she add to the burden of a man who was already carrying the welfare of Europe on his shoulders? Wilhelmina tartly thanked Gentz for minding her business for her, but something the little redheaded chevalier said struck home. She had her chasseur settle the bill, and in spite of a sudden heavy downpour, she returned to Vienna. That night Wilhelmina slept badly, had nightmares about Clemens, and awoke earlier than usual. Her mind made up, she sent the chancellor a little note asking when she might find him at home. Back came a reply as fast as his footman could carry it. And Wilhelmina flew to him.

Metternich loved Wilhelmina far too deeply to have abandoned hope of possessing her, and he was watching for her from a side window of the chancellery. Impatiently, he rushed to help her down out of her carriage himself, before his startled lackeys had a chance to do so, and that Monday, July 25, he would later refer to as "the first day of my life."

In the late afternoon, Clemens drove Wilhelmina in the four-seated barroccio he had brought from London through the Kartner Gate to his Italianate villa on the nearby Rennwegg, where he and his family spent spring and fall when the Ballhausplatz apartments were too damp and chilly for habitation. The sun, reflected on the tributary's muddy waters, was setting, and the bells from the Silesian convent opposite were already calling the nuns to vespers as Metternich wheeled the well-matched bays to a halt. He was anxious to show her the new ballroom that was being added for the forthcoming congress, which, Clemen's oldest daughter claimed, was as big as some people's houses. Several details remained to be settled in the great domed pavilion, and Metternich desired Wilhelmina's opinion. Then, in the lengthening twilight, they wandered along the gravel paths bordered by well-kept hedges, past carved stone deities and animals, while Clemens, who was an avid gardener, showed off some of his exotic blooms.

Wilhelmina no longer wondered if she had made the right decision in coming to Clemens, although "made" was not, perhaps, the correct word. For Wilhelmina persuaded herself that it was Fate—a euphemism for Alfred's absence from Vienna—that had decided for her, as there, beside the splashing fountains, she told Clemens what he was waiting to hear. Yes, she loved him and would belong to him alone. "For at least six months?" Clemens felt confident enough to ask her, teasingly, in a little note before he retired later.

Next day, the pair stopped back at the white-stone chancellery so Wilhelmina might examine the work that was also in progress there. For like everything else in Vienna, the Ballhausplatz had gotten shabby during the long years of war. There were new wall coverings, new stucco ceilings, even new fireplaces, a rarity in Austria. The chancellor had also solved the unsolvable by having a door constructed for each sovereign, to avoid any protocol crisis over which crowned head should enter the remodeled audience chamber first. That lovely room, heavy green damask from top to bottom, with gilt moldings, dark carved woodwork, and white-and-gray marble busts, was to be the nerve center of the congress.

When Clemens left her off at the Palm palace, Wilhelmina hastened to put in writing her long-sought pledge of fidelity while the memory of the blissful past hours was still fresh. Unable to find a clean sheet of paper at her desk, she quickly tore off the bottom of an unfinished letter and scribbled a few lines—She would belong to him as he wanted her to belong to him. Clemens had her word. But he, in turn, must trust her—which her out-of-breath lackey rushed to hand to the chancellor just as he was stepping into his carriage to rejoin his family at Baden. Wilhelmina would follow later.

By establishing Vienna as the congress locale the previous spring, the farsighted chancellor had automatically assured himself of its presidency, a trump for any negotiator. The extensive Austrian secret police, which dated from Maria-Teresa's day, and the imperial postal service's board of censors were other important cards in the international poker game that lay ahead. Nothing —if Clemens could help it—was going to compare with the Congress of Vienna, which must not only remake the face of Europe but celebrate the peace suitably. Since he intended that Austria should regain her former Continental prominence, the chancellor must demonstrate that the Hapsburg star was not setting in a sea of bankruptcy after so many lost battles and had survived the ignominy of the arch-duchesses Marie Antoinette's and Marie-Louise's ill-fated marriages to Frenchmen. Not given to delegating authority, Metternich was bogged down with a myriad of tasks, but with both his family and, now, Wilhelmina settled at Baden—she had taken two suites at the Eichelberg mansion to have adequate space—he commuted as often as possible.

The succeeding weeks slipped into a heavy, easy pattern for Wilhelmina. She drank the curative waters daily and took the baths for pleasure rather than for need. When Hännchen brought her three foster daughters out on their vacation, Wilhelmina donned the de rigueur tentlike flannel shirt and had swimming lessons with them. Picnics in the nearby woods ranked high on their list of favorite pastimes, and once their *"Chère Maman"* took them as far as Raühenstein to admire the ruins, which seemed more romantic than ever, that day, because of an unexpected thunderstorm. Another time, Wilhelmina and her family slowly climbed the foothills in an open carriage and stopped along the way to admire different views of the beautiful Saint Helenen Valley. Clemens often met the group at the floral clock beside the Plague Column in Baden's town square and accompanied them for a stroll along the the shady walks in the Kürhaus's lovely formal grounds.

In the evening, friends who dropped by informally for tea found Clemens seated at Wilhelmina's elbow while she poured. There were dinner parties outdoors, with a string group playing background music behind the shrubs, and, later, cards—generally *l'hombre,* a centuries-old Spanish game that Wilhelmina enjoyed. There was also dancing nightly at the casino with scores of eager young army officers for waltzing partners, but Wilhelmina, knowing Clemens would take a jaundiced view of such goings-on, never appeared.

Wilhelmina's path constantly crisscrossed with that of the

princess von Metternich, but Clemens's wife was delighted to have her husband home, and since she had no choice, sharing must do.

When the chancellor went briefly to castle Persenberg to consult with His Apostolic Imperial Majesty, he wrote Wilhelmina:

> I do not know if the Emperor is in love with you, or if he is trying to please me, but one of his first questions when we met was to inquire if you would be in Vienna for the Congress. I assured him you would. "Good," he replied, "because I regard the Duchess of Sagan as one of the most essential ingredients of the Congress." "Yes, she will be very helpful," I answered. I would have embraced him, if I had not feared to make him suspicious whether so much ardor might not be inspired by some other motive than politics.

Those of the crème who had summered elsewhere were congregating in Baden to enjoy the last of the season, and the tiny spa's one inn added an extra service but still could not handle its regular clientele at dinner.

Alfred—as well as Wilhelmina's favorite young English attaché, Frederick Lamb—appeared shortly before Metternich went up the Danube. Windischgratz found the duchess of Sagan, whom he had not seen since Prague at the outset of the Allied campaign, more attractive than ever. The young prince was filled with remorse at breaking off all ties, and he took advantage of the chancellor's four-day absence to plead for renewal of their affair. She was not strong enough to endure so much suffering again, Wilhelmina replied in a long letter. Nonetheless, like leaves in a strong wind, malicious tongues fluttered.

The chancellor had scarcely time to unfasten his traveling cloak before talebearing Gentz was whispering the latest Baden gossip in Clemens's ear: "Prince Windischgratz is holding the duchess's fan." "The prince is fetching the duchess's shawl." Small wonder that when Metternich encountered Wilhelmina a few hours later at a soirée, surrounded by the usual circle of admiring swains, he wore the sulky expression Wilhelmina most disliked—until she assured him she had not stopped thinking about him during his entire absence, except when she was asleep.

Increasingly that late August and early September, when

Clemens showed up with the draft of several official letters that he intended to read aloud for her criticism and comments, he no longer found Wilhelmina alone. Her rooms were filled with visitors —among them the young Britisher Lamb and a persistent, ever-hopeful Alfred.

An Austrian general returning from a special mission to Saint Petersburg brought word of d'Armfelt's death from a stroke at Tsarköe-Tselo, the tsar's summer palace outside his capital. (Gustav was governor of the Russian province of Finland and a member of Alexander's inner circle at the time he was stricken.) Wilhelmina considered his demise a stroke of luck that should expedite retrieval of her daughter, and Clemens, who had not forgotten his promise to help Wilhelmina regain Vava's custody, agreed to do what he could to speed a decision as soon as Alexander arrived. But these matters moved slowly at best, and Wilhelmina had yet to receive the necessary documentation from Finland and Russia.

Metternich had planned to hold the Allied ministers' preliminary sessions—primarily to resolve the fate of Poland and Saxony, the most crucial issue confronting the delegates—in Baden, but the pregnant wife of the Russian foreign minister was afraid of a miscarriage and refused to leave Vienna, and her husband would not quit her side. So the chancellor transferred the meetings to the capital.

He and Wilhelmina had had their ups and downs these past weeks. Clemens was often consumed with jealousy, and he had resumed his disquieting, wearying dissection of their mutual feelings. Still, on the whole it had been a happy time. In a farewell letter, he declared that the two months spent together since the day Wilhelmina promised to be his alone had decided the destiny of his life. It was inseparable from hers.

Dorothea, the duchess of Dino. Portrait by Dubufe. (Bibliothèque
Nationale, Paris)

Talleyrand. Engraving by
I. B. Chapuy, after a painting
by Pierre Paul Prud'hon.
(Bibliothèque Nationale, Paris)

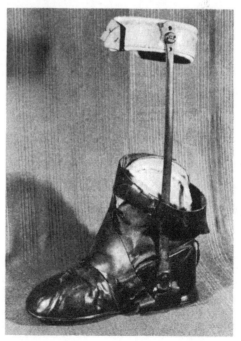

The orthopedic boot
Talleyrand always wore.
(Collection of the
Château de Valençay)

Comte Edmond de Talleyrand-Périgord   Count Karl Clam-Martinitz

The Palm Palace, number 54 Schenkenstrasse, Vienna (Historisches Museum der Stadt Wien, Vienna)

The castle at Nachod in Bohemia. A contemporary lithograph by
A. Hann. (Dr. Maria Ullrichova)

Schloss Ratiborzitz, where Wilhelmina preferred to stay when she
was at Nachod. The Three Kings Salon, as it appears today.
(Dr. Maria Ullrichova)

CHAPTER ELEVEN

The Grand Duchess, Dorothea, & Talleyrand; Wilhelmina & Metternich
1814 - January 1815

EXHAUSTED BY THE ENDLESS ROUND OF entertaining, Anna-Dorothea had retreated to her country estate, the Château Neuf in Saint Germain-en-Laye, for a few days of rest the instant the sovereigns and her daughters had departed for England the summer of 1814. She was indulging a hobby for which she never had time in the capital—arranging fragrant bouquets of garden-fresh originals below the sixteenth- and seventeenth-century floral still lifes of them hanging on her salon walls—when Charles-Maurice was announced. The tsar was furious at Louis XVIII for a variety of reasons, personal as well as political, and because Alexander blamed Talleyrand for persuading him to restore the Bourbons, His Imperial Majesty had refused to see Charles-Maurice before he crossed to England. Since it was imperative that Charles-Maurice make his peace with the Tsar of All the Russias before their fall meetings in Vienna, he brought along a preliminary draft of a letter to Alexander in which he mentioned the grand duchess, and he wanted her approval before sending it off.

As a defeated nation, France's situation at the forthcoming congress was precarious at best, and made more so by Alexander's unpredictability. Talleyrand's task—as foreign minister he would head the French delegation—was the most challenging of his entire career, and for the first time in years, he had forgone his cure at Bourbon-l'Archambault, which did a world of good for his bad right foot, in order to prepare for this difficult mission. Since Talleyrand had been the prince of Bénévent because of a minuscule papal state Napoleon had given him, and it would never do to have the Bourbons served by a minister with an imperial title, Louis XVIII elevated him to hereditary prince. Louis XVIII and Talleyrand might not be in sympathy personally, but they understood each other completely and were in thorough accord on the line to be adopted and developed. Both were committed to work for moderation and a balance of power.

Charles-Maurice had already chosen the principal members of his Vienna staff. His second-in-command, the duke of Dalberg, the former Baden minister who had served in his provisional government, was related to the handful of great families who owned half of Central Europe; he had enough centuries of blue blood to look down his nose at anybody, and with his mother-in-law at Schönnbrunn palace as Marie-Louise's mistress of the robes, he should have ready access to whatever news came from Elba.

Another equally capable diplomat was selected to do the basic staff work. Charles-Maurice was also taking along one of the principal aides-de-camp of the comte d'Artois, the king's brother. Since the Ultras—as the overly reactionary returning Royalists were called—did not trust Talleyrand, and the comte d'Artois as their leader would insist Charles-Maurice be watched abroad to make sure he toed the accepted line, Talleyrand preferred to pick the spy himself. The quartet was rounded out by a young aristocrat of distinguished lineage and social graces, who was so handsome the ladies would love him. His lack of brains was immaterial; he would do very nicely for signing passports.

One of the most important things still bothering Charles-Maurice—and perhaps this was the real reason he had come to see Anna—was the question of who was to be his hostess. For most decisions at the congress would be made in the drawing rooms and ballrooms rather than around a green baize-covered table. With diplomacy the prerogative of the privileged class, European power rested in the hands of a relative few, and the French embassy, to be effective, must be a focal point of that elite.

In order to remove the prejudice and fear, the bad taste left by France's Revolution and subsequent imperial adventure, which still lingered, especially in Vienna, the embassy's salons must be more ancient regime than any of those of Vienna's crème. Its hostess must not only help restore France's reputation in the circles where it had suffered most; she must also hold her own, through looks, breeding, and intelligence, in the web of political intrigue that would underlie the distaff side of the congress's life.

The role was tailor-made for the grand duchess of Courland and would be a fitting climax to her life. All Europe—that is to say, all those who mattered in Anna's eyes—was already packing for Vienna, and with Europe at peace after more than two decades of war, the five or six weeks of the meetings promised to be exceptionally brilliant. Anna knew she could be of help to Charles-Maurice with difficult Alexander. But as much as she longed to be his hostess, she realized this was impossible.

Mme. Malàprop—Catherine de Talleyrand, Charles-Maurice's wife—still presided at the hôtel Saint Florentin, and Charles-Maurice remained impeccably correct toward her. As he was fond of quoting to Anna, "A witty woman often compromises her husband; a woman without wit only compromises herself." Custom decreed that he take her to Vienna but political expediency said no. A married bishop and his wife in that Catholic stronghold, the former seat of the Holy Roman Empire of German States? Especially lumpish, blowzy Catherine, with her pretentious airs? Throwing Catherine to the wolves would be more merciful than placing her in the midst of that snobbish, arrogant society for whom frontiers did not exist, only bloodlines—and where everyone knew everybody else, or was related to them. Another insurmountable hurdle was Catherine's earlier, widely publicized affair with the Spanish princes' equerry. That duke was now an important figure in Madrid government circles, and Catherine's presence at Talleyrand's side could make him a laughingstock as a cuckolded husband—not that Charles-Maurice personally prized marital constancy.

The irregularities of Talleyrand's past life—political, religious, and social—provided enough handicaps to overcome in Vienna without Catherine's presence to add to them. But the grand duchess could not preempt Mme. de Talleyrand's place there. And it is doubtful whether Anna and Charles-Maurice ever discussed this possibility. Some things were better left unsaid. But both knew that even if Louis XVIII had been willing to shut his eyes—which was wishful thinking—Emperor Franz was a family man and never would have. Certain proprieties had to be observed, at least superficially, by His Most Christian Majesty's envoy. But even though Anna could not accompany him—and to go in anything but the number-one spot was beneath her—dear Charles-Maurice would not be without Courland cohorts. Wilhelmina's leading political salon would be at his disposal—an enormous asset for a man in Talleyrand's delicate situation—and Paulina, too, was in a position to be helpful. Her husband, Friedrich-Hermann-Otto von Hohenzollern-Hechingen, would be one of several south German princes attending, and the field marshal who was her present lover was slated for a leading part in the negotiations.

It is quite possible that the initial suggestion to take the youngest Courland princess as Talleyrand's hostess stemmed from Anna, as part of her ceaseless effort to make herself and her family useful to Charles-Maurice—not that Talleyrand needed help when it came to using the opposite sex for his personal ends. The grand duchess hardly considered her twenty-one-year-old daughter a potential rival, and by birth and education, Dorothea, like her sisters, had entrée and could hold her own in any gathering of European blue bloods. Furthermore, since she was Talleyrand's niece by marriage, society would countenance his taking her.

Talleyrand was still worried about Dorothea, who had remained locked in a shell of grief ever since her child's death in mid-May. Talleyrand was extremely fond of his niece, and after the funeral, busy as he was, he had tried to visit her time and again, although Dorothea refused to see anybody, even him. Grudgingly, she had moved, at *l'oncle*'s insistence, to the rue Saint Florentine. He felt a change of atmosphere would do her good and hoped the continuous activity in the great mansion might distract her. But Dorothea never set foot outside her ground-floor apartments and hardly saw her sisters throughout their Paris stay. Something else was needed to draw her out of herself. The change and excitement in Vienna would help assuage her grief, and it was time that Dorothea, who had already done her duty and assured the continuance of the Talleyrand line by producing two sons, had some compensation for her unhappy marriage.

Dorothea had come to trust *l'oncle,* and she had been drawn closer to him by his silent comprehension of her sorrow. The knowledge that he cared for her and was the one person she could count on had given her a sense of security those past harrowing months. She must have been pleased to learn there was something she could do to help him. Besides, Dorothea had nothing to lose. Her little girl's death had irrevocably widened the gulf with Edmond. The right husband might have helped Dorothea through this difficult period. Instead, her original indifference to Edmond deepened into aversion, and her marriage was at an end on any but the most formal terms.

Dorothea had been a model wife for five years. But her deep sorrow evolved into rebellion, and drastic decision though it was, she accepted without a backward glance the opportunity to escape that *l'oncle* offered. Nor did Talleyrand include Edmond in his legation in some minor capacity, as a sop to convention, which he surely would have, had Dorothea wanted him along. For Talleyrand to take Dorothea without her husband was a serious matter. But *l'oncle*, too, was heartily tired of his nephew's follies and extravagances, and he was serving notice that as head of the Talleyrand family, he was on Dorothea's side, not on Edmond's.

Surely one of the shabbier incidents in Talleyrand's long life was the ignominious manner in which he set forth on his most important mission. Rather than risk an unpleasant public scene with his unpredictable wife, the grand seigneur met Dorothea clandestinely in the countryside outside of Paris in mid-September. Catherine did not learn that Dorothea was to accompany him until the pair were already rolling eastward at top speed.

The tsar and the king of Prussia were already on their way, and Talleyrand was determined to precede them and marshal his forces before their arrival. So chasseurs on fleet-footed horses raced ahead to assure that the time spent at each relay post was kept to a minimum, and they made only two stops, in Strasbourg and in Munich. With horses pushed to the limit by the postilions' cracking whips and loud halloos, pine-clad foothills soon yielded to tiny medieval towns huddled in deep valleys amid snowcapped mountains. But there was ample time for *l'oncle,* settled comfortably back in the luxurious velvet-and-morocco-lined interior of the great berlin, his hand, framed in point de Bruxelles lace, playing mechanically with his gold-headed cane, to brief his niece on what lay ahead.

Talleyrand's task was to reinstate France to her rightful place alongside the other great powers, with equal rank and voice, and restore the country's lost prestige. He was also concerned about any undisclosed understandings that might have been reached between the Allies when they were in London. Napoleon's downfall had freed half of Europe from French rule, and both Louis XVIII and Talleyrand were in accord that the eighteenth-century Law of Nations and the same principle of legitimacy that had put the

Bourbons back on the French throne must prevail, rather than the Bonaparte policy that might makes right, when the Napoleonic spoils were redistributed.

France was still the richest nation in Europe, both in men and material, and its dominant role before Napoleon had been based not on military power but on cultural contributions and the power of its wealth. These were the aspects *l'oncle* intended to emphasize to dazzle and seduce Vienna and revive French influence. But since France had been the Continent's problem child for the past quarter of a century, it would take a near miracle to entice the crème and the leaders of the Congress in the Austrian capital.

As she listened, Dorothea could envisage her role. For like her mother, the grand duchess, and her sister, Wilhelmina, she refused to be window trimming. A love of political intrigue was in Dorothea's blood. She wanted to be a participant and contribute to events even more now than she had years before when she was engaged to Prince Czartoryski.

The pair covered the six hundred miles in a record-breaking seven days, and Dorothea gazed with anticipation at the Austrian capital's many church spires glistening in the distance. "Vienna! The whole of my destiny was in that word," Dorothea would write in her *Souvenirs*. Here was the green room for her debut on the European stage.

Talleyrand had selected the Kaunitz palace for his delegation because that Italianate residence with its three vast wings was one of the handsomest there. It stood at 1029 Johannesgasse, a narrow street in the section known as "the old city," almost in the shadow of the Cathedral of Saint Stephan, two steps from the Church of Saint Etienne, a short walk from the Hofburg, the Ballhausplatz, and busy, central Kartnerstrasse. The Kaunitz had rarely been occupied for several decades and required more attention than anticipated. Its mattresses were ruined by maggots, and there were moth-eaten rugs, bedding, and drapes, but these were housekeeping details. The interior was exuberant Viennese Rococo— sheer fantasy—in sharp contrast to its forbidding, gray-stoned exterior. Frolicking cherubini abounded in Dorothea's suite. Four chubby little figures gaily supported a chiming clock; others, two fat-bellied rosewood chests. More encircled each rock-crystal chandelier.

Dorothea had time only for a short nap. Then she and *l'oncle* were trotting along the Leopoldstrasse, where the torches of their running footmen, preceding them, illuminated the theatrical livery of the doormen with their mighty staffs and bandoliers in front of the great palaces lining the way. Tomorrow the pair would begin the round of calls prescribed by protocol which would require eight to ten days, since the entire imperial family and the diplomatic corps must be visited. Meantime, no one could question the propriety of Dorothea's wish to see the duchess of Sagan immediately. Although Dorothea had always been intimidated by her older sister and had never felt close to her, she knew it was imperative for *l'oncle*'s sake to establish the pattern of informal daily access to the left wing of the Palm palace.

Entering her sister's salon on Talleyrand's arm, with one of *l'oncle*'s favorite—and more cynical—dictums ringing in her ears, "Never trust your impulse because it is good," Dorothea caused a stir, as the ubiquitous Austrian secret police were quick to note. And the impression *l'oncle* and his niece made as they walked slowly—because of his bad right foot—the length of the salon to greet Wilhelmina was the one Vienna would always retain of them. Both emanated elegance: he so old—Talleyrand was now sixty— and so tall; she so young and so small. It was evident at a glance that Dorothea, though she had the delicate, overly long Medem nose, was far too exotic a bird for the Courland aviary, with her striking black hair and huge dark eyes—a paternal heritage. She was not conventionally pretty, even with her pale oval face fleshed out. But a small, delicate head set on a long slim neck enhanced her distinguished carriage, and her innate dignity and grace of bearing added inches to Dorothea's height. Her slight stutter when she was excited would never desert her, but her deportment and gestures now formed an enchanting ensemble.

"Leave it to that old scoundrel to bring that pretty young thing along as a decoy," somebody muttered.

"As a Courland Princess she will force doors that would not otherwise open to the ex-Bishop of Autun. Look, do you see what I mean?" One guest nudged another. For as the brother of the Prussian ambassador to Vienna entered, Wilhelmina gestured toward Dorothea, and the distinguished scientist hastened over to kiss her delightedly on both cheeks.

"Why shouldn't the baron be pleased to see her? He knew her as a child when she was growing up in Berlin."

"That's true, but see, he's talking to Talleyrand, too. One of the foremost leaders of Prussian resistance to French tyranny, talking to Napoleon's former right-hand man! I never thought I'd live to see the day."

On September 25, Wilhelmina was awakened by a blast of cannon announcing that Alexander had left the border town of Nikolsburg, two and a half hours away. The Austrian emperor had gone only as far as Schönnbrunn to greet the other sovereigns, but today he was going farther, to the left bank of the Danube at the end of the Tabor Bridge. The Tsar of All the Russias might be miffed at Metternich and at odds with the British prince regent, but he was the hero of the day to the Viennese for leading his country, with its vast military resources, out of centuries-old isolation to participate in the Continental crusade against Bonaparte. And His Apostolic Imperial Majesty was prepared to give Alexander his due.

Wilhelmina was tired from a late evening and would have liked to sleep, but by 10:30 A.M. she was dressed and ready, adjusting her fashionable new *charivari* with its enormous packet of gold charms better to show off her slender waist. Clemens had taken pains to procure her a front-row seat to witness the high point of the opening pageantry of the congress, Alexander's entry into the inner courtyard of the Hofburg, and she must be there promptly. Vienna's many church bells were pealing when the imperial cortege swung into the somber, weather-beaten palace grounds, where the visiting royalty—four kings, one queen, two emperors and empresses, two hereditary princes, three grand duchesses, and three princes of the blood—were already housed and waiting. Drums rolled and soldiers presented arms. The richly caparisoned, aristocratic Hungarian guards led the way, their commander astride a turquoise-studded saddle and outfitted in a priceless jewel-encrusted uniform, with pearl pendants adorning his boots and a huge aigrette of diamonds tucked jauntily into his headgear. Then the masters of the north, Alexander and King Friedrich-Wilhelm III, who was accompanying him, trotted in side by side. This heavy-handed emphasis of their political solidarity did not bode well for Metternich if Alexander remained as capricious as he had been in London.

The chancellor had to cancel an afternoon tryst with Wilhelmina at the last minute because the tsar wanted to see him. Knowing she would be concerned about their first interview, Clemens scribbled Wilhelmina a little note upon leaving the august presence. All had gone well. He was to dine with the tsar at the Russian embassy and accompany him to the gala at the Kartnertor Theater. They would be later than usual and miss most of the opera, but at Alexander's request, they expected to arrive in time to see the highly touted French ballerina, la Bigottini, in the ballet *Zephyr and Flora*. Clemens was looking forward to meeting Wilhelmina at the supper for the two newly arrived rulers afterwards, and concluded, "Devote a single tiny thought to me and end your reply with the answer to the following very small word—*Mein?*"

Metternich's subconscious reversion to German—the billet was in French, as was all their correspondence and conversation—revealed the depth of his feelings, and if Wilhelmina had been vexed earlier at his failure to appear as promised, she must now have been touched.

The next evening, the Austrian imperial couple gave a gala reception for their guests. Talleyrand sat in the great mirrored ballroom as isolated as if he had the plague, waiting for his niece to return from dancing a *tempête*. When she came back, she brought her partner with her—young Crown Prince Wilhelm, her childhood playmate in Berlin. Politeness forced His Highness to greet Talleyrand, and bystanders, who were eagerly watching and unsure what line of conduct to follow, were no longer afraid to be seen speaking to the pariah—a representative of defeated France. Through them Talleyrand learned that his worst fears were justified. In secret agreement to keep the direction of affairs in their own hands, England, Russia, Austria, and Prussia were meeting daily in the Ballhausplatz and intended to present their decisions as a fait accompli when the congress was called into session.

Talleyrand was determined to call a halt to the Big Four's game. Like an old war-horse sniffing gunpowder, he invited the Spanish plenipotentiary and various of the smaller powers' emissaries for dinner. Talleyrand also included the prince de Ligne, the patriarch of European society, although he did not represent any country. A living legend and the quintessence of the eighteenth century at its best, the prince could be counted on to discuss the superlative menu in mouth-watering detail and to spread the guest list, sowing apprehension in the Allied embassies and making them wonder what the wily statesman was up to. To round out the party, at Talleyrand's request Dorothea asked several members of the local crème who were Maman's old friends. Prince and Princess Nicolas Esterhazy would find it hard to refuse, and their presence would dispel the unpleasant rumor that none of the Austrian aristocracy would set foot in the Kaunitz after the way France had treated a Hapsburg archduchess. Imagine beheading Marie-Antoinette!

Talleyrand had warned his niece that it would never do to treat the less powerful nations as second best, and the dinner tendered them was as fine as if nothing but crowned heads were seated around the long sparkling table. The soups were excellent and not too filling, the trout was as fresh as the morning dew, the larded roast plover was succulent, the *brioches en couronne* had the proper texture, and the other pastry was equally breathtaking. Instead of discussing high politics, as Dorothea anticipated, she heard *l'oncle* praising the merits of brie, "the king of cheeses," as he helped himself to some which had arrived by special courier from Paris. On Dorothea's left, the British ambassador was commenting on the superb place settings the prince de Metternich had used at the Ballhausplatz the night before. "I understand it's a service for one hundred and fifty," the Englishman added, "and was a gift from Napoleon I for the Chancellor's help in arranging his marriage to Marie-Louise." "A service for a service!" the witty prince de Ligne chuckled, above the clatter of the gold-and china-ware and the clinking of glasses.

As Talleyrand suspected, those present were resentful of their treatment by the Big Four. The congress had been called to make decisions as a group, with each country having an equal voice—not to be dictated to by the Great Sanhedrin. The fact that France was the only one at the congress that wanted nothing for itself —its boundaries were fixed by the recent Treaty of Paris—made these disgruntled delegates Talleyrand's natural constituents. They looked to him as their patron saint, and Talleyrand reported to Louis XVIII that the English plan of isolating France was doomed to failure. The Big Four might ignore defeated France, but they could not readily turn their backs on a France that was the champion of the rest of Europe.

As he swung into action, *l'oncle* battened down the home

hatches. Forewarned by years of living under the shadow of Napoleon's secret police, Talleyrand had brought his entire household staff from Paris, including an army of assistant chefs, pastry chefs, and sauce chefs. When he was alerted that the *Oberste Polizei und Censu Hofstelle* planned to place a spy among his vegetable peelers, he took the necessary precautions, and temperamental sulks notwithstanding, his "Cher Maître"—Chef Carême—had to await a replacement from Paris. Talleyrand would not tolerate any local domestics. He did not want his wastebaskets searched, the ashes from each porcelain stove sifted. As it was, his number two in command would leave enough love letters scattered around for a dozen major scandals. He always did. That should suffice to keep the secret police busy and titillate Emperor Franz. (Despite Talleyrand's efforts, the Austrian secret police did place on their payroll three Kaunitz doorkeepers and chambermaids, as well as a minor legation official.) Talleyrand also ordered that informants be placed in most of the embassies and instructed his men to welcome warmly the countless dissatisfied Saxons and Wurtembourgeois, not to mention the dispossessed natives of Nassau and other small German states, who were anxious to volunteer information.

A few days after their first dinner party, Dorothea was amazed upon entering Talleyrand's bedchamber to find *l'oncle,* who was propped up in bed still wearing his nightcap, a sort of percale tiara gathered with pale ribbon and fastened to a headband jammed down low over his brow, giving orders to dispense with his sacrosanct levee.

That levee was famous as a spectacle. It began at eleven every morning, and business of greater or lesser magnitude was freely discussed with total disregard for the listening ears of the army of servitors who attended him. Under the watchful eye of Courtiade, his veteran valet, attired in powdered wig and silk stockings, one subordinate held a huge bowl under Talleyrand's chin. While his doctor and familiars respectfully watched, Talleyrand inhaled several large glassfuls of water, gargled, and then ejected the liquid as noisily as an elephant through his trunk. One by one, favored friends dropped in, and Talleyrand acknowledged their appearance with a nod. Various notables often silently joined the scene.

His ablutions finished, the prince bathed his feet in a pail of foul-smelling Barrèges water, exhibiting with cynical indifference the distorted claw that served as his right foot. At the same time, his abundant hair was dressed. Two hairdressers, their gray uniforms covered by large aprons, bustled from side to side with curling irons, like mechanical dolls, then blew a powder, lightly perfumed with amber, over the finished project. Simultaneously, Talleyrand sipped a cup of chamomile tea—to tide him over until dinner—told stories, signed papers, dictated, and settled matters with new groups of advisers. Nearby at a large table, a secretary leafed through journals, cutting articles, speeches, and opinions that might interest the prince, then reading them aloud whenever there was a lull in the conversation.

Finally, Talleyrand stood up to dress—a series of elaborate maneuvers that lasted another hour, during which he faced his audience and continued to converse unperturbed. The procedure was so elegantly performed, under cover of so many robes, that there was nothing to make any lady present blush.

This two-hour feudal ritual was such an integral part of Talleyrand's day that Dorothea was consumed with curiosity as to why he had forgone it, but she had long ago learned not to ask importunate questions. So she took the thin porcelain cup brimming full of café au lait that a footman handed her and perched silently on the edge of the magnificent Maria-Teresa bed. Elaborate silver ornamentation framed the deep alcove where she sat, swirled out over the lemon-colored panels of the walls and doors and edged the long windows; the scent of amber was pervasive.

After signing several dispatches for an aide-de-camp who was standing respectfully alongside, *l'oncle* explained he must get dressed at once because he had just received a note inviting the French—and the Spanish—plenipotentiary to a meeting of the Big Four at 11:00 A.M. in the Ballhausplatz. His plan to parlay France's weakness into strength was paying off. First, Bavaria and the other minor German states had come flocking when they learned the French statesman was backing their cause. And now the Big Four wanted to see him.

Dorothea accompanied her sisters across the Danube on the famous Schlägbruecke, gaily painted in the Austrian national colors, black and yellow, to visit the imperial crypts in the Kapüziner Kirche in Mëhl-Grub, but she managed to be home to greet Talleyrand when he returned. *L'oncle* savored the retelling of his initial encounter with the Allied ministers. He put them on the defensive from the start and did not give Metternich a chance to recover. In an adroit scene between the two most skilled diplomats in Europe, one which Gentz would never forget, the sixty-year-old Talleyrand hopelessly scuttled the forty-one-year-old Metternich's plans. But more important from *l'oncle*'s point of view was his discovery that the coalition entente was weak. The Big Four buckled under and abandoned any intention to dictate to the congress.

Emperor Franz entertained again. There was a party afterwards at Wilhelmina's. Metternich spent the night and was still at the Palm at noon the next day, while impatient dignitaries and heads of state tapped their heels in his Ballhausplatz anterooms, astounded that the chancellor should not be available until mid-afternoon.

Instead of continuing with the rest to Wilhelmina's in the left wing of the cavernous palace's second floor, Alexander had turned in the opposite direction and gone to his cousin Katya the princess Bagration's apartments in the right wing. (The palace was vast enough to accommodate three or four families without their ever meeting.) Whatever transpired between His Imperial Majesty and Katya—whether Alexander spent the time questioning her minutely about Metternich's affair with the duchess of Sagan, as the omnipresent Austrian secret police claimed—the crème had their own ideas and hurried to Wilhelmina's drawing rooms the next evening anxious to draw blood.

"Everyone else left the princess's at dawn, but His Imperial Majesty didn't leave until 7:00 A.M.," someone snickered.

"Honi soit qui mal y pense," a loud voice retorted from the back of the crowded salon.

Startled, Wilhelmina turned to her tormentors. "What a pity it took so long! The poor darling. Did you know, there's no such thing as an impotent man? Only an inept woman." If her prestige as a hostess was not hurt by the tsar's absence from her supper— and by her failure to snare his first tête-à-tête in Vienna—Wilhelmina's pride as a woman could easily have been. For Katya, the princess Bagration, had scored a resounding victory in the opening rounds of her scramble with the duchess of Sagan for the lion's share of the Congress of Vienna dignitaries.

Wilhelmina and the "Naked Angel"—Katya, the young blonde widow of General Bagration, the elderly Russian war hero, affected daring décolletage—shared not only the coveted distinction of being the capital's leading political hostess but the second floor of the palace—and Metternich. A twelve-year-old-daughter, brazenly named Clementine, attested that the intriguing, ambitious Princess Bagration had been Wilhelmina's predecessor in the chancellor's affections. Because the princess had been born on the steps of the Russian throne and her quarters were the center of the important local Russian colony, it was imperative for Metternich to remain on friendly terms with so valuable a source of information concerning the Romanoff court. And so the chancellor had resumed visiting Katya in Baden these past months.

To have Clemens, the man on whom the fate of the congress depended, in love with her rival, Wilhelmina, overwhelmed Princess Bagration. She thirsted for revenge on the faithless chancellor and set out not only to provide Metternich's domestic opponents with fresh ammunition in their efforts to force his resignation, but to deprive him of Wilhelmina. Sensing that the tsar was no longer on the best of terms with the chancellor and was vexed that the duchess of Sagan, whom he considered a Russian princess, should still be Metternich's mistress, Katya deliberately fanned imperial displeasure with the chancellor in an effort to force Wilhelmina from Clemens's arms.

Because Katya nurtured Alexander's fear that Wilhelmina would repeat his every word to Metternich, the tsar prudently avoided the left wing on the Schenkenstrasse. By so doing, he placed Wilhelmina in a dilemma. Her salons provided the chancellor with an indispensable locale for discreet informal discussions with many important visitors and delegates with whom Wilhelmina had family or personal connections—including Talleyrand. But Wilhelmina's consuming desire to regain her lost Vava dictated that she not upset her cordial personal relations with the volatile tsar who should, normally, be her habitué also.

This Gordian knot involving two foreign women, the tsar, and the chancellor, and composed in equal parts of political and social ambitions and boudoir rivalries, earned Wilhelmina and Katya the widest coverage—after the crowned heads—in the Austrian secret police dossiers, which were avidly read daily by scandal-loving Emperor Franz over his morning café au lait. Since Metternich's nightly presence was assured in the Schenkenstrasse palace's left wing, the secret police labeled it the "Austrian Camp," as opposed to Katya's "Russian Camp" in the right.

Talleyrand, who kept one ear to the ground, visited them both; he believed in keeping his options open. Besides, he wanted the gossip-loving Katya to repeat whatever he chose to tell her.

To further complicate the scenario, Prince Windischgratz was creeping back into Wilhelmina's good graces. Storm warnings were again hoisted between Wilhelmina and Metternich, and there were hateful scenes. For now, when Clemens deserted the Ballhausplatz and a jammed appointment calendar to walk briskly through the busy streets and across the Minoriten Platz to be with Wilhelmina at 11:00 A.M.—"his hour"—to discuss the latest news and brief her on the day's activities, it was a major feat to squeeze inside Wilhelmina's packed pink-and-white boudoir. And Alfred and Frederick Lamb were always under foot like pet dogs.

On October 5, exactly four days after the twelve hours Clemens spent with Wilhelmina at the Palm that he labeled as "a day of the greatest happiness of my life," Windischgratz gave a small dinner for Talleyrand and Dorothea. A glowing Wilhelmina presided as hostess, and something occurred—no one has ever pinpointed what—to indicate that Alfred was once more enjoying her favors. The crème was agog, and an outraged Clemens reduced Wilhelmina to tears when he taxed her with being unfaithful.

The chancellor was having equally difficult sailing on the diplomatic front. The congress's official opening, initially scheduled for October 1, was continuously postponed while the Allies tried to resolve the Polish-Saxon conundrum on which the two northern sovereigns stood adamant. The sole thing the Big Four agreed upon unanimously was not to present this prickly question to the three hundred rank-and-file delegates, with their wide range of interests, until a solution was found to suit themselves. The principal stumbling block was Alexander's iron-clad determination to use additional plunder—to be taken from the defeated Saxon king, who had made the mistake of remaining loyal to Napoleon when the others switched sides—to barter, first, for Prussian acquiescence to Alexander's seizure of Saxony's duchy of Warsaw, already blanketed by 200,000 Russian troops, and second, for Prussia's large Polish provinces. Taking a different tack, Austria and

England were trying to buy Prussian assistance to stop the tsar's plans for a reconstructed, Russian-dominated kingdom of Poland.

On Sunday, Berlin shrewdly raised the ante to include all of Saxony with its two and a half million inhabitants and the city of Mainz-on-the-Rhine. That evening, as Metternich sat in the imperial ballroom watching Wilhelmina perform in a quadrille of the four elements with other society belles, he was still trying to digest the Prussian chancellor's staggering memorandum. Enthusiastic applause drew Clemens's attention back to the sextet representing Earth, who were gliding effortlessly back and forth, finishing an intricate figure they had rehearsed with the ballet master from the opera. To his prejudiced eyes, the duchess of Sagan, in brown velvet and diamonds and carrying on her head a golden basket filled with jeweled fruit, was easily the most beautiful woman on the floor.

Clemens knew Wilhelmina was flattered to have the Austrian man of the hour consult her—this was part of his appeal for her—and he would have liked to discuss Prussia's incredible new proposal with her. Would Wilhelmina be as astounded as Clemens was at the Prussians' unheard-of asking price? The performance was almost over, and he was soon mingling with Dorothea and the others crowding forward to congratulate the dancers.

Dorothea met *l'oncle* later in the adjacent gallery as planned. They had arrived at the ball separately because the tsar had summoned him. When she found Talleyrand, he was playing whist with his customary partner, Empress Maria-Ludovica. The Austrian empress looked wanner than ever, and the game broke up when she got a bad coughing spell. *L'oncle,* with his niece on his arm, was dragging himself slowly into the large salon where the buffets and tables with seats for the ladies were located—the men stood at these affairs—when Talleyrand observed Castlereagh, the British foreign secretary, and excused himself to confer with His Lordship about his meeting with the tsar. Alexander had invited Talleyrand to come for a friendly talk—informally. But it was far from friendly. The tsar had accused Talleyrand of playing the minister of Louis XIV, the great Sun King, rather than the minister of Louis XVIII, a king who owed his throne to Alexander. And Alexander had refused to change his position.

The unending flow of guests streaming into the Ballhausplatz apartments for his regular Monday reception prevented Metternich from a private word with Wilhelmina. To see her leave on Alfred's arm chatting happily and smiling up into his face was unbearable. At the one moment when Metternich needed a clear mind, perfect composure, and complete self-confidence to face down Berlin and the tsar, Clemens was shattered by the thought of losing the woman he loved above any other. Instead of going to bed after the footmen lowered the great crystal chandeliers and snuffed out the candles, Metternich sat down dejectedly to write Wilhelmina. His ego refused to admit that she could prefer Alfred or that she might have deceived him. So Clemens rationalized his status and salvaged his pride by withdrawing. He claimed he did so to save Wilhelmina's honor: "I love *your honor* 100 times more than *your life.*" But Clemens could not break with her completely, and assuring Wilhelmina he would remain her friend forever, he left the door open for reconciliation. As he scrawled his signature, somewhere a clock chimed out what could be the hour, or a fraction of it. Metternich had lost track of time.

Raised as Grand Duke Peter's spoiled, pampered pet, Wilhelmina had never learned to resist temptation—or, as Clemens expressed it, to use willpower—and Windischgratz apparently had little trouble regaining her intimacy. Perhaps the secret of the dark, curly-haired officer's charm was the paradoxical way he radiated sheer animal magnetism and yet touched a maternal chord by remaining a small, overgrown boy for her, although admittedly he could never satisfy Wilhelmina's appetite for participation in the events of the day.

Wilhelmina bedded down as casually as others dined, and sleeping with Alfred did not mean she cared less for Clemens. But she could not ignore Windischgratz since he still wanted her too, and apparently he was a better bed-partner.

Tuesday, the eleventh, when the chancellor called with the letter of renunciation, Wilhelmina managed to take him aside to ask whether he might not broach the matter of her daughter's custody with the tsar now. His Imperial Majesty was so restless he would surely depart the instant the Polish-Saxon controversy was resolved. Their conversation was interrupted by the appearance of luncheon guests. Silently, Clemens handed Wilhelmina the envelope that was burning a hole in his heart and returned to the Ballhausplatz.

Before dusk, Wilhelmina sent word that as luck would have it, her legal adviser had just come from Prague. He was armed with the long-sought papers pertinent to Vava's custody and was accompanied by a trustworthy steward who was prepared to continue on to Saint Petersburg if necessary. Could Metternich find time to see them? So obsessed was Wilhelmina with Vava that she barely acknowledged Clemens's grief-stricken communication, and a subsequent note the following morning, would indicate she had not yet had time to more than glance at it.

Three additional days passed before Wilhelmina could bring herself to answer fully Clemens's heartbroken outpouring— point by point, as he requested. Yes, her feelings for Alfred were rekindled. Yes, she had broken her promise to Clemens. She could not help herself, she confessed, and the tear-spattered sheets attested to her inner turmoil. She hoped the chancellor would judge her with indulgence. After the congress was over, she was going to Ratiborzitz, alone, to try to sort out her feelings.

> Adieu, dear Clemens—pardon me for the wrong I do you.
> God knows it is despite myself and believe that nobody
> is more truly attached to you and devoted than I.

Her letter arrived on Saturday, while Clemens was still at breakfast. Although Metternich spent most of the day in an extensive reevaluation of the Polish-Saxon problem, his mind wandered repeatedly to the duchess of Sagan. Frequently he would break off in the middle of a sentence to ask Gentz, in a worried tone, "What is happening to the Duchess and me?" Each time the chevalier disconsolately fished out his snuffbox, took a pinch, sneezed, pulled his heavily perfumed lace handkerchief from his sleeve, wiped his nose, then his dark glasses, and settled back to listen to still another analysis of the chancellor's disintegrating love affair. When Metternich assigned him to work out the details of the Courland steward's proposed trip to Russia, the crusty redheaded chevalier was indignant. How could so much of the chancellor's valuable time, not to mention his own—as secretary to the Congress of Vienna, Gentz was the most important second-string man present— be wasted on personal trivia? But there was always a chance,

Clemens kept telling himself, that Vava's return to Wilhelmina's arms might bring Wilhelmina back to his.

Later, at the conclusion of yet another fruitless parley with the tsar about Eastern Europe, Metternich raised the question of Wilhelmina's daughter. Then he hurried to the Palm palace to report that Alexander would not stand in the way of Vava's return to Wilhelmina. However, the tsar felt the girl's wishes should be respected, and the last time His Imperial Majesty had seen her, she preferred to remain with her foster mother. So Metternich felt it imperative that Wilhelmina's steward go east, as planned, and talk directly to Vava.

That same Saturday afternoon when Dorothea returned from a long ride in the Prater, which was sweet with the odor of decaying leaves and noisy with the waltzes played by countless little bands, a message awaited that *l'oncle* wanted to see her as soon as she came in. Gentz had been complaining to Talleyrand of Metternich's lack of leadership and confided that the chancellor was so upset over a threatened rupture with Wilhelmina that he was paying more attention to the duchess of Sagan than to Austria's reply to the Prussian-Russian demands. Talleyrand had good reason to believe the chevalier. For last night, when he tried to talk to Metternich about the need to preserve Saxony, the chancellor was so engrossed in showing Wilhelmina some engravings she had requested him to bring—in order to help her choose a costume for the Metternichs' forthcoming masked ball—that Talleyrand could not squeeze in a word. Talleyrand was very disturbed. How could the chancellor contemplate handing Prussia on a silver platter the eventual means to challenge Austrian hegemony among the German states? Farsighted Talleyrand was even more concerned about an enlarged Prussia as a future threat to European stability than he was worried about a kingdom of Poland—a Russian toehold in Western Europe—under the tsar's thumb. Therefore, Talleyrand had asked Wilhelmina, at noon, if she might arrange a family dinner with Metternich, and *l'oncle* and his niece were expected shortly at the Palm palace to dine.

On Tuesday of the following week, October 18, the first anniversary of the Battle of Leipzig was celebrated by a great parade and festival in the Prater to honor the military and by the Metter-nichs' ball. In response to Wilhelmina's request that she be at one of the supper tables facing that of the sovereigns, Clemens sent her a plan for the seating arrangements and told her to mark the table she desired. He also enclosed the extra tickets she had asked for; with 1,500 guests, 3 more could not make any difference, and Wilhelmina wanted to fetch her daughters from Mme. de Brévil-lier's Institute for Aristocratic Ladies. They were old enough to witness the spectacle.

There was so great a crush that the twenty-minute drive to Rennwegg took almost two hours, and when Wilhelmina was helped out of her carriage the chancellor, his wife, and the leading officials of the Austrian court were already assembled under a canopy decorated to resemble a tent to greet the honored guests. Quickly mounting the steps, Wilhelmina noticed the buttons and braid she had bought for Clemens in London on the new livery of the jägers.

A balloon arising from the drive released fireworks, forming the arms of the tsar, the Prussian king, and Emperor Franz, to open the fête. Strolling through the extensive grounds, which were beauti-fully illuminated with the great pots of fire that the Turks call *machal,* Wilhelmina watched a ballet in the sunken gardens, listened to a choral group in an arbor of late-blooming roses, and saw a tableau vivant before a Temple of Minerva. Then a pic-turesque line of dancers—Wilhelmina and the other women who had been requested to appear in the symbolic colors of peace, blue and white, with olive or oak leaves in their hair, to match the eve-ning's decor—christened the sumptuous new ballroom, twining round the great circle of pillars in the inevitable opening polonaise.

Congress affairs were never far from the statesmen's minds, and Wilhelmina noticed the tsar steer the Prussian chancellor into a back salon, later, for a private discussion. She was watching Talleyrand and the consumptive, waxen-faced empress, Maria-Ludovica—her matchstick-thin arms so heavily weighted down with Hapsburg jewels that she could hardly lift them—playing whist, when Alex-ander reappeared and encountered Clemens talking with several ministers. "You diplomats make decisions and then we soldiers have to let ourselves be shot into cripples for you," he fired at the startled Austrian chancellor. Wheeling abruptly, the tsar encoun-tered Wilhelmina and added, loudly, in a withering tone, "I find it demeaning, Madame, for a duchess to be seen with a scrivener." Alexander's angry remarks were overheard by many, as His Imperial Majesty intended them to be, and greatly upset Wilhelmina. If Alexander felt that bitter toward Clemens, was the chancellor the best person to have intercede for her daughter? Could someone else do better?

Sometime during the next forty-eight hours, while Metternich, with his final reply to Prussia still hanging fire, found time to meet with Gentz and Wilhelmina's Prague counsellor to discuss her steward's forthcoming departure, Wilhelmina decided on a different approach. She must appeal to Alexander herself. Then and there. For time was growing short.

Wilhelmina was dressed in red—her favorite color—at Thursday's ball in honor of the tsar and tsarina. The elaborate gown was one of her new Leroy creations that Clemens had helped her select, and she wore no jewels except a large pear-shaped emerald, a Biron family heirloom which Mellerio, the French imperial jeweler, had reset to dangle from a delicate golden circlet on her forehead. Wilhelmina was in the main salon talking to Metternich and several others when she saw Alexander approach. Seizing the opportunity, she turned and made a deep curtsey. "Sire, will you grant me an audience? I have a favor to ask."

"My dear Wilhelmina." Alexander took her by the hand and raised her to her feet. "There can be no talk of an audience between us. I will visit you. Only name the day and the hour. Shall it be tomorrow, at 11:00 A.M.?" Clemens, who was at Wilhelmina's elbow, paled. Nothing could have wounded him more than to hear Wilhelmina ask a favor of his adversary. And to make matters worse, Alexander, who was well briefed by the princess Bagration concerning the chancellor's habits, specified the very hour which Metternich still thought of as "his." His heart lacerated, the chancellor silently turned on his heel and immediately ordered his carriage. Wilhelmina knew she had committed an unforgivable sin in Clemens's eyes—a personal betrayal—but she had had no alternative. And, no doubt, she was too relieved by Alexander's cordial response to think twice about the time selected.

Friday dawned chilly and damp, but the porcelain stove in Wilhelmina's salon gave off a cheerful warmth, and the table for two was set close by. Moreau, the Empress Maria-Ludovica's favorite French decorator, had hung the walls throughout the duchess of Sagan's suites with pale silk damask to provide a suitable ambiance for her lush blonde beauty. The muted color scheme served as an admirable foil for the fine old Turkish pottery from Iznik, which was displayed in a large cabinet and came closer to Western tastes with its broad design and somewhat gaudy colors than many other items her father, Grand Duke Peter, had collected. While one footman frothed and poured the strong Spanish chocolate, another passed hot, freshly baked *Blätterteig, Kaffeeküchen,* and high-crowned *Kugelhopf.*

Alexander helped himself, then piled *schläg* generously on his steaming cup. He was at his charming best and promised to meet Vava the minute he got back and see what could be arranged. They also discussed Maman's continuing financial embarrassment, and Alexander vowed to attend to that at once. Alexander had promised the same thing to Anna in Paris and had promptly forgotten about it. This time the tsar promised to send Nesselrode, his foreign minister, around for details. Then he was gone.

Wilhelmina slipped a wool cloak with a hood over her flowered *sacque* and hastened to brief her sisters; she also sent the chancellor a few lines relating Alexander's promises. Gossip would quickly concoct more versions of her two-and-a-half-hour tête-à-tête than there were days in the week, but even His Apostolic Imperial Majesty's ubiquitous secret police never—either then or later— uncovered the secret of Wilhelmina's illegitimate daughter.

Metternich postponed crossing the Rubicon for a full day, and it was not until Saturday morning that he sent Wilhelmina the soul-searching pages he had written in the wee hours, upon leaving her so abruptly. This letter shut the door his earlier one had left open:

> You have brought me more pain than the whole universe could ever repay me for. . . . You have compromised my existence at a moment when the future of my life is bound up with questions that decide the future of whole generations —*mon amie,* I forgive you everything. . . . I shall pronounce my own sentence. Our relationship no longer exists.

Wilhelmina was not surprised. Perhaps it was better this way. Perhaps Clemens was right and she lacked the willpower to relinquish Alfred. Perhaps, if she had been able to keep her promises and not seen Alfred again, she would have been able to love Clemens the way he wanted her to. Perhaps . . .

When Clemens met Wilhelmina at a ball that same evening, he asked whether she had received his letter. She nodded. Had she read it? She had. All of it? She had. When might he expect a reply? If he was to live with himself, Clemens must know where he had failed.

Wilhelmina was so upset by Clemens's remarks that this time, it was she who left the ball precipitately. Faithful Hännchen was waiting up, as always, to undress her, but instead of going to bed, Wilhelmina put on her robe, walked into the salon, and, pushing up her frayed-at-the-elbow sleeves, sat down at the great Riesner desk her father had bought. As she did so, she was phsyically reminded of Clemens. He had purchased the now faded robe for her in some town along the path of the Allies' victorious march west and taken great pains to select one made of fabric that would age quickly. Clemens knew that Wilhelmina preferred comfortable, well-worn clothes about the house, and he wished her to use it often. He had wanted the things he gave Wilhelmina to become an intimate part of her life, the way he hoped to be.

Hännchen silently replaced the dwindling candle stubs more than once before she retired, leaving Wilhelmina still there, the only sounds in the Palm palace those of her scratching quill. It is indicative that Wilhelmina, who rarely bothered to date her letters, did so now: "The night of October 22–23." She too was writing finis, at last. Wilhelmina was vexed at Clemens's constant interrogation, for she had already written a detailed reply to his previous agonized letter. Since he was still not satisfied, she was answering him, once and for all, reviewing their relationship from the beginning.

Wilhelmina was sorry she had not been able to love Clemens as deeply as he wanted:

> In marriage, friendship supported by duty is doubtless
> enough. In a liaison, one must find something to silence
> duty. I did all in my power. . . . But beyond the enthusiasm
> of friendship all remained calm within me. Even this
> misfortune could have been met—if instead of so much
> passion, I had found in you more art.

As she wrote, Wilhelmina's mood softened, and she concluded on a tender note:

> My dear Clemens, may God protect you—I should have been too happy, perhaps, if I might have been the means by which He repaid you for so many virtues and so much grief. . . . Please let your best friend tell you how much she cherishes you!

The moment was ill chosen for a woman who craved being center stage in the world of power politics to make an irrevocable break with Metternich. As Austrian chancellor and president of the Congress of Vienna, he alone could offer Wilhelmina so much backstage involvement in the affairs of the day and an opportunity to influence them in the only way possible for her—indirectly. Obviously, something else had assumed more importance. What? As some of her correspondence of the period shows, and in the light of subsequent events in her life, Wilhelmina was apparently tired of being a woman alone. And she knew Clemens would never marry her.

That may have been reason enough to break with Metternich. But why, after more than four years of an on-again-off-again liaison with Alfred, did she pick up the traces with him at this point? Had he that much renewed appeal? Or, as one biographer suggests, had the young prince—and also Wilhelmina's sisters, who had known Alfred before Wilhelmina did and were friendly with his family—intimated there was finally the possibility of a Windischgratz marriage? There is no way of knowing.

Saturday, when the chancellor sent Wilhelmina his final letter, was also the day he drafted a reply to Prussia's outrageous asking price for support against the tsar in the Saxon-Polish impasse. Metternich had been brooding over his memorandum, which has been called one of the most critical of the entire congress, for almost two weeks, his concentration unquestionably shattered by his rupture with the duchess of Sagan. Ignoring instinct and disavowing the crème's opinion, which was slowly crystallizing in the opposite direction, the chancellor finally sided with Britain and agreed to the sacrifice of Saxony—with certain important stipulations.

On Sunday, the tsar restated his position to Talleyrand and the British foreign secretary. He would not budge from his original stance.

On Monday morning, it was Metternich's turn with the tsar. In a stormy two-hour session, Alexander lost his self-control and so violently abused the chancellor that Metternich expected to be tossed bodily out of the window.

Guests at the Metternichs' regular Monday soirée were shocked at their host's appearance—there were deep circles under his blue eyes and he had trouble stifling yawns—and came up with their own answers. Word of Clemens's definitive break with Wilhelmina had already seeped out. Recalling his tumultuous discussion with the tsar, earlier in the day, and Wilhelmina's previous tête-à-tête with Alexander, they were convinced that they were witnessing cause and effect, and that the duchess of Sagan had become the tsar's mistress. Clemens himself wondered whether Alexander might have demanded as a quid pro quo that Wilhelmina break with him in exchange for assistance with Vava. He must know. But when Metternich tried to have a few words alone with Wilhelmina, she refused.

They met at the Palm palace the next morning instead, at his request, and Wilhelmina set his mind at ease. No strings were attached to the tsar's offer of help. She had seen to that.

Wilhelmina counted on Clemens's friendship, she reminded him in a follow-up billet. She had always been Clemens's friend. She still was—his best friend.

My heart remains completely the same towards you—while all is changed in you, nothing is in me.

In the weeks ahead, the only other topic dominating the salons as much as the burning issue of Poland and Saxony was the forthcoming carrousel at the Spanish Riding School. A nostalgic glance at the age of chivalry, this was to be, literally, the fête to end all fêtes, for with Advent approaching, it was the last great social event scheduled for the year. Echoing the old prince de Ligne's latest bon mot, "The congress dances, but it does not march," most of the delegates sincerely hoped that a stop in the frolicking might finally enable them to convene.

The carrousel participants were from the elite of Hungary, Bohemia, and Austria, with the single exception of the two Courland sisters. Wilhelmina took it as her due to be selected. But Dorothea was not yet spoiled by adulation, and she was ecstatic. Weeks of preparation were required, and the rehearsals were half the fun. Talleyrand wrote Anna what a great coup it was for the French embassy to have Dorothea chosen and asked her to please see that the official *Moniteur* carried an account of this brilliant affair.

The night of the spectacle, the regular Hungarian palace guards, resplendent in their tiger-skin calpacks, were reinforced by special squadrons of mounted police, but they were still inadequate to hold back the curious throngs who gathered, well ahead of time, in spite of the cold, to catch a glimpse of the guests as they were handed out of their carriages in front of the Spanish Riding School. The mirrored galleries of the immense, baroque parallelogram, built by Fischer von Erlach for Charles V, were a rippling river of light, reflecting thousands of shimmering candles, with one of the two long sides reserved for the Austrian-Hungarian nobility, the other for foreign dignitaries and the top echelon of the military. The chief of protocol, with an eye for decorative value, seated the prettiest and most elegant women in the first rows directly behind the red velours-draped balustrades. In back of their plunging, jeweled and flower-bedecked bodices surged a sea of gold-and-diamond-studded dress uniforms, wtih a cardinal's scarlet robes, a pasha's turban, and the multicolored caftan of an African leader supplying unexpected accents.

Promptly at 8:00 P.M., amid a rustle of anticipation and the murmur of fans, heralds-at-arms sounded a fanfare of trumpets. The orchestra, which contained every musician of note in Vienna, burst into festive seventeenth-century music, and Dorothea, Wilhelmina, and the rest of the queens of love entered. Veiled from head to foot, they circled the huge arena before being seated at the far end. When a second trumpet flourish announced the sovereigns' appearance, opposite them, the queens rose in greeting. Throwing back their veils in unison, the stars of the evening revealed their identity in a blinding blaze of color, covered, as they were, with rubies, emeralds, sapphires, and diamonds. The young women had commandeered every precious stone to be found in Central Europe, including some that had not seen the light of day in decades, and it would be a miracle if every piece was returned to its rightful owner intact afterwards.

The carrousel was on. Mounted on superbly harnessed black Hungarian horses, Dorothea's paladin, a count who was the son of the Lord Grand Master of the Horse, and Wilhelmina's—Prince Windischgratz—and the others trotted in, wearing scarves given them for good luck by their respective queens. Talleyrand must have chuckled when he observed the poppy-red foulard sprinkled with masses of golden fleurs-de-lis—the Bourbon emblem—fluttering around the arm piece of his niece's gallant, the son of one of the highest Hapsburg officials: subtle propaganda for an eventual Austrian-French accord. The paladins held long lances propped against one knee and were preceded by pages deploying their personal banners; equerries followed carrying their tilting shields.

Fine horsemanship was still among the most admired of skills, and Dorothea, who like the rest of her family was a fine rider, was thrilled at the dazzling display. Sawdust flew and chairs shook as the knights, galloping full speed, speared rings strung from the ceiling with their lances, threw javelins at turbaned Turks' heads suspended on posts, cut apples hanging on ribbons loose and split them in midair with their scimitars. The grand finale was an exhibition of dressage, the medieval army maneuvers for which the imperial Lippizaner horses were famous.

At the banquet that followed in the Hofburg proper, the participants sat at a table of honor to the right of the crowned heads' dais. Strolling minstrels, singing lays of courtly love, entertained until it was time to open the ball with the much-talked-about, much-rehearsed quadrille. The forty-eight performers were divided into four units of twelve, and each group wore identical authentic seventeenth-century costumes of the particular country they represented. Wilhelmina and Alfred were in green, as were the others in Austrian attire; red was the Polish color; and blue the Hungarian. Dorothea and her paladin were in black for the French group. Dorothea's partner had a waist-hugging black velvet tunic decorated with multiple buttons and frogs and with wide, satin-trimmed sleeves; his tight-fitting trousers were encased in half-length yellow riding boots with gilded spurs. Gold-embroidered gauntlets were in matching black velvet, as was his broad-rimmed hat, wide peaked in front, with a big diamond buckle. Dorothea's costume mirrored his. Her enormous black velvet skirt was held open in front with ruby and diamond clips to disclose an underskirt of white satin; a bodice of the same peeked through the slashed sleeves of her long black tunic, and her small black toque was paved with diamonds. The elaborate steps executed were patterned after those performed to Lully's music.

When Dorothea hastened up, her pale face flushed with excitement, to get *l'oncle*'s approval of her performance, the elderly prince de Ligne was standing talking to him. "Tell me, Madame," the witty patriarch said as he glanced mischievously at her. "Does M. de Talleyrand still dazzle with the same conversational pearls he has always strewn about?"

"As long as they are pearls, I don't care," Dorothea deftly countered—and the secret police duly recorded.

The carrousel's resounding success—it would be repeated twice to overflow audiences—was another triumph in Talleyrand's campaign to sell France as the cultural center of the universe, and amply justified his insistence that the artist Isabey accompany him to Vienna. For *l'oncle* had arranged to have the famous painter appointed its artistic coordinator.

As winter tightened its grip, France's position as an outcast was further ameliorated by Talleyrand's strong stand on behalf of the old Saxon king. The crème was noticeably friendlier as its members switched to concur with *l'oncle*—not Metternich—in the ever-changing behind-the-scenes shifts of stance occasioned by this ongoing dispute. For Talleyrand's main concern was to avoid an enlarged Prussia, which he saw as a grave threat to the Continental balance of power, whereas Metternich's position was colored and compounded by his need to resolve the Polish question.

No longer was the Kaunitz palace filled with solely delegates of the small powers and unimportant, lower-rung Austrian officials. The best indication that the corner of acceptance had been turned was when Gentz admitted, publicly, to having eaten two meals the same evening. Talleyrand's invitation came too late to decline a previous one, but since Talleyrand dined earlier than others in Vienna, the chevalier was able to accept both—with the help of a digestive powder. For where else in the Austrian capital could one eat like a god and have the best conversation this side of Paris?

The disposition of Talleyrand's chef, Carême, brightened proportionately, although he had not yet had any crowned heads to taste the gastronomical miracles he was performing with the fresh Danube fish, hard firm apples, and other seasonal delicacies available—or to immortalize with a special dish or sauce. Anyone listening to Talleyrand and his Maître daily analyze the evening's forthcoming repast might be excused for thinking the famous chef had missed a second calling. He was a born diplomat. The popularity of the delegates, and the progress of the congress's negotiations, could be measured—from Carême's point of view—by the absence or presence, and relative position, on the dinner menu of the culinary chefs d'oeuvre honoring each one. Carême would no longer consider serving "Nesselrode Pudding," which had been dedicated to the Russian foreign minister, or "Charlotte Russe," with its molded exterior of lady fingers, two sublime concoctions that the great chef had created when the tsar was a guest at the hôtel Saint Florentin and the French-Russian honeymoon was in full force. Here in Vienna, the dish might be the same with perhaps a subtle variation of the sauce, but it would bear a good Austrian name, like "Bombe à la Metternich," or "Clam-Martinitz Torte." For Carême was not above playing cupid, and like the rest of the legation household, he knew of Dorothea's love for the dashing Count Karl Clam-Martinitz.

Dorothea's former fiancé, Czartoryski, had arrived in Vienna at almost the same time as she did. Since the Poles, as a nation, persistently raised their heads after being trod upon, Prince Adam's influence—he was once again the tsar's chief Polish adviser—could not be underestimated. Consequently, Dorothea had promptly invited him to call so that *l'oncle* might talk to him informally, without raising suspicions about what "old Talley" was up to. Because the pair had not seen each other since Prince Adam was in Mitau at the time of the Tilsit conference—the only occasion, in fact, they were ever together—it is a fair assumption that they made some kind of accounting about the past. Dorothea's reaction when she discovered how Maman had tricked her into marrying Edmond and her amazement upon learning that Czartoryski was not—and never had been—engaged can be imagined. Still, it was little use to recall the shattered dreams of yesteryear or to realize that, but for Maman, she would now be the princess Czartoryska. The whole focus of Dorothea's existence had changed. Today, her one aim was to serve *l'oncle*, and he was opposed to the reconstruction of the Polish kingdom, the cause to which Prince Adam had devoted his life. (Adam would eventually marry the young cousin his mother had been grooming as his bride.)

Unquestionably the revelation, on top of the bruises inflicted by her unhappy marriage and by the tragic death of her little girl, would have supplied additional stimulus for Dorothea to snatch from life what could be had for the taking. In a Vienna honeycombed with amatory intrigue, with the example of her three sisters in front of her nose, it was only surprising she had not taken a lover sooner. For, as worldly-wise Talleyrand suspected, among the forget-me-nots and roses nestled sensuality.

It was Gentz, with his matchmaker's soul, who introduced Dorothea to Count Karl, the handsome scion of a powerful Bohemian family. His mother was a good friend of Wilhelmina's; he was the favorite aide-de-camp of the commander in chief of the Austrian forces and was posted to serve on the tsar's guard of honor at the congress. Clam-Martinitz also boasted the most rakish sideburns Dorothea had ever seen, a magnificent dark brown set that stretched across his face almost to his nostrils. The count had seen and admired Dorothea's performance in the carrousel, and he decided that to possess the elegant Comtesse Edmond de Talleyrand-Périgord, whose father had been an ex-ruler, maecenas, and crack shot and whose mother was an international beauty and grande dame, could only add luster to a career that was most distinguished for a young soldier only a year Dorothea's senior.

Count Karl courted Dorothea with the same vigor and determination that had already made his name in the military. Ambition quickly yielded to love, and he haunted the Kaunitz. *L'oncle* might comment, cynically, that "love is a reality in the realm of the imagination," but for Dorothea, it belonged very much to the here and now. And she succumbed to his ardent assault.

Her every wish was his command. Dorothea had promised Talleyrand's dog, Carlos, a romp? Count Karl bundled Dorothea, warmly wrapped in a long squirrel-lined hood and cape, and the King Charles spaniel into his little cabriolet and took them out to a deserted meadow in the great Prater Park, where the dog spent an intoxicating afternoon chasing the startled deer through the snow-flecked fields and woods. Dorothea wanted to visit Isabey's studio near the Café Jüngling in the Leopoldstadt? Count Karl took her across the Danube Canal to his atelier, its walls already plastered with preliminary sketches for portraits of the congress notables. Dorothea desired some local food? Clam took her to the famous Kaiserin von Osterreich for noodle soup, schnitzel, and *gespritzten*—or for a Viennese breakfast of boiled beef and *marillen knödel* at popular Papperl's. And paid the magic-lantern vendor they passed, trudging along the Johannesgasse, to unstrap the machine he was carrying on his back and set it up so that Dorothea, standing on tiptoe, could peer in and see the show.

Swept off her feet by the high-spirited officer, Dorothea's inhibitions were discarded like winter clothing at the coming of spring. A passionate new Dorothea emerged, surrendering to life with a greater abandon because her emotions had so long lain dormant. Once she, too, had a lover, she felt more at ease with her older sisters, and the pair frequently rounded out intimate dinners in Wilhelmina's cheerful, flower-filled dining room at number 54 on the Schenkenstrasse. Paulina still had her field marshal and Joanna, a stocky Dutch mynheer who flung himself from one comfortable chair to another "with the abandon of a discarded mask from last night's ball"—as some insensitive soul graphically described him. Joanna was trying to wheedle the Austrian chancellor's help for her *ami,* who wanted the Dutch embassy in Vienna but had little to recommend him for his country's most important post other than the newly acquired ability to clamp a monocle firmly in his right eye.

Wilhelmina was usually attended by either Windischgratz or Lord Stewart, the English ambassador to Vienna, who had been a serious admirer since the Prague days. Should these two be out of town—or out of favor—Gentz, who was carrying on a wild, but platonic, flirtation with Joanna, was happy to fill in.

The congress still had not opened and continued to play. Because Alexander was laid low for almost two weeks—too much night life and running after women was the Austrian secret police's diagnosis—the Saxon-Polish question hung suspended over the delegates' heads, frozen in midair, like Dorothea's breath those crisp mornings when she and Count Karl joined other fashionables for a canter in the Prater. Advantage was taken of several unexpected days of good weather to schedule additional hunts, for many of the titled guests were avid sportsmen. Wilhelmina gave her annual servants' ball, and Dorothea and their friends peeked from behind a curtained gallery on their maids, seamstresses, and lackeys frolicking below.

At a children's party given by Princess Maria Esterhazy, which Dorothea attended with Wilhelmina and her three foster daughters, Katya Bagration had illegitimate Clementine in tow, and Clemens's wife appeared with the youngest Metternich. Even there, protocol raised its troublesome head, and one of the tiny highnesses threw a temper tantrum because a pretty playmate of lesser rank was asked to lead the opening polonaise with the tsar. When Alexander, fresh from his sickbed, gallantly rectified the situation by dancing with the offended child—then with every other little girl present—Dorothea was afraid he might have a relapse. That was the first day the imperial physicians had allowed their patient out, and she hurried home to report to Talleyrand that His Imperial Majesty seemed hale and hearty once more. This was important news, for it meant the Polish-Saxon negotiations could resume, and should be included in the evening's dispatch, which *l'oncle* was waiting to finish with Dorothea.

What had started as an occasional exercise—Dorothea's copying certain pages for *l'oncle* for the sake of secrecy, because Talleyrand hated writing lengthy letters personally—had become routine. *L'oncle* did his entire correspondence to Louis XVIII with his niece, and he counted on these frequent sessions with her to turn the rough draft, prepared for him from his notes, into a finished report. Since His Most Christian Majesty prided himself on being a man of letters, Talleyrand took pains to prove himself a master of the French language, and warmly wrapped in a purple velvet dressing gown lined in sable, he limped slowly to and fro, dragging his bad right foot across the Aubusson rug and the parquet, across the parquet and the Aubusson rug, reading, then rereading the amended, amplified sheets. The only other sound was the clock ticking away in the belly of a small bronze Venus atop the desk's elaborate mahogany-and-ormolu *cartonnier*. Not until they had "fought the battle of words," as *l'oncle* expressed it—after each sentence was weighed, rejected, replaced, each phrase and nuance carefully adjusted—was his niece able to lay down her quill, snap the inkwell shut, and rush off to the Hofburg for the opening of the empress's tableaux vivants, Maria-Ludovica's favorite form of entertainment.

The present series, depicting paintings by contemporary artists then on exhibit in Vienna, was intended as a diversion for Advent, when the official tempo of entertainment of necessity slackened and was more subdued. Wilhelmina starred as Marie of Burgundy, wearing Clemens's Golden Fleece, a decoration she had borrowed for the occasion, though Metternich had sent her as an alternative a fifteenth-century chain and crucifix which, he pointed out, would be more authentic, since a woman could never be awarded the Golden Fleece. Dorothea had only a supporting role, but *l'oncle* proudly wrote the grand duchess:

> Dorothea is proving herself an actress. She plays as well as Mlle. Mars in one of her best nights at the Comédie. In fact, Dorothea does well anything she tries.
>
> After the performance when the music started, the prince de Ligne complained that to waltz in formal attire seemed inappropriate. He regretted the elegance of the old-fashioned minuet and, when he discovered that some of the younger generation present had never seen it danced, he selected Dorothea as his partner and led her through the stately measures of my youth.

A short time later, the Prince de Ligne caught a chill while awaiting a rendezvous with a tardy young thing on the ramparts and died—not long before his eightieth birthday. Since every other form of entertainment had been exhausted, the prince, with characteristic thoughtfulness, chose to break the monotony with the great spectacle of a field marshal's funeral.

The *London Morning Chronicle* was telling the truth when its Austrian correspondent reported:

> We learn from high sources a project is made,
> How Vienna's grand Congress the Christmas will spend,
> Since public affairs have so long been delayed,
> They may very well wait til the holidays end.

Dorothea suggested to *l'oncle* that they celebrate the festive days ahead as she had growing up in Berlin. Several long consultations were held with the majordomo, and soon the smell of marzipan and butter cookies mingled with the heady fragrance of pine emanating from the public rooms and *l'oncle*'s study, which were gaily decorated with boughs, swags, and bow-tied wreaths. Count Karl took Dorothea out into the countryside to the foot of the Köhlenberg, where they searched among the snow-tipped evergreens on its slopes for two that she judged to be the right size and shape for the spacious main entrance hall and her little sitting room. Because this was the first year Vienna had ever seen Christmas trees, she supervised when the bigger one was hauled in and placed under the curving ceremonial staircase, and oversaw festooning it with multicolored garlands and lit candles.

Christmas Eve, Dorothea and *l'oncle* gave a large party for the embassy and household staffs that concluded with singing merrymakers gathering under the great fir, where Dorothea handed each one a brightly wrapped package from its spreading branches. Continuing to celebrate in the German fashion—in France, gifts were exchanged on New Year's Day instead—Dorothea gave *l'oncle* her present as soon as they were alone. She knew how often Talleyrand consulted the time when a conference proved long and tedious, so she had ordered a Bréguet watch from Paris and had Isabey place inside it a miniature of his newest portrait of her. Now, when *l'oncle* opened his watch, he would discover Dorothea smiling out at him. In exchange, Talleyrand gave his niece a cashmere shawl, as delicate in color and design and as large and fine as any in Marie-Louise's extensive former collection at the Tuileries. There were also two fragile Meissen pieces, *The Fish-Woman* and *The Song-Merchant,* to add to her growing series of small porcelain replicas of eighteenth-century Parisian street vendors.

As dawn was breaking, less than a week afterwards, Talleyrand was awakened by the alarm drum of Vienna's fire squad. He had rolled over to go back to sleep, when his faithful valet hurried in. The superb palace of Count Andreas Razumovsky, the Russian ambassador, which was one of the capital's most sumptuous and had taken twenty years to complete, was ablaze, and Dorothea, who had gone there to a soirée with Count Karl, had not yet returned. In no time, Talleyrand was dressed and hastening in a light phaeton through the narrow streets which were already jammed with sleepy curiosity seekers and late revelers magnetized by the great glowing light on the horizon. Progress was agonizingly slow, affording Talleyrand ample time to relive the catastrophic conflagration at the Austrian embassy gala for the newlywed Napoleon and Marie-Louise years before, in which he and Anna had been trapped and scores of Paris society had perished tragically. *L'oncle* would never forgive himself if something happened to Dorothea.

By the time he arrived, the stately residence on the Landstrasse had been fanned by a strong wind into an incandescent volcano, belching sparks in every direction. The fire, which had started in the pipes laid in the floors and walls—a modern heating system that was the wonder and envy of Vienna—was raging out of control, and everything possible was being tossed indiscriminately out the windows—the count's breeches and shirts along with his incomparable collections, which he had spent a lifetime amassing. Masterpieces of oil painting—works by Titian, Raphael, Rubens, Van Dyck, Corregio, Claude Lorrain—priceless medieval and Byzantine manuscripts, the finest classical sculpture spewed forth, only to disappear in the deep mire created by the water, melting snow, and milling crowds or to be greedily snatched by pilferers. The city's number-one fire buff, Emperor Franz, a sable cloak thrown hastily over his nightshirt, a cap of velours jammed down on his tousled head, arrived and, taking a quick professional look, ordered out several infantry battalions to help. Even the tsar appeared. But where was Dorothea?

The great central copper roof, glowing a fiery red, tore apart with a thunderous roar, and in the unearthly glare cast as the flames shot skyward, *l'oncle* finally located his niece, watching the spectacle from a safe distance with Count Karl and other friends. He reached her side just as there was an earsplitting crash and still another ceiling collapsed in a shower of sparks. "That's the gallery that held the Dutch genre paintings! I sat in it for supper," Dorothea exclaimed, shuddering. Was it then, when he discovered how near he had come to losing her, that *l'oncle* realized for the first time how very important in a special way his niece was becoming for him?

The sun was high in the sky before Dorothea's head touched a pillow, but she was still able to go with Clam to the Palm palace for dinner that Saint Sylvester's Eve. Later that evening, before she left Wilhelmina's to continue on elsewhere, her sister took her aside to show her the handsome chased-gold bracelet that a jeweler's apprentice had delivered, according to Clemens's instructions, precisely on the stroke of midnight, when Wilhelmina and her guests were toasting each other with champagne. It was inlaid with four large gems. The diamond represented love; the emerald was Metternich's birthstone; the amethyst, Wilhelmina's; the ruby stood for fidelity. There was also a *G* engraved on the back of each stone and, on the reverse of the bracelet, a *15*—for the year about to start.

What Dorothea did not see was Clemens's accompanying billet:

> —11 P.M. December 31st
> I designed this gift for you last fall. . . . The "G" signifies
> the words I had hoped to say as I fastened it on your wrist
> this evening—*Gott gebe Gnade, Glück, Gedeihen* [God give
> you grace, happiness, prosperity].

He went on to request that if Wilhelmina chose not to wear his bracelet—and, he emphasized, wear it always—she was to return it. Poor Clemens. How much easier it would have been if he and Wilhelmina could have made a clean break once they decided to go their separate ways. This, of course, was an impossibility as they ran into each other almost daily. Although Metternich was not yet completely cured, the bitterest moments when he seemed tormented, silent, and withdrawn were now a thing of the past. Gentz's *Journal* noted that the chancellor was once more in control of himself and reasserting his leadership. Nevertheless, Metternich's relationship with the tsar was worse than ever. On December 11, Metternich and the tsar had had their most explosive encounter. After Metternich as good as called the tsar a liar, and Alexander declared his intention to challenge the chancellor to a duel, Emperor Franz had had to step in. Alexander refused to deal any more with the chancellor, and now, whenever their paths crossed, he looked straight through Metternich as if he did not exist. Princess Katya Bagration and others in the Russian camp were instructed to entertain on Mondays, so Alexander would have an excuse not to appear at the Metternichs' weekly receptions, and the tsar had doubled his efforts to outshine the chancellor socially.

By the the time Dorothea and Clam arrived at their Saint Sylvester's Eve Ball, the orchestra had stopped tuning up and was starting to play. The tsar led off the polonaise, and the two latecomers joined the long line that was soon undulating through the various drawing rooms and halls into the distant cardroom where Talleyrand was. *L'oncle* looked up, annoyed at the disturbance. The whist players were tucked too far away for the music to be audible, and only mischievousness could cause the tsar to snake through there. Or imperial displeasure at the growing rapprochement between Talleyrand and Metternich and at the way Talleyrand, too, was doing his best to thwart Alexander's Polish plans.

Talleyrand finally got up from the card table, and the British foreign secretary took him aside to complain about the Prussian chancellor's threat of war if Berlin's Saxon demands were not unequivocally granted. When Milord angrily declared that England had no intention of being dictated to, Talleyrand, who had been awaiting this moment for a long time—he had always favored a British as well as an Austrian alliance—soothingly suggested a defensive pact between France, Austria, and Britain.

"Why not," the British diplomat replied, "since we three agree on the rights of the Saxon king."

A secret tripartite agreement—each was to come to the aid of the other if attacked—was finalized in a matter of days. By skillfully exploiting the discord provoked by the exorbitant claims of Prussia and Russia, Talleyrand had broken the coalition originally formed against France, and, like a magician, transformed the pariah into a member in good standing of this new alliance formed to defend the balance of power in a free, stable Europe.

Diplomats are flesh and blood, too. And it is permissible to think that the culminating crisis of the chancellor's tension-fraught love affair with the duchess af Sagan the end of October and early November was a blessing in disguise for Talleyrand. Coming at that particular moment, when Metternich needed full control of his faculties and powers of concentration, their breakup must have affected his decisions. Aside from the blow to his self-esteem, his physical exhaustion after round after round of meetings followed by sleepless nights spent writing Wilhelmina long probing letters could not have helped but impair Metternich's powers of perception. There seems little other explanation for what he did.

The Prussian chancellor's ultimatum was the watershed. Had Metternich rejected it out of hand and insisted, then and there, on the preservation of some part of Saxony, the impasse of the congress would have been broken weeks before. Instead, by prolonging the stalemate, one of the gravest errors of judgment he ever made, Metternich handed Talleyrand a golden opportunity: the time and the wedge with which to manipulate this secret tripartite agreement.

The evening of January 3, after the covenant had been initialed, Dorothea helped *l'oncle,* as usual, write the dispatch describing his diplomatic breakthrough. If Talleyrand did not order the footman, who came in to lower the chandelier and snuff out its candles, to bring champagne instead of his usual madeira, he should have. For surely a private celebration was in order. It was ironic that it should be Wilhelmina, the great Francophobe of the Courland family, who indirectly paved the way for Talleyrand's triumph.

This only confirmed what *l'oncle* was always telling his niece: "What are politics, if not women?"

CHAPTER TWELVE

Dorothea & Talleyrand
January-June 1815

THE VIENNESE INTERPRETED the heavy snowfall the first week of 1815 as an omen indicating that the new year was to start with a clean slate, like the fresh snow. Carriages swept along the narrow streets to the swishing accompaniment of the runners that had replaced their wheels. The days were cold and clear, and the Graben and other public squares were crowded with visitors and delegates who were out, like the natives, for a breath of fresh air.

With Dorothea's help, the French embassy was now one of the focal points of life in Vienna—concrete evidence, as Talleyrand had intended it to be, that France was as rich and powerful as ever. The Kaunitz's ancien régime atmosphere, carrying with it the ultimate felicities of life, created an ambiance that neither the magnificence of Emperor Franz's Hofburg nor the oriental splendor of the Razumovsky palace, where Alexander had done his official entertaining before the fire, managed to convey. Talleyrand and his niece had become the most famous couple in Vienna. A certain *parfum de scandale* helped, and the fact that he was so old and she so young made the whispers more titillating. Although Dorothea's liaison with Count Clam-Martinitz was an established component of the social scene and encouraged by *l'oncle*, insiders claimed this was mere window dressing. The secret police noted, "With those scandalous Courland princesses, anything goes." And in Gentz's *Journal* these days, the four sisters were referred to on every other page as the "Courland whores," for Joanna had jilted him.

Advent was past, and the delegates' extracurricular activities, which had been dampened by the death of the old prince de Ligne and the agitation generated by the Saxon-Polish crisis, resumed in an atmosphere of increasing boredom and satiety. The inventiveness of the empress's festival committee was as strained as the imperial exchequer, and the man in the street, for whom the novelty of so many crowned heads strolling informally on the ramparts had long since worn thin, was worried that he would soon be taxed to raise the 50,000 guldens per diem their board alone was costing.

Since Vienna was the music capital of the world, with a great many talented composers, and more, and more generous patrons than elsewhere on the Continent, musical events were on an exceptional scale, and one evening, Dorothea heard one hundred pianos in a joint recital under the baton of Antonio Salieri, the first kappelmeister of the Austrian court. A German-born American doctor, Dr. Justice Bollman, the sole overseas visitor to attend the congress, was much in demand for his ghost stories. And in a form of inverted snobbism, the crème fought over invitations to Gentz's exclusive little dinners, although his apartment on the Seilergasse was so tiny that even after the chevalier had had the doors removed, everyone was still squeezed, and the servants had to place the dishes on the table instead of passing them.

Because there was little other way readily to exert pressure on congress affairs, Wilhelmina's apartments remained crowded. The rulers of the small principalities, not to mention important foreigners who needed recommendations and contacts, flocked to the Schenkenstrasse to seek her widespread influence. Distinguished men who enjoyed her superior mind and respected her opinions swarmed round. As a result of the secret tripartite treaty, the inner council had become a committee of five—Talleyrand was admitted at the insistence of Metternich and the British foreign secretary, Castlereagh—and Talleyrand, Metternich, and the British met in the left wing of the Palm regularly to discuss plans before turning them into decisions. When the rest left, the widowed Lord Stewart stayed on to enjoy the pleasures of his fair hostess's bed.

On January 21, the twenty-second anniversary of Louis XVI's death on the guillotine, both his body and Marie-Antoinette's, which had lately been discovered in an unmarked common grave in Paris, were to be reburied ceremoniously in the Bourbon family crypt at Saint Denis, outside of the French capital. Seizing this as a splendid opportunity to consecrate the principle of legitimacy —and the need for it to prevail in the resolution of the fates of Saxony and Poland—Talleyrand planned a requiem mass in the martyred rulers' memory in Vienna on the same day. As a gesture of sympathy, Emperor Franz volunteered to foot the expenses and forbade any entertainment in the city for twenty-four hours. With Dorothea's enthusiastic help, nothing was spared to make the solemn occasion reflect the grandeur of the French crown. The painter Isabey was again in charge of the overall artistic effect, and with the help of Empress Maria-Ludovica's interior decorator, the entire nave of Saint Stephan's was hung with black drapery richly embroidered in silver. Talleyrand's personal music director composed special orchestral music and a requiem without instrumentation for a choir of 250 voices. To guarantee there would be room for those he most wanted to impress, Talleyrand made the service invitational and took pains to assure the Prussian king and the tsar and tsarina prominent places. *L'oncle* did not want them to miss the point he was making—or to forget that the Saxon king they were trying to despoil was a cousin of the late Louis XVI.

In an abrupt change of mood, the imperial sleigh ride was scheduled for the next day, after numerous postponements due to recurrent thaws. Thirty-two sleighs, elaborately decorated in emerald green velvet embroidered and fringed in gold, with more gold on the axles, were lined up on the Josephsplatz awaiting the guests, while their impatient steeds, caparisoned in tiger skins and other rich furs, with ribbons and bows braided in their manes and nodding ostrich plumes on their heads, champed at the bit and pawed the air. Around 2:00 P.M., after the usual confusion, a large detachment of cavalry set off to lead the way, followed by a six-horse sledge of trumpeters and drummers. The sovereigns followed, then twenty-four pages in medieval costume, a squadron of the imperial guards, and the rest of the party, including *l'oncle* and his niece. Bringing up the rear was another sledge with a group of court musicians in Turkish garb.

The cavalcade proceeded at a walk through the winding streets so the crowds waiting on the ramparts might enjoy the show. Once they crossed the Danube, the horses were given their heads, and they dashed along the country lanes, the myriad bells in their elaborate harnesses tinkling. After circling through Schönnbrunn's elaborate grounds—with a brief, distant glimpse of l'Aiglon out sliding—and a long stop for a figure-skating exhibition on the main lake, the group entered the palace for a banquet. Later, the imperial opera troupe presented a German version of *Cinderella,* which Marie-Louise also witnessed, sight unseen, from a specially prepared, concealed cubbyhole.

As they reentered Vienna, their way illuminated by the thousands of new, pear-shaped glass lanterns that were Emperor Franz's pride and joy (even though they were filled with a foul-smelling mixture of linseed oil and pork drippings), the wind shifted and the thermometer dropped. Dorothea had forgotten how cold Central European winters could be and got thoroughly chilled. The minute she reached the Kaunitz, she tossed her cloak imperiously at the first footman she saw and hastened to *l'oncle*'s study, where she casually raised the back of her elaborate skirt and layers of lace petticoats to warm her derrière in front of the porcelain stove. Only lackeys were present. They did not count as men, and Talleyrand was *l'oncle*—and only that, despite the gossip.

Metternich's favorite cousin, pretty Countess Flora Wrbna, who was in the tsar's sleigh, was almost as frozen as Dorothea and got into an argument with Alexander about the amount of clothing men and women wore. Alexander claimed that he wore as much as the countess but, he added with a touch of bravura, "I can dress faster." Flora accepted the challenge, and a few nights later, the competition was held at the Zichys' with mock pomp and ceremony. Flora and the tsar were in ordinary street clothes to start with and solemnly revealed their underpinnings, so that neither one could be accused of cheating. At the stroke of ten, the pair and their witnesses disappeared. In eleven and one-half minutes, to be precise, the tsar, who had held a carefully rehearsed trial run that morning, strode back with a self-satisfied smirk. There was a suppressed giggle. He wheeled round, astonished. Flora was complacently fanning herself, dressed like a whiff of the past in an ancien régime French court costume, with *mouche* powdered hair, high heels, small gauntlets, even a bouquet. Other guests arrived in clothes of the same period, and the evening ended with a costume ball.

The duke of Wellington's arrival on February 4 to replace the British foreign secretary breathed fresh life into the dying social season, and Talleyrand snared the plum of introducing the distinguished Britisher to the capital. Sitting between the two imperial consorts—the Austrian empress on one side, her frail, consumptive body again weighed down by the awesome Hapsburg jewels; the ash-blonde, sad-faced tsarina, overrouged by all but Saint Petersburg standards, on the other—Talleyrand, in his superbly elegant long-tailed plum velvet suit, aglitter with the stars and orders of the sovereigns who were his guests, personified power. Across from him, gowned in Leroy's stiff white brocade with ropes of the Courland pearls wound round her neck and arms and in her ink black hair, Dorothea presented an enchanting picture as she leaned over the top of her great white ostrich-feather fan to address the tsar in his good ear.

Destined by nature and birth to do the honors of a palace, Dorothea had been honed by her experience as a lady-in-waiting at Napoleon's court. But she was still treated as the baby of the family, and she must have gotten great satisfaction that evening showing off to Paulina and Joanna and, especially, Wilhelmina, who considered herself—and was considered by the Courland princesses—the outstanding hostess among the four, if not in all Vienna. With a reassuring grace, Dorothea tempered the gravity of political matters when a note of levity was required, and the tsar laughed appreciatively when she directed the conversation skillfully away from a potentially dangerous subject to safer ground. *L'oncle's* music director and musicians lulled the ear with music by Haydn, then Mozart; Beethoven, who had recently conducted the premiere of his Seventh Symphony in the Kartnertor Theater, was too controversial for such an evening. And a succession of white-wigged footmen in the aubergine Talleyrand livery passed an endless procession of epicurean delights, although Maître Carême regretted it was no longer January, a month the great chef preferred because of the variety and quality of foodstuffs to be had in Vienna's markets.

Talleyrand never allowed dinner to last more than an hour, and tonight was no exception. In the Kaunitz's great salons, which opened one onto the next and had been transformed into a solid mass of white carnations and azaleas, stars of the diplomatic world, the congress, and the crème awaited the sixty dinner guests. The painter Isabey wandered about doing sketches—Wellington, who was conscious that his hatchet nose was a cartoonist's delight, stipulated he must be drawn face on—and later, a trio of famous French ballerinas, whom Talleyrand had insisted appear in the Austrian capital during the congress, performed. A ball followed, and it was very late when the final measures of the old-fashioned *"Mon Grandpère"* were danced in the traditionally stiff, formal way as a finale.

February 8, the day after Mardi Gras, was Wilhelmina's birthday. Clemens sent a gift—a beautiful pair of small vases, made of different kinds of lava, to go with the other things he had given her for her desk—and a note to her early, while she was still eating breakfast, in order to be the first to congratulate her. Wilhelmina thanked Clemens at once and invited him to call that afternoon. But Metternich refused. Before, he could not bear to see Wilhelmina when others were around; now, it was too painful to be alone with her. All four sisters celebrated together at a dinner in Wilhelmina's honor at Alfred's. In an age when life expectancy was short, Dorothea and her contemporaries considered the duchess of Sagan middle-aged at thirty-four. Abloom with the radiance of youth and aglow with her first love and the triumph of her Wellington dinner, Dorothea was slowly nudging Wilhelmina out of the spotlight and emerging as one of society's uncontested new queens.

While toasts were being drunk to Wilhelmina in the Windischgratz palace, glasses were being raised at the Ballhausplatz to celebrate the resolution, that same evening, of the marathon Polish-Saxon controversy. Wellington's arrival had set the creaking machinery of the congress into rapid motion. And with Britain, France, and Austria in accord, the impasse disappeared like snow in June. The tsar was to retain the bulk of the duchy of Warsaw, which was to form a new kingdom of Poland, with constitutional principles drawn up by Czartoryski, and King Friedrich-Augustus I of Saxony was to keep something less than half of his original territory. In a triumph for Talleyrand's principle of legitimacy, the old Saxon king, who was still being held as a prisoner of war in Berlin, must give his consent for his immolation in behalf of the general peace.

Never had the forty days of abstinence before Easter seemed so essential to salvation as after the festivities that year during Fashing, the six traditionally merry weeks preceding Lent, and Dorothea was anxious to hear the poet Zacharias Werner, a

Lutheran libertine turned Roman-Catholic abbé, who was setting the capital agog with his graphic weekly lectures on carnal sin. She and Count Karl set forth with Talleyrand's warning, "Beware a reformed rake in the surtout of a secular priest," ringing in the ears. No one could be more prickly where the Church was concerned than *l'oncle*, the former bishop of Autun.

Haiduks and little blackamoors in gaudy livery, armed with prayer books and cushions, had scurried to stark, high-vaulted Saint Etienne hours ahead of time to hold down seats for their aristocratic mistresses. So Dorothea and Clam had trouble finding places. The semiobscurity of the frigid interior, unalleviated by any sunshine, afforded a suitably sepulchral setting as the emaciated Werner, with flying hair and leathern features, stained clothes and down-at-the-heel shoes tied with string across the insteps, launched into a dramatic attack on his listeners' morals. Ranting, raving, shedding tears, the pale-faced evangelist raked over his spellbound audience as he built towards a climax. "Repent, o ye sinner!" he exhorted. "Beware that tiny piece of flesh, that abomination, the most dangerous appurtenance on a man's body that has brought all the ills into the world!" He paused dramatically. "Shall I name you that tiny piece of flesh?" In the horrified silence that followed, women could be heard fumbling in their reticules for smelling salts. "Shall I show you that tiny piece of flesh?" the Savonarola of the congress thundered, easing himself from behind the pulpit. There was an agonizing pause. A sly smile slid over Werner's perspiring face. "Ladies and gentlemen, behold the source of all our sins!" Leering, he stuck out—his tongue.

"O ye sinners, let us pray the Holy Spirit for his blessing," Werner cried. Throwing himself to the floor, he cradled his forehead in his hands to give himself time to think how to conclude his sermon and release his overwrought congregation.

With the subdued social activities dictated by Lent, and the burning question of the day resolved at last, the delegates—each with a pet project to push—settled down with scissors and paste for the tidying-up process. The end of the congress was in sight.

Talleyrand's letters to the grand duchess were full of "our girl's" triumphs, and Anna's to him of the rising unrest in France, where Louis XVIII was looking less and less like a Sun King and more like a paper lantern carried by a foreigner. Meanwhile, the French consul in Leghorn kept reporting rumors about the former emperor's suspicious activities on Elba. But Alexander refused to consider moving him.

On Tuesday morning, March 7, Dorothea was perched on a corner of *l'oncle*'s great canopied bed, petting Carlos and chattering about a final dress rehearsal of Kötzebue's *Old Love Affair*. Their conversation was interrupted by a knock at the door, and a footman entered with a note that had just arrived from the chancellor. "It's probably to advise me of the time of our meeting today," Talleyrand commented, handing the envelope to Dorothea to open.

"Napoleon has escaped from Elba!" she cried, reading it at a glance. "Oh, *mon oncle*, what about my rehearsal?"

"It will be held on schedule, of course," he blandly reassured her.

"And the performance this evening?" Would all her work be wasted?

"Life goes on, even if the heavens fall in."

Something in *l'oncle*'s voice caught Dorothea up short. Suddenly the enormity of the news penetrated—and the childish selfishness of her reaction. Anxiously she demanded, "What is going to happen now?"

L'oncle shook his head. How he wished he knew. He had committed a cardinal sin. There had been plenty of warning, but he had not believed the accumulating evidence. "What audacity!" he concluded admiringly. "History affords no example of such a challenge to the human race."

Talleyrand was the first of the ministers to arrive at the chancellery. Metternich handed him the six-line dispatch from the Austrian consul-general at Genoa advising that the former French emperor had disappeared on board the *Inconstant* with a thousand men. The chancellor recalled, in his *Memoirs,* the laconic conversation that ensued:

TALLEYRAND: "Do you know where Napoleon is going?"
METTERNICH: "The dispatch says nothing about it."
TALLEYRAND: "He will disembark somewhere on the coast of Italy and throw himself on Switzerland."
METTERNICH: "He will go straight to Paris."

The chancellor had already notified Emperor Franz, met with

the Prussian King, and then with the tsar—his personal difficulties with Alexander forgotten in the urgency of the moment. Once the others assembled, it was quickly agreed to resume military operations. Special couriers were sent scurrying to the commander in chief of the coalition forces and the scattered Allied commands, but the sensational news was temporarily withheld from everyone else. Even Gentz, the secretary of the congress, was not informed and spent the morning leisurely soaking—he was afflicted with rheumatism—in the Diana Baths' thermal waters.

That evening, the harp and the flute were playing the overture, and the sovereigns were assembled in the Hofburg's great ballroom, where a temporary stage had been set up, surrounded by sweet-smelling boxed orange trees in bloom, when an aide-de-camp of the tsar appeared and whispered in his ear. Alexander immediately got up and followed him out. The candles in the massive silver torchères were being extinguished and the stage curtains slowly pulled open by the time he was back. His Imperial Majesty murmured a few words of apology to the countess on his left. She turned and said something to her neighbor, who turned and said something to hers. The news spread like the sails of the bark taking Napoleon from Elba. Spring was early this year, and the Eagle was returning—as he himself had predicted—with the violets.

The tsarina clutched her pearls convulsively. The superb collar broke, and the guests, who were glad to have something to do to relieve the tension, stooped under their chairs to retrieve the marble-sized beads. "Don't trouble yourselves," Her Imperial Majesty pleaded. "They're not worth the effort."

The play was beginning. The young stars, Dorothea and Metternich's seventeen-year-old daughter, Marie—his favorite child and the debutante of the season—sensed they had lost their audience and made a valiant effort to recapture their attention, but no one was interested in the play, or in the tableaux vivants or the ballet that followed. Afterwards, those present crowded round to commiserate with Talleyrand. Napoleon's flight was not conceived as a threat, but they concurred that this time when the former emperor was seized, he must be sent some place farther away, so he could never again disturb Europe's peace.

A consummate cardplayer, impassive **Talleyrand** acted as if he held a full flush and bluffed his way through the evening with customary aplomb. Dorothea tried to copy him with less success. When the two returned to the Kaunitz, she had a hard time sleeping. The same moon that was streaming through her partially opened louvers was also shining on Napoleon. But where?

Less than a week later Dorothea found out. She and *l'oncle* were at the Metternichs' Monday supper when a courier from the king of Sardinia arrived at the Ballhausplatz, travel-stained and weary after crossing the Alps by forced marches. His message, "Napoleon has landed at Cannes!" transformed Talleyrand once more into a pariah before the eyes of the astounded gathering. The orchestra tried to coax somebody back onto the floor, but no one felt like dancing. Until this moment the congress and the Viennese, with no news other than that of the fugitive's disappearance, had been making book on Napoleon's capture and death within a fortnight. Suddenly the still-fresh memories of the past twenty-five years—the capitals invaded, the industries paralyzed, the battlefields piled high with corpses—came flooding back, and everyone huddled in worried little groups talking.

The Prussian king motioned to the duke of Wellington, and both left, with the tsar and Emperor Franz hard on their heels. Their precipitate departure made the rest of the company uneasy, and one by one, the others followed suit. As he watched the spacious salons emptying prematurely, Talleyrand commented to Metternich, "Napoleon, not wishing to finish by a tragedy, will finish by a farce." The chancellor, in turn, excused himself to follow his master for any instructions occasioned by this surprising turn of events, leaving Dorothea and Talleyrand standing there alone. *Sic transit gloria mundi*. Trite but how true. Dorothea put her arm through *l'oncle*'s, as if to say they would see this through together, and *l'oncle* and his niece left, too—slowly, with Talleyrand dragging his bad right foot.

The next few days, Talleyrand worked feverishly to convince the signatories of the Treaty of Paris to brand Napoleon an outlaw, subject to public vengeance, and to label France, under the lawful government of Louis XVIII, his first victim. This was the only way to put the former emperor's escape into proper perspective and to save France from dismemberment once Napoleon was again defeated.

"Wait here for me, Madame," *l'oncle* urged, when Dorothea and the entire legation staff anxiously accompanied him to the door of the Kaunitz to wish him luck as he set off for the decisive meeting. "Watch for my return. If I triumph, you will see me, through the carriage window, wave the treaty on which will depend the fate of France—and of Europe."

Hours later, he returned, brandishing the proclamation plastered with black and red seals. "I don't believe another such document has ever been written," he exulted. "History furnishes no example of a similar rejection by all mankind."

But Talleyrand's elation did not last long. Rumors poured in. And all bad. Fearful that Napoleon might have his son, l'Aiglon, kidnapped from Schönnbrunn, Emperor Franz ordered his grandson moved into the safety of the Hofburg and dismissed the boy's French governess. To show imperial appreciation of her services, the emperor selected as a farewell gift Wilhelmina's sapphire parure —a transaction discreetly arranged by Clemens, who knew that Wilhelmina was momentarily hard pressed for funds. If the delegates remained much longer, not only the duchess of Sagan but most of the crème would end up in debtors' prison. La Bagration was so hard pressed that her chef had to foot the food bills, and her creditors placed her under house arrest for fear she might flee town before money to settle her accounts arrived from Russia. Alexander was tightfisted, as usual, where money was concerned, even with his cousin.

Dispatches reported that French regiments were defecting in droves; dismissed officers, seething over unpaid pensions, flocked to the imperial colors. Town after town, displeased with Bourbon ineptitude and the Ultras' vindictiveness, were swinging to the eagle-headed standards as Napoleon passed through en route north. Recent visitors to Elba might describe the former emperor as a middle-aged man with a too-tight waistcoat, a bloated yellowish face, and sparse hair, but to the Frenchmen who were clearing his passage toward the capital, he was surrounded with the aura of a superman and appeared seven feet tall, young and handsome.

Wellington's last night in Vienna before setting forth to take command of the Allied forces in the west was spent in the left wing of the Palm with Talleyrand and Metternich. Wilhelmina's youngest foster daughter could not take her eyes off the resplendent red uniform that she had not seen the duke wear before. Creeping up behind him, she gently stroked his magnificent gold epaulets, but her new British friend did not feel like their usual romp.

Wellington was the first to leave, kissing each lady good-bye and arranging a rendezvous in Paris with one and all. Like so many others, he too had fallen under Wilhelmina's spell, and the next morning as a final adieu, he sent her a gold memorial coin that had been struck off with his portrait.

Metternich, although he was the mainspring of the reformed coalition, found time to help Count Karl and Dorothea perpetrate an elaborate April Fool's Day joke on Gentz. Climbing the narrow, rickety stairs to his Seilergasse flat on April 1, the young couple was greeted at the door by the chevalier's valet and, peering over his shoulder, a half-dressed, wild-eyed Gentz. He was enormously relieved to recognize Count Karl and too upset to be surprised at seeing Dorothea there at that unseemly hour. But he automatically pulled his dressing gown round his shivering, birdlike frame and clapped a hand protectively on his naked pate as he ushered them into the tiny salon, which was strewn with half-packed luggage. His departure seemed imminent.

"My dear count, what do you make of this?" The distraught redhead shoved a copy of the *Wien Zeitung* at Clam. "Look at the front page! I've got to get out of town." He sat down in a state of bewilderment. "Read it out loud." Gentz seized a tumbler, dumped in one of his innumerable powders, added water, stirred, then needed both shaking hands to raise it to his lips, while the count read:

> Reward, 10,000 ducats. To whosoever delivers Friedrich von Gentz, the well-known publicist, dead or alive, or simply produces proof of his murder.
>
> —Napoleon

As his friends well knew, Gentz had been suffering from insomnia for days, terrified that the French emperor, once he was back in power, might take revenge on the secretary of the congress for drawing up the declaration Talleyrand had pushed through outlawing Napoleon. This thundering broadside justified the chevalier's worst fears. Watching the strange little figure twitching with agitation over the counterfeit journal concocted by the chancellor, Dorothea, who was trying desperately to keep a straight face, choked and gave the game away.

The grand duchess, who was not one to panic, had not left

Paris until the Bourbons themselves prepared to do so—when Napoleon was only hours distant—and then came, like a homing pigeon, to the Kaunitz. She had arrived on Good Friday, around midnight. While official entertainments had ceased with the emperor's dramatic return, social life was not completely stagnant, and with Anna in Vienna, there were now five Courland "Graces" to sparkle and charm. The crème no longer spoke of the duchess of Sagan and her sisters, or of the comtesse Edmond and hers, but of the grand duchess of Courland and her daughters. Even when her petite, blonde older girls elected to do a sister act, as Wilhelmina, Paulina, and Joanna often did—gowned and coiffed alike, staying close together to produce a dazzling effect in triplicate— fifty-four-year-old Anna more than held her own. Seeing her again for the first time after a number of years, her ex-son-in-law, Prince Louis de Rohan, remarked that the elegant grand duchess, in her devastatingly cut Paris gown, outshone every lady present, his former wife, Wilhelmina, included.

Of course, to continue to do so took more time and more doing. Anna had long since had her fabulous pearls strung into a wide choker to hide the telltale lines around her neck. And here in Vienna, she spent additional hours each morning letting her maid administer a new miracle jelly of herbs, moss, and honey to her face and other crucial areas. While she had resumed, at least on the surface, her former intimacy with Charles-Maurice, she had already heard in Paris rumors that *l'oncle* was more attentive to his niece than the situation warranted. And Wilhelmina's idle quip, "At least the great man's kept in the family," overheard by chance shortly after her arrival, was indelibly stamped on the grand duchess's brain. Exactly what did her oldest daughter mean? Anna was too old a hand at the delicate shadings of love not to have detected a subtle change in Talleyrand's attitude toward her youngest daughter. Perhaps it was the way Charles-Maurice put his hand under Dorothea's elbow to help her to her seat. Perhaps it was the way the timbre of his voice changed when he addressed her.

Anna's feelings as a mother were not shocked at the idea of Dorothea's possible seduction by Talleyrand. Men would be men, as the old adage went, and Charles-Maurice had already bettered Don Giovanni's *mille e tre*. It was ironic, though, that it should be Dorothea who interested Talleyrand. Wilhelmina, it was true, had snatched Baron d'Armfelt from her years before, but Wilhelmina was one of the grand duchess's "duty offspring"—as Anna thought of her three girls by Grand Duke Peter—whereas Dorothea was her love child, Batowski's daughter. Small wonder Dorothea had stirred the old Adam in Charles-Maurice. For here in Vienna, surrounded by admirers and with Count Karl firmly in tow, she was unfurling like a petal in the noonday sun.

However interested Talleyrand was, Dorothea had eyes only for Clam. Since it took two to waltz and her relationship with Charles-Maurice was the most precious thing in the autumn of her life, Anna was well able to turn a blind eye to anything she did not wish to see.

Talleyrand's personal feelings about the mother and her youngest daughter might be the enigma one would expect of so sphinxlike a man. On the other hand, his public life was an open book. In four short months Talleyrand had brought defeated France back onto an equal footing with the Big Four, but Austria, Prussia, Russia, and England were once more meeting without him. The French statesman was isolated on an island of mistrust that grew increasingly desolate each time the newfangled semaphore telegraph's arm waggled with additional news from Paris—provided the weather was clear enough to see the signal. The government Talleyrand continued to represent existed solely in the bulging person of an elderly Bourbon, his gout-swollen feet encased in velvet slippers, who had fled without soldiers or prestige into the Low Countries. To add to Talleyrand's problems, Napoleon had lost no time in confiscating Talleyrand's property and vast holdings in France, and Vienna's bankers refused Charles-Maurice credit. But when Napoleon sent a lifelong friend of Talleyrand's to Vienna to try to bribe him back into the imperialist fold, Comte de Montrond returned after three weeks empty-handed. In Talleyrand's eyes, Napoleon was now an adventurous brigand whose second reign would soon burst and disappear like a brilliant meteor.

Finances posed a problem to the luxury-loving Talleyrand, for whom poverty was a state worse than death, until Britain came to the rescue with a subsidy adequate to remain at the Kaunitz, provided expenses were dramatically trimmed. So Talleyrand sent Maître Carême and the entire legation staff home, except for his faithful valet, one secretary, and two clerks, and filled in with a few local domestics. It made little difference, anymore, if the latter were spies for the Austrian secret police.

Serious by nature, Dorothea had worked too closely with *l'oncle* since coming to Vienna and taken too profound a satisfaction in their joint successes—social and diplomatic—not to be upset by the turn of events beyond his control and by his present precarious situation. But she was determined to let nothing cloud what remaining time Count Karl had before he rejoined his military post. Those lovely May days, the pair often drove through the blossoming Prater out toward Freudenaum, Nussdorf, Nödling, Laxenburg. Sometimes they went as far as Semmering to spend the night in a charming inn Wilhelmina and Lord Stewart had discovered near the old guesthouse in Reichenau that Stewart had redecorated, as a surprise, for his own trysts with the duchess of Sagan.

Wilhelmina's affair with Alfred was definitely terminated, his place preempted by the British ambassador, who had the added attraction for Wilhelmina of being a widower. He was also the diametric opposite of the complex, metaphysically inclined Metternich, the pleasure of whose company Wilhelmina was once again enjoying—with none of the heartache. Almost seven months had passed since the letter of rupture, dated "the night of October 22–23." The passage of time had transmuted Clemens's love back into friendship, and he walked over to the Palm palace almost daily—casually, as in the days before their liaison—to discuss politics and divulge the latest news from France.

Most of Vienna's 100,000 visitors were leaving, and with summer premature, society was trekking to the countryside earlier than ordinary. The Metternich family, including their new pet, Polly the parrot, cut short their customary spring stay at the Rennwegg villa and proceeded to Baden a few days before the chancellor set off with the emperor and the other Allied sovereigns for general headquarters.

Then it was time for Lord Stewart and Count Karl to depart. Europe's armies were again on the march, moving west in a giant crescent from the Alps to the North Sea, and processions of young Viennese boys and girls from the working class marched daily with banners and flags to the city's different churches to pray for victory.

On June 3, Dorothea was off, supposedly to attend to matters concerning her Prussian estates but actually to be as near Clam-Martinitz as possible. Like a ship at sea that has lost its compass, Dorothea was not sure in which direction port lay. Her husband, Edmond, no longer figured in her calculations. Her two small sons—her one obligation—were in France, which was in a state of chaos; Clam was with the Austrian army; *l'oncle* was about to join the exiled king.

Talleyrand had hoped to dissuade his niece from the folly of following her lover. It was one thing to have an affair; the present trip he deemed madness. Whether he was already in love with Dorothea—as Anna feared—is anyone's guess. But one thing was certain. Dorothea, whom Talleyrand had brought to Vienna to pamper, amuse, and make use of, was leaving the city as *l'oncle's* trusted friend, a counsellor with an intuitive understanding of the personalities she was in contact with, and on whose judgment he was to depend increasingly for the rest of his life.

When the grand duchess left, in turn, for Karlsbad to meet her sister, Elisa, and take her annual cure, her three oldest daughters heaved a sigh of relief. The formerly self-reliant, confident grand duchess had become like a child who thinks that if she talks enough about something she does not want to happen, she can prevent its occurrence. And Wilhelmina complained about hearing Maman discuss "nothing but that old cripple who is taking it into his head to play the fool at sixty-one!"

Early in June, Talleyrand and the other delegates initialed the General Act of the Congress of Vienna in their first, last, and only plenary session. And Talleyrand, too, set forth, headed westward.

CHAPTER THIRTEEN

Dorothea, Talleyrand, & the Grand Duchess
1815-1821

ON JUNE 18 NAPOLEON WAS DEFEATED at Waterloo by Wellington and Blücher before the Russian troops had time to join forces. With the three Allied sovereigns still at general head-quarters in Heilbron, on-the-spot Wellington served as coalition arbiter. The former emperor was quickly dispatched to Saint Helena in the South Atlantic, and plump Louis "Dix-Huîtres"—so nicknamed by pun-loving Parisians because of his passion for oysters (XVIII is Dix-Huit; *dix huîtres* is ten oysters)—reentered his capital with the English troops, for he was the legitimate French ruler, and at the Congress of Vienna, Talleyrand had persuaded the Big Four to accept the principle of legitimacy. The British were also convinced that the Second Restoration was the administration most likely to ensure the tranquillity of Europe, even though the Bourbon cause did not command unanimous support within France.

Talleyrand entered the capital on the same day, but he did so inconspicuously, in an unmarked carriage and by a different gate. Unlike his sovereign, the wily statesman refused a public entry with the help of foreigners. The brief campaign of 1815 had raised a number of thorny problems, and Wellington had decided that the diplomat who knew all Europe, and whom all Europe knew, should remain as foreign minister and assume the presidency of the council, as well. Louis XVIII acquiesced grudgingly—he was no longer master in his own house. His Majesty did not consider Talleyrand indispensable and was displeased to hear Talleyrand's enemies repeat Talleyrand's alleged boast that it was he who had again set the Bourbons on the throne.

Anna hurried back at Charles-Maurice's urgent request. He hoped she might once more help placate the tsar, who was now his implacable enemy. For Napoleon, on his return to the Tuileries, had discovered a copy of that January's secret tripartite treaty, which was largely Talleyrand's work and directed against the Russians, and he had wasted no time in forwarding it to the tsar.

Her first evening at the hôtel Saint Florentin, Anna looked around with interest, recalling Napoleon's confiscation of Talleyrand's property. Except for a heavy coat of dust, she found everything as Talleyrand had left it; even the great malachite bowl for burning the amber he loved was still in place—and filled with ash.

With Paris it was a different story. The city again housed the Allied sovereigns and their general staff. But there any resemblance to the previous June ended. The Champs Elysées had been converted into a white-tented town for the British military, and English troops were also bivouacked in front of Notre Dame. Marshal Blücher and his numerous dogs were billeted in Marie-Louise's former suite at Saint Cloud—with its delicate feminine decor—while his regiment of chasseurs' musicians fished insolently in the château's lake in front. And Louis XVIII was threatening to sit on the Pont d'Iéna and be blown to bits with it, should the Prussians persist and destroy this new span across the Seine because it was offensively named after one of their most humiliating defeats at Napoleon's hands.

Administratively speaking, there was as little change on the surface as at the rue Saint Florentin. For Talleyrand was again the master of the hour, face to face with a backbreaking task. There any resemblance to 1814 ended. In 1815, Talleyrand must not only calm the savage political passions unleashed by Napoleon's "Hundred Days," further aggravated by Ultra intrigues and compounded by the Allied occupational forces; he must also strive for peace conditions that did not strike the integrity and honor of France, and rid the country of foreign troups as fast as possible.

One of the last things Napoleon had said after abdicating was, "If the Bourbons are wise, they will only change the sheets on my bed and continue to give employment to the men I have trained." Of course, they did not. But if His Majesty had learned from past events and was willing to recognize some of the errors that had led to Napoleon's return, the comte d'Artois, his brother and heir, remained the ringleader of the troublemaking, reactionary

Royalists. The Ultras were once again headquartered in "Monsieur's" apartments in the Tuileries's Pavilion Marsan, and they blamed the recent catastrophe on Louis XVIII's weakness for survivors of the First Empire—starting with Talleyrand.

Dorothea reappeared in Paris soon after the grand duchess did and reinstalled herself and her two small sons in her former ground-floor apartments at the hôtel Saint Florentin. Count Karl was due there shortly, and she had no intention of returning to her husband. She was determined to cut herself loose from so unhappy a union, although divorce was impossible for Catholics—Dorothea had converted several years before—and a legal separation was hard for a woman to procure.

The evening of Dorothea's arrival, when the great doors of the Salon de l'Aigle opened and an usher tapped the floor with his staff and announced, "His Grace, the duke of Wellington," she was the first to greet him. "My savior!" Dorothea cried, carried away with a rare public display of enthusiasm and oblivious to the icy reaction of the French guests present. Few of the Faubourg Saint-Germain regretted Napoleon's downfall, but a chasm existed between politeness and that warm a welcome to the leader of the foreign troops who had wrought this miracle.

Feelings waxed strong in the lovely gilt gray-and-crystal salon, and Talleyrand interceded. "But, Messieurs, you want to bring back the ancient regime, and that is not possible."

"Monseigneur," an Ultra reposted, "who would dream of making you once more the bishop of Autun? What foolishness!" For the first time on record, Talleyrand did not have the last word.

The French capital resumed its role as the Continent's mecca, and Europe strolled the boulevards. At Lord Stewart's invitation, Wilhelmina arrived—to stay at the grand duchess's—bringing her oldest foster daughter and coming the scenic route, by way of Salzburg and Arlberg, for the girl's benefit.

The tsar, too, was finally back, but anxious as Anna was to help reinstate Charles-Maurice in Alexander's good graces, she hardly laid eyes on His Imperial Majesty this time round. Alexander had rediscovered religion, and his free moments were spent with Baroness Julie de Krüdener, the Riga mystic. If Anna as a girl had not known the tall, willowy blonde who was almost her exact contemporary and a near neighbor on the Baltic shores, the grand duchess assuredly had in the heyday of her salon at 7 Unter den Linden in Berlin. There Julie had cut a notorious swath, not only with her boast that she had compared measurements on a recent Italian trip and her figure was the equal of Florence's Venus de Medici's, but also with her best-selling autobiographical novel, *Valérie*, based on her many scandalous affairs. Since then, Mme. de Krüdener had seen the light and converted to pietism. Introduced to Alexander at Heilbronn through a cunningly contrived accident, Julie's vague mysticism and mixture of sincere exaltation and charlatanism enthralled susceptible Alexander, and he had invited her to Paris. The Baltic prophetess convinced the tsar that he was "the Elect of God," destined to regenerate the world. This new title as Europe's moral leader was a timely one, for Alexander was jealous of Wellington's social success and military laurels. His Imperial Majesty had a door cut in the wall of the Elysée palace so he could slip into the adjacent hôtel Montchênu nightly for further sibylline pronouncements.

Tout Paris flocked to Mme. de Krüdener's "celestial witches' sabbaths." At these times the streets outside Julie's apartment were impassable, with carriages of every size and description lined up in the front. Inside, the several rooms, opening one onto the other, were without carpets, pictures, or mirrors. But in the semiobscurity, many prominent people were recognizable, often including the king of Prussia, learning back, ill at ease, in a straw-covered peasant's chair. An unearthly silence reigned, broken by an occasional whisper. With theatrical flair, Julie remained in the room farthest from the entrance, reclining motionless on a divan that ran along the wall. At her back were crimson velvet cushions that dramatized her stark white, flowing robe and heavy blonde locks streaked with silver. She would stare with a fixed gaze into space. Then she would slowly arise, take a step forward, and wave her arms. "Let us pray." She had a low, heavily accented voice. "All sinners that ye are, sink upon your knees and beg for forgiveness from the God of Heaven." Everyone present, including the tsar, who materialized from the gloom alongside the baroness, even the footmen who had been passing refreshments, followed suit. And arms uplifted, head thrown back, Julie would pray in burning language.

Metternich had an even odder experience. Clemens told Wilhelmina that the evening before she arrived in Paris, he had been invited to dinner at the Elysée and found the table set for four: the tsar, Mme. de Krüdener, Metternich—and Our Lord, Jesus Christ.

Religion or no, Alexander, like the other coalition leaders, was taking a much stiffer line with France than he had the previous year, when only two months were required to conclude the First Peace of Paris. The Allies expected a heavy price for Louis XVIII's restoration, and while the present talks involved most of the same negotiators who had participated at Vienna and whom Talleyrand knew well, eight weeks passed and they were still far apart.

Anna had never seen Charles-Maurice so distraught. Talleyrand was not and never had been a detail man, and the dossiers on domestic affairs that came across his desk as president of the council spilled over onto the floor, unattended. It was not surprising that Louis XVIII was annoyed. Only the foreign ministry was functioning properly—because the British foreign secretary, Wellington, Metternich, and the Russian foreign minister dined regularly at the hôtel Saint Florentin.

Lifelong colleagues found Charles-Maurice a changed man. "It it age?" some asked. One prominent diplomat hinted at the cause in letters and a memoir, but only the minister of justice in Talleyrand's cabinent dared make the obvious comment that Talleyrand's mind was elsewhere. At the very moment when new elections returned a hostile chamber of Ultra deputies, when Talleyrand lacked the king's support and had a powerful enemy in the tsar, what could be keeping that worldly, perspicacious sexagenarian's thoughts from his staggering dual responsibilities? Most contemporaries concluded that by one of those imponderables of the human heart, *l'oncle* was in love with his niece.

The grand duchess had had ample time to adjust. For as his seraglio bore ample witness, Charles-Maurice never completely severed a liaison. A mellowing, middle-aged Anna was sadly discovering what Clemens's wife had learned long ago: When you have no choice, sharing must do. And there was still the faint hope that it was all a nightmare of her imagination and life might revert to its pre-Vienna status quo. For Dorothea was still focusing on Count Karl, whose reappearance in Paris emphasized how infinitely superior he was to Edmond.

In Vienna, Dorothea's liaison was only another of those Slavic sisters' amours, but it created a furor in Paris because of the prominence of the Talleyrands. In early August, Edmond, whom his uncle had recently persuaded the king to promote to brigadier general, felt honor bound to challenge Count Karl to a duel. He had his face slashed open from his nostrils to one ear for his pains, while Clam received no more than a scratch. That night, someone at dinner at the hôtel Saint Florentin mentioned to Talleyrand how much she admired his niece. "Ah, yes," Talleyrand replied. "She is charming and very intelligent. There's nothing young about her except her freedom from affectation." Pleased with his bon mot, *l'oncle* repeated it to Dorothea when they went into the small salon for coffee. In response she kissed him on both cheeks, which so delighted Talleyrand that he fed her mocha from his cup with his own spoon—a disgusting performance in the eyes of one guest, Frances, Lady Shelley, who recorded the incident, but failed to mention whether Anna was present.

Afterwards, Dorothea went to a great ball given by the duke of Wellington in Paulina Bonaparte's former hôtel on the rue Faubourg Saint Honoré, which Wellington had purchased for the new British embassy. The gathering was predominantly male because most Parisians refused to dance in the victor of Waterloo's residence. But Dorothea was, as always, a law unto herself, and she had come there purposely to muffle, if not silence, any talk about the dawn's affair of honor. So she waltzed the night through, pretending that nothing had happened in the Bois de Boulogne. Interestingly enough, while a spy of the Austrian secret police sent a report of the duel to Vienna, identifying Clam-Martinitz only as an "Austrian officer," no account appeared on the local police blotter. Presumably *l'oncle,* who could not bear to have the family name besmirched, had all mention of the affair expunged.

A few days later, as Dorothea and Count Karl were crossing the Seine in a carriage, they noticed a large angry crowd being held in check by a troop of national guard and a regiment of Austrian infantry. Approaching as close as possible, Clam descended to investigate. He discovered Wellington perched atop the Arc de Carrousel, lending his great personal prestige as a protection for the removal of its four bronze horses. Allied demands for restoration of the wagonloads of art that Napoleon had systematically looted from The Hague to as far as Rome were bitterly resented by the French, and these magnificent steeds that Napoleon had pillaged from Saint Mark's Square in Venice were a popular favorite. When Dorothea reported the scene to *l'oncle,* he shook his head sadly and said, "The army is in the same sorry state as the Louvre. Nothing remains in either one except *les vieux cadres"* [the old frames = the lists of old officers].

At least Talleyrand had not lost his sense of humor. These were difficult days for *l'oncle*—quite outside his personal situation— with the terms of the peace treaty still unresolved and the country paying over a million francs daily for the Allied occupation forces. Everything was going so badly, he confessed to Anna, that he kept telling himself it could not continue.

Early fall was the season for military reviews. One day the duke of Wellington sat his horse in the Place de Concorde and, with drawn sword, took the salute from lines of British infantry marching smartly past. The next weekend it was the tsar's turn, with a two-day affair on the Plain of Vertus, near Châlons-sur-Marne, where some 200,000 Russians were camped. Talleyrand claimed that Alexander was flexing his muscles to get his way in the peace talks, and putting on a spectacle to bolster his ego. Dorothea's feelings are not known in the matter, but Wilhelmina did not consider it a privilege to be invited. Rather, she felt commandeered and complained about the small room she and Dorothea were expected to share, for space was strictly limited, even in the lodgings provided for special guests like themselves.

The two sisters were in the select group on horseback that trailed Friedrich-Wilhelm III, the tsar, and the Russian general staff as they followed maneuvers, while Anna and her generation watched from reserved armchairs, protected from the broiling sun by a canopy. Sunday, September 11, Alexander's name day, the troops were deployed around seven large altars where mass was sung simultaneously. The tsar then led the Ambassadress from Heaven, Mme. de Krüdener, and her acolytes from one altar to another to consecrate his armies to God.

When the Austrian commander in chief returned to Vienna, taking his favorite aide-de-camp, Count Karl, with him, Dorothea considered moving there. Not only did she miss Clam-Martinitz, but she found herself under unexpected attack from several quarters. To begin with, the Allies this time round were acting as conquerors in Paris. The unchecked Prussian forces, with grudges to repay, were the worst behaved of the lot, and Dorothea, who had been born and reared in Berlin and had an Austrian officer as a lover, suffered the barbed consequences. In addition, many friends who had served with her at the French imperial court were alienated because of her subsequent role with the Bourbon legation at Vienna. The public scandal of Count Karl and Edmond's duel estranged some, and the Faubourg Saint-Germain openly sympathized with Edmond, whose previous indifference toward his wife had shifted to bitterness. Dorothea was tugged in one direction by family obligations and loyalty to her children and in another by her love for Clam. Restless and miserable, she lay stretched out on a chaise longue with her vinaigrette, a little articulated fish filled with rosemary and rue, never far from her nose.

Marie-Thérèse, the princess Tyskiewicz, Anna's old friend who was perhaps the most devoted of Charles-Maurice's seraglio, was forever running across from her apartment at 7, rue Saint Florentin to smother him with attention and often bore the brunt of his peevishness. One day, when she asked him for the tenth time, "How are your legs?" Talleyrand, who was thoroughly annoyed, stopped twirling his gold-and-ivory lorgnon, stared pointedly at her glass eye, and snapped, "As you see, Madame."

The prince was in this frame of mind when negotiations with the Allies reached a final stage. If the minister of justice was surprised, earlier, at Talleyrand's apathy, this time it was the minister of transportation, a more reliable witness than the malicious justice official, who was flabbergasted by his old friend's strange indifference to public affairs. A reconciliation with the tsar, who was against any serious dismemberment of France, would supply the key vote to back up the moderate British and Austrians against the revenge-bent Prussians. Yet suave Talleyrand, who possessed more skill than anyone at surmounting this type of obstacle, was too preoccupied to exercise his unfailing charm and had done nothing to woo Alexander all summer, except to lend Maître Carême once again for the duration of His Imperial Majesty's stay. Just as Metternich was distracted by Wilhelmina at a crucial period during the Congress of Vienna, now Talleyrand was suffering from a curious mental lassitude so foreign to the veteran statesman that stupefied colleagues could only attribute it to late-blooming, unrequited love.

The peace terms were painful and humiliating. Talleyrand,

who was more at odds with the king daily, and fighting a down-hill battle with the Ultras, saw no reason to bear the odium of signing an unpopular treaty and resigned on September 24. His regret at going was tempered by the belief that he would not be out of power long. He was too indispensable. But he was fooled. When the king received the resignation, he stared at the ceiling a long time in silence. Then His Majesty replied, with an air of complete indifference that would have done Talleyrand himself proud, "Well, I suppose I shall have to find another cabinet."

When the duc de Richelieu, who had served as Russian governor of Odessa for twenty years, was appointed his successor, Talleyrand quipped cynically, "Assuredly a good choice. Richelieu is the Frenchman who knows the Crimea the best." That might well be, but Richelieu was the tsar's protégé, and he quickly concluded the stalled peace treaty.

Wilhelmina had some last-minute shopping to attend to in Paris. She needed to locate some sheer stockings for Maria-Ludovica to match a sample the Austrian empress had sent the emperor, which His Majesty in turn had passed on to Metternich. She also bid an affectionate, sisterly farewell to Prince Windischgratz, who was in the French capital pursuing her relentlessly. But Alfred belonged to the past—like Clemens. Then Wilhelmina and her foster daughter set off for Milan to rejoin Lord Stewart, the British ambassador, who had preceded her. Paulina was already there to participate with them in the gala festivities attendant upon the restoration of Austrian rule in northern Italy.

Count Karl was also in Milan to help arrange for Emperor Franz's forthcoming visit. And Dorothea, too, was Milan-bound—with *l'oncle*'s approval. This made it easier for Dorothea to leave behind at least temporarily her two young sons, for she was confident that *l'oncle*, as the head of the family, would never permit them to be taken from her.

Very little is known about the next few months of Dorothea's life except that after the first of the year—1816—she and Count Karl were in Vienna. Talleyrand refused to admit that Dorothea, who had become an integral part of his life, might have disappeared from it forever, and realized that only by appealing to his niece's conscience and her sense of accountability could he draw her back to Paris. An endless stream of letters and go-betweens flowed eastward. *L'oncle* also deployed Gentz. The shrewd little chevalier made it a point to see Dorothea frequently to plead Talleyrand's cause, and he soon wondered if her rose-colored glasses might be turning cloudy. On the eve of Count Karl's departure to rejoin the Austrian general staff in Milan, he and Dorothea had tea as well as dinner with Gentz.

Exactly why Dorothea decided to leave Vienna and return to Paris is impossible to say. Members of Clam's family said that before his last weeks with Dorothea he was already deeply in love with Lady Selina Meade, the beautiful Irish girl he was later to marry. But a series of letters Count Karl wrote Dorothea when he came back from Italy and found her gone and in which he pled with her to reconsider gives the lie to that.

The deciding factor may well have been Wilhelmina's return in mid-February. Unfortunately, there is no trace of any conversation between the two sisters, although it is known that Talleyrand enlisted Wilhelmina's assistance to return the stray to the fold. Before, Dorothea had been too young to appreciate the tragedy of the duchess of Sagan's life—the limited role society permitted Wilhelmina, in spite of her intelligence. To find Wilhelmina increasingly unhappy and dissatisfied after disappearing with Lord Stewart into the Italian hill towns for a protracted idyll following the Milan celebrations shocked Dorothea. Wilhelmina's wasted capabilities and empty existence despite her vaunted independence were disturbing—a possible preview of what Dorothea herself might be like ten, fifteen years hence.

Several days passed. Dorothea had another confidential talk with Gentz and gave a farewell ball. The next morning, the chevalier arrived with an armful of the latest journals and a box of dragées that Dorothea adored—they were a Courland family weakness—and bade her farewell. Dorothea was headed west. Her decision was clear-cut, based on man versus man, and the life each offered. The choice was between her contemporary, Clam-Martinitz —handsome and more mature than Edmond, but cut of the same cloth, with a world limited to battles and balls—or the highly complex Talleyrand, the most fascinating political brain in Europe, who because he was thirty-nine years Dorothea's senior, possessed the added attraction that age had always held for her. Count Karl was part of the never-never world that had been the Congress of Vienna; Talleyrand represented responsibilities— and her children. And Dorothea was incapable of irresponsibility, although there would be several interludes in which the hot Slav blood of the Courlands took over.

For the day-to-day fulfillment Dorothea sought, no tie could permanently bind her unless her mind was involved. As a girl, infatuated with Czartoryski, Dorothea's ambition had been to govern a famous, powerful man, but she was not getting this with Talleyrand. Although *l'oncle*'s name rang throughout Europe and he held no peer as a diplomat and statesman, at the moment Talleyrand was benched, in complete disfavor with Louis XVIII, with nothing to indicate he had any immediate chance of a return to high office. Nor did Dorothea delude herself that she could ever be his Egeria. But strong intellectual ties still bound her to Talleyrand, and perfect mutual understanding. This could have stemmed, subconsciously, from scars inflicted on them both in loveless childhoods, similar wounds that produced the same con- suming pride as a defense to hide a feeling of inferiority—*l'oncle* because of his crippled right foot, the niece because of her illegiti- macy. For while Dorothea in her memoirs referred to Grand Duke Peter as her father, it is hard to believe she did not know the truth from nursery days when her older sisters teasingly called her "Mlle. Batowska." To be the by-blow of a ruling monarch was one thing. But for Maman to be the grand duchess of Courland and Dorothea the offspring of a refugee Polish nobleman was quite another matter. So Dorothea preferred to ignore the facts and push them out of her mind.

L'oncle's fervent appeals to Dorothea to return were so out of character with the restraint and strength she associated with him that they must have struck her like a dash of cold water. They bore out Gentz's repeated assertions that *l'oncle* needed her, and gave her the sense of security and significance that comes from the knowledge that one is indispensable. Dorothea had probably been too wrapped up in Clam to analyze *l'oncle*'s feelings for her before. And if she had bothered to reflect that the easy atmosphere of mutual trust and affection that had so happily existed between them in Vienna in the beginning had subtly changed, in all likeli- hood she attributed it to Maman's reappearance on the scene and the resumption of her romance.

Maman. Time might have brunted the bitterness of Dorothea's

early relations with her mother, and her affair with Count Karl temporarily obliterated whatever Prince Czartoryski may have revealed about the grand duchess's exact role in their aborted engagement. Still, veiled animosity lay between daughter and mother. And Dorothea was going back—to *l'oncle*. That Talleyrand might derive great pleasure from the grand duchess's company Dorothea could accept. But that Maman or anyone else should henceforth play the leading role in Talleyrand's life was unthinkable.

Dorothea's sons did not belong to Dorothea as much as to the great house of Talleyrand-Périgord, whose heirs they were, so for them to reside permanently with their mother in the hôtel Saint Florentin was in one sense perfectly acceptable. On the other hand, Edmond, from whom Dorothea was neither legally nor financially separated—an important consideration in the Catholic, ancien régime Faubourg Saint-Germain—was still domiciled in the rue Grange-Batelière residence that he and Dorothea formerly called home, and his wife and two boys' proper place was there.

As patriarch, Talleyrand was anxious to shield the sensibilities of Paris society, and fortunately the enormous size of the hôtel Saint Florentin enabled him to maintain the fiction that it was a multiple family residence. Living there already were *l'oncle*'s adopted daughter and her husband, with a baby on the way; his resident musician, wife, and children; and the head of his secretarial staff and his wife.

When decorators arrived to redo Dorothea's ground-floor apartments in Indian paper and white silk damask, Anna reminded herself that one must accept life, without wishing for the impossible. Rather than give up Talleyrand, she accepted him on his terms—as he knew she would—and was more warmly cherished than ever. It is impossible to read Charles-Maurice's continuous billets to the grand duchess, with their constantly reiterated protestations of affection, or recall his unfailing, innumerable attentions, and not believe in his sincerity. His love for her was simply no longer all-inclusive.

Talleyrand might craftily orchestrate a peaceful modus vivendi between Anna and Dorothea—living under separate roofs—but had the hôtel Saint Florentin been as large as Versailles, it could never accommodate both Dorothea and his wife, Catherine, simultaneously. There was no possible give and take between the pair.

Talleyrand had returned after Waterloo to find Catherine still in London, where she had fled during Napoleon's "Hundred Days." So *l'oncle* instructed the marquis d'Osmond, his appointee to the Court of Saint James, to persuade Mme. de Talleyrand—for a significant sum—to remain there and to divide her time, whenever she crossed the Channel, between Brussels and Pont-des-Sains, a Talleyrand estate in the Ardennes in northern France. In the intervening year, Mme. de Talleyrand had grown restless, and she wrote early that summer complaining that the pea-soup London fogs were bad for her health. Talleyrand apparently sent the letter on to his niece, who was briefly in the countryside at Rosny with her children. Reading between the lines, Dorothea suspected that one fine morning Catherine would suddenly materialize in the hôtel Saint Florentin. Dorothea, who knew that the return of the red-faced, heavyset Mme. de Talleyrand spelled annoyance and embarrassment for *l'oncle*, sensed the kill and cruelly counseled:

> The only proper thing for you both is that she should be made to stay in England—assuming that Europe must continue to possess this treasure. . . . Forgive me for being so bold, but let me give you some advice which will spare you a painful conversation of the kind you most dislike. . . . The Princess [Tyskiewicz] and I have often discussed this problem and she agrees with me. . . . Since money motivates all Mme. de Talleyrand's actions, send . . . M. Perrey [Talleyrand's secretary] to her at once, armed with a letter of credit and instructions to tell Mme. de Talleyrand that she is not to touch one more sou of the income you give her until she crosses the Channel and that she will forfeit it all if she leaves Britain again. Have . . . M. Perrey accompany her as far as the packet and not return until he sees it sail with her on board.

Unbeknown to Dorothea, Talleyrand did not follow her vindictive instructions. Catherine was paid off, handsomely, as she deserved, without any stipulations whatsover, and never again crossed the threshold of the hôtel Saint Florentin.

Although life was as brilliant as ever, its table, under Carême's magic direction, still the finest in Europe, and every person of mark passing through Paris automatically signed the guest register, Dorothea found *l'oncle* was not as resigned to removal from public office as he pretended. Talleyrand had played too active and important a role for the past quarter of a century not to be keenly displeased at his present inactivity. Confirmed cynic though he was, Talleyrand refused to believe that Louis XVIII, upon whose head he had twice set the French crown, could be so ungrateful. But the monarch, who had appointed him grand chamberlain, the same high, purely ceremonial post Talleyrand held at the close of the empire, had conveniently wiped the painful years of exile from his memory, as Dorothea well knew. For His Most Christian Majesty also chose not to recall dandling her on his knee at Mitau.

Talleyrand ostentatiously attended to his personal affairs, which had been grossly neglected, and dictated his *Mémoires* to his secretary. But one weather eye was always on the government scene, and he delighted in the failure of his foes, repeating, "In politics, the important thing is not to be right but to succeed." When Chateaubriand, the famous diplomat and writer who never saw eye to eye with *l'oncle* on anything, complained of becoming deaf, Talleyrand explained to Dorothea, "He only believes he is deaf because he no longer hears anyone mention his name."

With warm weather, the seasonal exodus to the countryside was in full swing. Anna moved out to her Château Neuf at Saint Germain-en-Laye, and Talleyrand and Dorothea set forth with a vast entourage, her two boys, and Carlos, Talleyrand's pet, on the twenty-hour trip to Valençay, *l'oncle*'s vast Berry estate. At their approach, the château's great gates were thrown wide, the cavalcade rattled over the drawbridge across a deep moat where trees and shrubs supplanted the water of an earlier century, traversed one enormous court, passed under a portcullis into a second, and came to a screeching halt. The household was lined up in front of the main door of the grandiose Renaissance structure to greet its absentee owner who had not set foot there in eight years—ever since Napoleon sent Talleyrand his two prisoners, the present Ferdinand VII of Spain and his brother, to lodge there. Quasi-feudal relations still existed between the hundred-room château and its domain of some 2,000 hectares and village, and Talleyrand intended to compensate for his neglect. Many of the master suites were in shambles. Talleyrand found more than fifty wolf traps nailed to the priceless paneling of one room; in another, the parquet floor had been ruined when Ferdinand VII and his brother tried the hydroculture of certain Spanish vegetables they missed. On the library walls, Dorothea discovered the charred ruins of a Spanish auto-da-fé in which the captive Catholic princes had burned the iconoclastic works of J. J. Rousseau and Voltaire.

Talleyrand's first act was to assign the bedroom of honor, called the Chamber of the King because of its previous occupant, to the grand duchess for her exclusive use. So Anna hastened out to inspect her new quarters and Valençay. The prefect of Indre, alerted by the minister of police to watch for any suspicious, conspiratorial behavior on Talleyrand's part, arrived unannounced and stumbled on an unexpected domestic tableau: mother, daughter, and *l'oncle* classifying and arranging endless stacks of books from Talleyrand's vast Paris collection. Charles-Maurice was no country squire and intended life at Valençay to be the lavish equivalent of that at the hôtel Saint Florentin. And it was.

When Anna departed for Karlsbad and Löbikau—to take her annual cure, see the various members of her family, and attend to estate matters—Talleyrand saw her off, comfortably settled in her vast traveling coach, with a hamper of the special pheasant pâté from his Périgord estates that she was so fond of nibbling. In a letter that awaited her at the first post stop, Charles-Maurice assured Anna that he intended to supervise personally the restoration of her room, to have the carpet taken up and everything cleaned so she could be comfortably installed there in the fall. He concluded, "It gives me the greatest pain to see you setting out on this long journey but I hope you will arrange things so that it will not be necessary in the years to come."

Talleyrand's warmly insistent letters brought Anna back several times to Paris, but age and increasing ill health banked the remaining, smoldering coals of her love, and the tedious trip to and fro loomed ever more formidable. The grand duchess's former dissensions and misunderstandings with Wilhelmina, Paulina, and Joanna had long since yielded to a sincere desire to enjoy her family, and the trio of Courland princesses, Elisa, and her shadow, the poet Tiedge, spent each summer with Anna. Her Löbikau house parties, an interesting mix of fifty to one hundred stimulating guests, became famous, especially for their amateur theatricals, and invitations were so widely sought that generous Anna had to build an annex to house the overflow.

Miss Mary Berry, a visiting British bluestocking, vigorously stirred her tea, then glanced up significantly at the large water-color of Dorothea, which had replaced Prudhon's charming draw-ing of Catherine de Talleyrand on the mantel of the Salon de l'Aigle by the spring of 1820. The celebrated statesman's great charm was undimmed, his witty fireworks still scintillated when he chose to exert himself—but today Talleyrand was enveloped in disdainful silence. The foreigner felt cheated not to witness in action this ex-bishop who treated his wife shabbily in order to live with his nephew's wife, who was also his former mistress's youngest daughter. Miss Berry shook her head, scandalized. Those Frenchmen!

Watching Dorothea preside—out of earshot—at the tea table, Miss Berry sniffed to the Princess Tyskiewicz, "I understand Comtesse Edmond is established here as mistress—in every sense that one usually attaches to that term."

"Haven't you heard?" the princess corrected her politely. In Anna's absence, Talleyrand, who was determined not to tarnish his household's patina of respectability, had assigned the role of chaperone-in-residence to the devoted Marie-Thérèse. "Thanks to Monsieur de Talleyrand, Dorothea is now the duchess of Dino." The king of Naples, out of gratitude for Talleyrand's past help, had presented *l'oncle* with this minuscule Calabrian domain. Dino was not much, as Mediterranean islands go—populated solely by rabbits, with a lot of anchovies offshore. But the titles, the duke and duchess of Dino, went with it, and at Talleyrand's request, the Neapolitan ruler permitted him to transfer them to his nephew and Dorothea.

"What a marvelous present in adultery's trousseau," the sharp-tongued spinster was heard to mutter.

Shortly afterwards, Edmond astonished the noble Faubourg by an ostentatious reconciliation with his wife, although there was no conspicuous revival of marital affection, and he moved into the hôtel Saint Florentin. Since he had already managed to dissipate his personal fortune, Dorothea had recently effected a property settlement to prevent his making inroads on her own estate and to protect their children's heritage. Now, *l'oncle* paid his nephew's considerable debts and procured his promotion to the high rank of Grand Officer of the Legion of Honor.

During the fall, Adèle de Souza, a member in good standing of Talleyrand's seraglio—the mother of his one acknowledged illegitimate son—was at Valençay and reported to her cronies in Paris:

> Mme. Dorothea has become a true mystic. Poor Edmond is a pitiable witness to this magical pregnancy conferred by the grace of God. He fears his uncle may force him to stay in bed when Dorothea is delivered. He sees their minds so disposed to believe in miracles that, for all he knows, he may be asked to suckle the infant.

Like Talleyrand, the grand duchess understood the importance of maintaining a facade for convention's sake and made one of her rare trips from Löbikau in time for the blessed event. Anna now found it fitting that one of the Courland princesses should be the comfort of dear Charles-Maurice's declining years. The grand duchess was satisfied that as one of Talleyrand's own generation, she shared a common denominator with him that no younger woman ever could. Deeply though Talleyrand might love Dorothea, the daughter would never wholly supersede the mother.

On December 29, 1820, little Pauline was born. Precisely who Pauline's father was has never been ascertained, but Talleyrand treated her as his. Edmond claimed the infant, but within the year, he and Dorothea got a legal separation, and he passed out of her life forever.

EPILOGUE

THE GRAND DUCHESS DIED AT LÖBIKAU the summer after Pauline was born. The mutual affection Dorothea and her mother shared for Charles-Maurice, and the love and devotion he lavished on them in return, had served as a belated bond between mother and daughter. Her death caused Dorothea sincere grief.

Anna's passing was a great shock for Talleyrand, who had never expected to outlive her. Years later, when Dorothea showed him a portrait of the grand duchess he had never seen before, *l'oncle* studied it at great length. Wiping away a tear, he remarked softly, "I do not believe there was ever a woman more deserving of adoration."

No name other than Dorothea's was ever again linked with Talleyrand. His needs absorbed her whole existence, and she consciously submerged herself to him in absolute devotion. If sex did enter their picture, it was not the most important part of their relationship.

Although he remained out of favor the next fourteen years, as one of the leaders of the opposition, Talleyrand became a major force to be reckoned with. He was constantly angling for power, and Dorothea worked ceaselessly to reinstate him. And as it turned out, Talleyrand had an important part of his career still ahead.

Without Talleyrand, the duc d'Orléans would never have mounted the steps of the French throne in the revolution of 1830. Installed as King Louis-Philippe, he appointed Talleyrand ambassador to the Court of Saint James. And Dorothea played a significant role there. When Wilhelmina went to Britain to visit, the duchess of Sagan's glamour seemed provincial in comparison with her young sister's high cosmopolitan polish. Dorothea's powerful analytical mind made her outstanding, even among the most sophisticated, fascinating charmers of Paris and London, and as a political muse, she exerted more direct influence than either her mother or Wilhelmina ever had.

After his final retirement in November of 1834, the niece and *l'oncle*'s last years together were happy, private ones. Dorothea heeded the call of more than one young stallion, as Talleyrand had known she would. But she lent, she never gave herself, and the heart did not play a major part in these discreet adventures. Society might whisper the name of a blurred shadow who flitted across Dorothea's path, but the proprieties were always observed, and the ties between Talleyrand and Dorothea endured.

When Talleyrand died in 1838 at the age of eighty-four and Dorothea's three children—Edmond's two boys and Pauline, the darling of Talleyrand's old age—were married off and their futures secured, the forty-seven-year-old Dorothea, who was more Prussian than French or Slavic, and always remained a foreigner in Paris, moved east.

Shunning Vienna and the world where she had once played so glamorous a role, Wilhelmina retired to her country estates. Lord Stewart disappeared from her life, she never gained custody of her daughter, Vava, and she eventually became Countess Karl Schulenberg. Since only one career, marriage, was open to women, for Wilhelmina to wed a simple major in the Austrian army was a clear admission of failure by society's standards, and her foster daughters sobbed uncontrollably throughout the marriage ceremony.

The duchess of Sagan's third marriage lasted little longer than her other two, and she ultimately moved back to Vienna to live quietly with her sisters. Metternich ruled Austria—and most of Central Europe—for close to half a century and visited her regularly to exchange political news and seek her valued opinion. She died in Vienna, almost two decades after the grand duchess, at the age of fifty-eight. It is not known whether Metternich attended her funeral, but a short time later, his wife bought for her husband, at auction, the desk at which Wilhelmina had written all those notes to him. Metternich survived another twenty years, until 1859. Joanna poignantly summed up the tragic life of the oldest Courland princess who never found a way to employ her faculties fully: "Whether, with all the gifts that Heaven bestowed on her, she was ever happy, I will not claim, and this doubt is painful to me."

Paulina passed away a few years later, and Joanna would outlive everyone else in the family.

Although known to posterity as the duchess of Dino, Dorothea bought the duchy of Sagan from Wilhelmina's heirs. She took a keen interest in this acquired domain, and as its ruling duchess—Sagan was a fief of the crown—she sat in the Prussian Estates. Except for an occasional trip to Paris, Dorothea divided her time between Sagan and Berlin, where her position as an intimate of the Prussian court was unique and unchallenged. With the crown princess of Prussia as her closest friend and ally, Dorothea arranged the marriage of her granddaughter Marie, Pauline's child, into the Prussian royal house. The match was a particularly pleasing one because the groom was the grandson of Dorothea's godmother, Princess Louisa of Prussia. It would certainly have delighted the grand duchess of Courland, for the Princess Louisa had been Anna's staunch friend.

Early in the summer of 1861, Dorothea was caught by a violent storm on the road from Günthersdorf to Sagan. The horses bolted and tipped the carriage into the ditch. Badly bruised and shocked, Dorothea crawled from the wreck. For an hour and a half, while the horses were caught and brought back, she lay exposed to a pelting rain and hailstones "as big as billiard balls," she later wrote a friend. She was running a high fever by the time she got home. The doctors put her to bed and for several days despaired of her life. Dorothea never fully recovered.

Dorothea was too ill to attend the crown princess's coronation as queen of Prussia the following year, and died a short time later, on September 19, 1862, at the age of sixty-nine—the happiest and most fulfilled of the Courland sisters, and the one most like her mother.

BIBLIOGRAPHY

It is difficult to know how much to include here; to cite all the works that have been consulted suggests unnecessary historical pretension.

Nothing has been published on the Courlands as a family, but there have been several works on individual members of the family.

ON ANNA-DOROTHEA, THE GRAND DUCHESS OF COURLAND:

Arrigon, Louis Jules. *Une Amie de Talleyrand—la Duchesse de Courlande.* Paris: Flammarion, 1945.

Günther, Elbin. *Macht in Zarten Händen—Dorothea Herzogin von Kurland.* Munich: Ehrenwirth Verlag, 1968.

Tiedge, Christophe Auguste. *Anna Charlotte Dorothea, letzte Herzogin von Kurland.* Leipzig, 1822.

ON WILHELMINA, THE DUCHESS OF SAGAN:

Brühl, Clemens. *Die Sagan: Das Leben der Herzogin Wilhelmine von Sagan, Prinzessin von Kurland.* Berlin: Steuben-Verlag, Paul G. Esser, 1941.

McGuigan, Dorothy Gies. *Metternich and the Duchess.* New York: Doubleday, 1975.

ON DOROTHEA, THE DUCHESS OF DINO:

Bernardy, Françoise de. *Le Dernier Amour de Talleyrand: La Duchesse de Dino.* Paris: Hachette, 1956.

Brandes, Georg. *Hertugindin af Dino og fyrsten af Talleyrand.* Kjøbenhavn Gyldendal: Nordisk forlag, 1923.

Bunsen, Maria von. *Talleyrands Nichte, die Herzogin von Sagan.* Stuttgart, 1935.

Feckes, Elizabeth. *Dorothea, Herzogin von Dino und Sagan.* Krefeld: J. B. Kleinsche Druckerei, 1917.

Ziegler, Philip. *The Duchess of Dino.* New York: John Day, 1963.

Unfortunately, only fragments of a few letters of the grand duchess survive. Wilhelmina's correspondence with Metternich appears in Dr. Maria Ullrichova's book, *Clemens Metternich—Wilhelmina von Sagan: Ein Briefwechsel 1813–1815* (Graz-Köln: Verlag Hermann Böhlaus Nachf, 1966), and in the McGuigan book listed above, which also draws extensively on unpublished correspondence in the Central State Archives at Prague (The Metternich Family Correspondence; the Metternich-Sagan Correspondence) and the State Archives at Pilsen (The Windischgratz Family Archives). The various published collections of Dorothea's letters are of no concern here, but her *Souvenirs* (Paris: C. Lévy, 1908) cover her life until her marriage.

The letters of Talleyrand that are of prime interest are those to the grand duchess, published by G. Palewski de l'Institut de France: *Le Miroir de Talleyrand: Lettres Inédites à la Duchesse de Courlande pendant le Congrès de Vienne* (Paris: Librairie Académique Perrin, 1976). They can be supplemented by those appearing in Georges Lacour-Gayet's *Talleyrand* (4 vols. Paris: Payot, 1928–1934), which is invaluable for the whole period of his relationship with the Courlands. Talleyrand's *Mémoires* (5 vols. Paris: C. Lévy, 1891–1892), in addition to the Plon edition of the first two volumes (Paul Louis and J. P. Couchod, Paris, 1957), are essential; Metternich's *Memoirs* (5 vols.), translated by Mrs. Alexander Napier (New York: Charles Scribner's Sons, 1881), are also interesting.

Certain scenes, like Talleyrand's levee and Zacharias Werner's famous sermon at the Congress of Vienna, surface time and again in contemporary memoirs and books of the period, especially French ones.

What follows is a selected listing that should prove helpful to the general reader who wants more information on the period and personalities involved. Because of the nature of Talleyrand's relations with the grand duchess and her daughter, they figure in the more gossip-prone lives of Talleyrand, a few of which are given below, along with some of the classical studies of the great French statesman. It would be folly for anyone interested in the Congress of Vienna not to consult Sir Harold Nicolson's *Congress of Vienna* (New York: Harcourt, Brace & Co., 1946), and also Albert Sorel's essay, *Talleyrand au Congrès de Vienne* in his *Essais d'Histoire et de Critique* (Paris: E. Plon & Cie 1895). Because so little was known of the duchess of Sagan's affair with Metternich until recently, the Metternich biographies are not up to date, with the exception of Antoine Bethouart's *Metternich et l'Europe* (Paris: Perrin, 1979).

Abrantès, Madame d' (Laure Junot). *Mémoires*. 18 vols. Paris: Ladvocat, 1831–35.

Almadingen, E. M. *Emperor Alexander I*. New York: Vanguard, 1964.

Bain, Robert Nisbet. *Last King of Poland*. London: Methuen & Co., 1909.

Bassanville, Anaïs (Lebrun) Comtesse de. *Les Salons d'Autrefois*. Paris: J. Victorion, 1870.

Berkis, Alexander V. *History of the Duchy of Courland*. Towson, Md.: P. M. Harrod, 1969.

Bibl, Viktor. *Metternich*. Leipzig und Wien: J. Günther, 1936.

Binzer, Emilie von. *Drei Sommer in Löbichau*. Stuttgart: Verlag von Spemann, 1877.

Boigne, Comtesse E. A. de. *Mémoires*. Paris: Mercure de France, 1971.

Bonsdorff, Carl V. *Armfelt*. 4 Bde in: Skrifter utgivna av Svenska Littera-tursällskapet, Helsingfors, 1930–1934.

Carrère, Casimir. *Talleyrand Armoureux*. Paris: Editions France-Empire, 1976.

Castelot, André. *Talleyrand ou le Cynisme*. Paris: Librairie Académique Perrin, 1980.

Cecil, Algernon. *Metternich*. London: Eyre & Spottiswoode, 1933.

Clary-et-Aldringen, Prince Charles de. *Trois Mois à Paris lors du Mariage de l'Empéreur Napoléon et Marie Louise*. Paris: Plon, 1914.

Coigny, Aimée de. *Mémoires*. Paris: Calmann Lévy, 1902.

Colmache. *Reminiscences of Prince Talleyrand*. 2 vols.: London: H. Colburn, 1848.

Cooper, Duff. *Talleyrand*. London: Jonathan Cape, 1954.

Corti, Egon Caësar. *Metternich und die Frauen*, Bd I-II. Zurich, Wien: Europa Verlag, 1948.

Coulmann, J. S. *Reminiscences*. Paris: 1862, 1869.

Curtiss, Mina. *A Forgotten Empress: Anna Ivanovna and Her Era, 1730–1740*. New York: Ungar, 1974.

Dard, Emile. *Napoléon et Talleyrand*. Paris: Plon, 1935.

Daudet, Ernest. *Un Drame d'Amour à la Cour de Suède, 1784–1785*. Paris, 1913.

Dussord, Jacques. *Les Belles Amies de M de Talleyrand*. Paris: Editions Colbert, 1942.

Eynard, J. G. *Journal*. Paris: Plon-Nourrit & Cie, 1914.

Ferrero, Guglielmo. *Reconstruction: Talleyrand à Vienne*. Paris: Plon, 1940.

Fournier, August. *Dei geheimpolizei auf d'em Wiener Kongress*. Wien: F. Tempsky, 1913.

Freska, Fred. *A Peace Congress of Intrigue: A Vivid Intimate Account of the Congress of Vienna Composed of Personal Memoirs of its Important Participants*. Translated by Harry Hansen. New York: Century Co., 1919.

Gaebelé, Mme Yvonne (Robert). *La Vie de la Princesse de Talleyrand:* Paris: la Société de l'Inde Française, 1948.

Grunwald, Constantin de. *Metternich*. Translated by Dorothy Todd. London: Falcon Press, 1953.

Hildebrand, K. *La Société de Berlin de 1789 and 1815*. Revue des Deux Mondes: March, 1870.

Joelson, Annette. *Courtesan Princess: Catherine Grand Talleyrand*. Philadelphia: Chilton Books, 1965.

Kielmannsegge, Countess of. *Memoiren der Gräfin Kielmannsegge über Napoléon I*. Dresden: Paul Artez Verlag, 1927.

Kraushar, Alex. *Les Bourbons en Exil à Mitau et à Varsovie*. Varsovie, 1899.

La Garde-Chambonas, Auguste, Comte de. *Souvenirs du Congrès de Vienne*. Paris: Vivien, 1901.

Loliée, Frédéric. *Du Prince de Bénévent au Duc de Morny: Talleyrand et la Société Française; Talleyrand et la Société Européene.* Paris: Paul, 1910.

Longworth, Philip. *The Three Empresses.* New York: Rinehart, Winston, 1973.

Madelin, Louis. *Talleyrand.* Paris: Flammarion, 1944.

Makanawitsky, Barbara Norman. *Napoleon and Talleyrand: The Last Two Weeks.* New York: Stein & Day, 1975.

Mazade-Percin, Charles. *Un Chancelier d'Ancien Regime: le Règne diplomatique de M. de Metternich.* Paris: Plon, Nourrit et Cie, 1889.

Missoffe, Michel. *Le Coeur Secret de Talleyrand.* Paris: Perrin, 1956.

Nicolson, Harold. *The Congress of Vienna.* New York: Harcourt, Brace & Company, 1946.

Nikolai-Mikhailovitch, Grand Duke. *Portraits Russes des 18e et 19e Siècles.* Traduit par M. Wrangel. Paris: Payot, 1931.

Noel, Léon. *L'Enigmatique Talleyrand.* Paris: Fayard, 1975.

Orieux, Jean. *Talleyrand.* Paris: Flammarion, 1970.

Paleologue, George Maurice. *Alexander I, un Tsar Enigmatique.* Paris: Plon, 1934.

————. *Romanticisme et Diplomatie: Talleyrand, Metternich, Chateaubriand.* Paris: Hachette.

Pichot, Amédée. *Souvenirs Intimes de M de Talleyrand.* Paris: 1870.

Rachel, Paul. *Elisa von der Recke: Tagebücher und Briefe aus ihren Wanderjahren.* 2 vols. Leipzig: Dieterich'sche Verlagbuchhandlung, 1902.

Remusat, Charles de. *Mémoires.* 4 vols. Paris: Plon, 1958–1962.

Rondeau, Lady. *Letters from a Lady Who Resided Some Years in Russia.* 1775.

Spiel, Hilde, ed. *The Congress of Vienna: An Eyewitness Account.* Translated by Richard H. Weber. Philadelphia: Chilton Books, 1968.

Talleyrand Intime, d'après sa Correspondence Inédite avec la Duchesse de Courlande. Paris: E. Kolb, 1891.

Tegner, Elof. *Gustav-Mauritz Armfelt.* 3 vols. Stockholm, 1887.

Thürheim, Countess Lulu. *Mein Leben: Erinnerungen aus Österreichs Grosser Welt, 1788–1819.* 2 vols. Munich: George Müller, 1913.

Vivent, Jacques. *La Vie Privée de Talleyrand.* Paris: Hachette, 1940.

Weil, Commandant Maurice Henri. *Les Dessous du Congrès du Vienne.* 2 vols. Paris: Payot, 1917.

Wulffius, Gerhard. *Aus dem Leben Herzog Peter* (of Courland). Sonderdruck des baltischen Deutschtums XXI, 1974.

INDEX